PROMOTING DIVERSITY AND SOCIAL JUSTICE

Promoting Diversity and Social Justice provides theories, perspectives, and strategies that are useful for working with adults from privileged groups—those who are in a more powerful position in any given type of oppression. The thoroughly revised edition of this accessible and practical guide offers tools that allow educators to be more reflective and intentional in their work—helping them to consider who they're working with, what they're doing, why they're doing it and how to educate more effectively.

New features include:

- A new chapter, "The Joy of Unlearning Privilege/Oppression," highlights specific ways people from privileged groups benefit from unlearning privilege/oppression and from creating greater equity.
- A new chapter, "Allies and Action," gives focus and guidance on how people from privileged groups can constructively and appropriately be involved in social change efforts.
- Updated Appendix of additional resources.

The theories and approaches discussed can be applied to a range of situations and audiences. This book is an excellent resource for professors, diversity trainers, teachers in classrooms and workshops, counselors, organizers, student affairs personnel, community educators, advocates, group facilitators, and any others involved with educating about diversity and equity.

Diane J. Goodman, Ed.D., is a trainer, college teacher, author, speaker, and consultant on diversity and social justice issues. For more information, see her website: http://www.dianegoodman.com.

THE TEACHING/LEARNING SOCIAL JUSTICE SERIES

Edited by Lee Anne Bell

BARNARD COLLEGE, COLUMBIA UNIVERSITY

PROMOTING DIVERSITY AND SOCIAL JUSTICE

Educating People from
Privileged Groups

Second Edition

Diane J. Goodman

Routledge
Taylor & Francis Group

NEW YORK AND LONDON

First published 2011
by Routledge
711 Third Avenue, New York, NY 10017

Simultaneously published in the UK
by Routledge
2 Park Square, Milton Park, Abingdon, Oxon OX14 4RN

Routledge is an imprint of the Taylor & Francis Group, an informa business

Typeset in by Bembo by Taylor & Francis Books
Printed and bound in the United States of America on acid-free paper by Walsworth Publishing Company, Marceline, MO

Library of Congress Cataloging-in-Publication Data
Goodman, Diane.
Promoting diversity and social justice : educating people from privileged groups / Diane J. Goodman.—2nd ed.
p. cm.
Includes bibliographical references and index.
1. Social justice. 2. Multiculturalism. 3. Upper class—Attitudes. 4. Social conflict. 5. Conflict management. 6. Social psychology. I. Title.
HM671.G66 2011
303.3'72—dc22
2011000308

ISBN13: 978-0-415-87287-4 (hbk)
ISBN13: 978-0-415-87288-1 (pbk)
ISBN13: 978-0-203-82973-8 (ebk)

To Halle and Kayla—who challenge me, inspire me, and give me hope that change is possible.

CONTENTS

SERIES EDITOR INTRODUCTION

Promoting Diversity and Social Justice: Educating People from Privileged Groups by Diane Goodman

The Teaching/Learning Social Justice Series explores issues of social justice—diversity, equality, democracy, and fairness—in classrooms and communities. "Teaching/learning" connotes the essential connections between theory and practice that books in this series seek to illuminate. Central are the stories and lived experiences of people who strive to critically analyze and challenge oppressive relationships and institutions, and to imagine and create more just and inclusive alternatives. The series seeks to balance critical analysis with images of hope and possibility in ways that are accessible and inspiring to a broad audience of educators and activists who believe in the potential for social change through education and who seek stories and examples of practice, as well as honest discussion of the ever-present obstacles to dismantling oppressive ideas and institutions.

What moves people from privileged groups to step out of our comfort zone and unsettle fundamental ways of thinking about the world and our taken-for-granted place in it? What do we stand to gain by challenging a status quo from which we often benefit in significant and material ways? In *Promoting Diversity and Social Justice: Educating People from Privileged Groups,* Diane Goodman engages just these critical questions through examining how privilege across a range of issues—race, class, gender, sexuality, religion, age, and ability—operates either to reproduce or to challenge the status quo. Using detailed examples gained through decades of work with people from dominant groups, Goodman shows how people can learn to see their/our own position within hierarchical structures and use social and positional privilege in the service of change for justice.

This important work disrupts what Boler (1999) calls "passive empathy," a safe and simplistic identification with less privileged others that does not require that we question our own position or challenge our own worldview.

> These "others" whose lives we imagine don't want empathy, they want justice ... What is at stake is not only the ability to empathize with the very distant other, but to recognize oneself as implicated in the social forces that create the climate of obstacles that other must confront. (p. 166)

This is a challenging concept, but one that is at the heart of the capacity to work for social justice and to build relationships of mutuality and equality.

Goodman writes with clarity and compassion about the ways that we resist knowledge of our implication in systems that harm others and the honesty required to acknowledge our role so as to be able to work effectively for change. Through numerous examples from her own teaching and training and interviews with other educators, Goodman traces a continuum of consciousness to illustrate how people from privileged groups become aware of their involvement in systems of oppression and then learn to act responsibly to challenge oppressive interactions and structures.

This book is an excellent resource for teachers, trainers, community activists, and others who struggle to create coalitions in which people who are differently positioned can work together to dismantle oppressive systems and create relationships and institutions based on equity and justice. Enlisting the power of privilege in the service of equality can be a powerful disruption of the status quo. Done effectively, with humility and honest self-reflection, people from privileged groups can have a constructive role to play in fostering social change. Developing our capacity to do so could be an antidote to the zero-sum politics currently creating gridlock in our government, and move us toward more inclusive practices of democracy in which we recognize our fates as intertwined.

Lee Anne Bell
September 2010

Boler, Megan (1999) *Feeling Power: Emotions and Education.* NY: Routledge, p. 181.

ACKNOWLEDGMENTS

This book evolved out of many years of learning and experience. There are countless people from whose work and lives I have benefited; some of them are referenced throughout the book. The students and workshop participants who have shared their stories and feedback are an invaluable part of this process. I continue to grow and be inspired by other educators, researchers, and activists.

First, I want to thank the people who reviewed parts of the manuscript for the first edition, upon which this second edition is built: Lee Bell, Robert Carter, Nan Frane, Pat Griffin, Ricki Mazella, Tema Okun, Nancy Schniedewind, Glen Weinbaum, and Charmaine Wijeyesinghe. I am particularly indebted and grateful to Rob Koegel who read the whole manuscript (at least once) and generously provided unflagging assistance.

For the second edition, I am indebted to the many people who shared their experiences with unlearning privilege/oppression, particularly to those whom I interviewed: Carlo Baldino, Jim Bonilla, Steven Botkin, Tricia Brainard, Bonnie Cushing, Robin D'Angelo, Steve Joseph, Joyce McNickles, Kathy O'Bear, Tema Okun, Tom Stern, Melanie Suchet, and Charmaine Wijeyesinghe.

I deeply appreciate the support and encouragement from friends and colleagues who helped me think about and write this new edition. I cannot express how much it means to me. To the people who generously gave their time to review parts of the manuscript, I thank: Lee Bell, Warren Blumenfeld, Carol Chung, Ann Marie Garran, Andrea Herrera, Tema Okun, Robin Parker, Anna Shabsin, Melanie Suchet, Glen Weinbaum, and Charmaine Wijeyesinghe. Charmaine has provided ongoing emotional and technical support throughout this whole project. Thank you as well to Catherine Bernard and Georgette Enriquez at Routledge for their skillful editorial assistance and feedback to help me get "unstuck."

My appreciation also goes to Kayla and Halle, who I love more than anything, for their patience and understanding when Mom had to be in the study working on her book. And finally, I am grateful to Glen, who after reading my work so much, is actually starting to sound like me. I feel blessed by his love and support which gave me the privilege of having time to write and helped make it possible for me to complete this book.

1

INTRODUCTION

In graduate school, my dissertation advisor told me, "People usually do research on the issues they're trying to work out in their own lives." That was true about me then, and it still is now.

Since the early 1980s, I have been doing what feels like my life's work, educating about diversity and social justice. I have done so in a range of contexts—universities, non-profit agencies, schools, women's organizations, and community groups; in different roles—as a professor, trainer, consultant, facilitator, and Affirmative Action Officer; and with various groups of people—students (of all ages), teachers, counselors, administrators, managers, staff, board members, police, local citizens, and activists.

This has been an ongoing learning experience, both personally and professionally. Issues of oppression and multiculturalism have complex histories and continually evolve. New concerns and manifestations of inequality emerge as social, political, and economic changes occur in our country and throughout the world. Demographics shift and social dynamics become increasingly complex. Personally, I am continually faced with trying to stay abreast of current issues, working on raising my own consciousness, and exploring the significance of my own social identities. Professionally, as the social climate changes, so does how we need to educate for social justice. People's attitudes about different groups shift, as do their ways of explaining inequalities. Different concerns become more prominent which evoke new sets of feelings and reactions.

One of the most challenging aspects of social justice education is working with people from privileged or dominant groups—those who are in the more powerful position in a particular type of oppression. At times, I have been impressed and humbled by their degree of openness, courage, and risk-taking. At other times, I have been frustrated, angered, and stymied by their unwillingness to consider new information, rethink assumptions, or express concern for others. It is in the latter situations that I, and many of my colleagues, have struggled with the most.

I believe it is critical that we are able to engage people from privileged groups in social justice issues. From a simple educational perspective, most educators will have a mix of people in their classes or groups, including those from dominant groups. In order for sessions to run smoothly and for learning to be maximized, ideally, all participants should be productively involved. From a social change perspective, people from privileged groups perpetuate oppression through individual acts, as well as through institutional and cultural practices. They have access to resources, information, and power that can either block or help facilitate change. People from privileged groups who are allies can influence decision-making, allocate funds, share needed skills and knowledge, and be role models for other dominant group members to support equity. It also helps to have people from privileged groups as part of the change effort. Even though more people from oppressed groups are likely to push for greater social justice, as people from privileged groups join in the struggle, it increases the critical mass needed to affect change. Furthermore, if we care about liberation, we need to care about liberating all people. As I'll discuss further, oppression diminishes all human beings.

My experiences, both positive and negative, and my commitment to justice, led me to write this book. In part, I was involved in a quest to more effectively understand and work with people from dominant groups on social justice issues. I wanted to be a better educator and change agent. I also wanted to share with others what I have learned and found useful. As I have presented some of this material at conferences, workshops, and classes, I have found people hungry for ways to think about and address diversity issues, especially with people from privileged groups. My choice to focus on working with people from dominant groups in no way implies that this is more important than working with people from oppressed groups. It is a response to my own experiences and to what I perceived as a need in the field. Some people have referred to the growing focus on educating people from privileged groups about and for social justice as "pedagogy for the privileged" (Curry-Stevens, 2007) or "pedagogy of the oppressor" (Kimmel, 2010).

I am extremely fortunate to have had graduate training in a program focused on Diversity and Social Justice Training (at the University of Massachusetts in Amherst). The courses on oppression theory, workshop design, psychological education, group dynamics, developmental theories, and workshops on racism, sexism, heterosexism, classism, ableism, and anti-Semitism were invaluable. And while not my only source of education, I am indebted to the faculty and students there who provided me with such rich learning opportunities (and who continue to be valued colleagues).

Many people educating about social justice do so with very little training in how to do this type of education. Often people are well-versed in content areas, but less trained or skilled in issues of pedagogy or process. Generally, people rely on their natural talent, intuition, and trial and error. These are indispensable. Yet, I find I am most effective when I can also draw on other theories and frameworks. These allow me to make better sense of what is occurring and inform my responses. This background helps me plan my approaches and anticipate reactions.

In this book, I share some of the theories, perspectives, and strategies I have found most useful when working with adults from privileged groups on diversity and social justice issues. It is written for practitioners who already have a commitment to these issues. I am not trying to convince readers of the existence of oppression or of the need to value differences and promote equity. My hope is that these theoretical tools will allow educators to be more reflective and intentional in their work—helping them to consider who they're working with, what they're doing, why they're doing it, and how to educate more effectively. The fields of education and psychology are heavily drawn upon. Yet, in doing so, I attempt to continually consider the individual in social context, to embed a psychological analysis within a structural analysis. I want to recognize the interplay between the external and the internal, how the socio-political context affects individual attitudes and behaviors, and thus our classroom dynamics.

Some general principles and practices are reviewed that are helpful in most educational situations, but they are discussed in relation to working with people from dominant groups. This is not a how-to book, providing detailed activities and exercises; nor is it a cookbook that promises that if you follow this simple recipe, you'll have a perfect educational experience. I offer educational and psychological perspectives to inform one's practice and increase one's options in addressing situations. I'll suggest approaches, but will not supply easy answers. There are none. I try not to be prescriptive, but in an effort to be concrete, examples and specific suggestions are offered. I encourage readers to take and adapt what is useful. This is not everything you need to know to teach about diversity and social justice. Readers are referred to the appendix for some additional resources, especially for ideas for particular activities. An explanation of the title will further clarify the focus of the book.

About the Title

Promoting Diversity and Social Justice

The term *diversity* has become a buzzword with a variety of connotations and synonyms. Schools are addressing *multiculturalism*, businesses are learning to *value diversity*, and our society is grappling with *cultural pluralism*. These efforts usually promote the understanding, acceptance, and appreciation of cultural differences. In order for people to live together in a caring and just world, this is important work. Consciousness-raising can increase an awareness of self and others. It allows people to challenge stereotypes, overcome prejudices, and develop relationships with different kinds of people. It can help individuals enlarge their narrow worldview and recognize that there are other legitimate ways of thinking, being, and doing. At times, diversity training allows people to work and live together more productively and peacefully.

Unfortunately, most diversity work stops here. It tends to focus on individuals and interpersonal dynamics. I add the words *social justice* to indicate that I advocate going further. Social justice also involves addressing issues of equity, power relations, and institutionalized oppression. It seeks to establish a more equitable distribution of power and resources, so all people can live with dignity, self-determination, and physical and psychological safety. It creates opportunities for people to reach their full potential within a mutually responsible, interdependent society. Working toward social justice requires changing unjust institutional structures, policies, and practices, and challenging the dominant ideology. Social justice educators seek to create the conditions required for a true democracy, one that includes the full and equal participation of all groups in the society. I am finding, in fact, that people are increasingly using the term *social justice* to indicate that they are addressing issues of power and privilege, not just cultural differences.

Educating

I use this term in the broadest sense. I do not limit education to only classrooms, or teacher–student relationships. Anytime we help people learn, think, and grow, we are involved in education. Educating involves increasing knowledge, developing skills, raising consciousness, and enhancing critical thinking. Social justice education takes many forms in many contexts, from lectures in formal classroom settings to conversations over the kitchen table to policy presentations in conference rooms.

This book is intended for anyone who educates others about diversity and equity. While the primary focus is on professors, teachers, and trainers in classrooms and workshops, others who are involved in social change—such as counselors, organizers, student affairs personnel, community educators, advocates, and group facilitators—may find this information relevant. The principles and perspectives discussed can be applied to a range of situations and audiences. Therefore, I will use a variety of terms to reflect different contexts and relationships: teacher, facilitator, educator, trainer, as well as student and participant. I hope the language (i.e., teacher and student) will not interfere with translating and applying the concepts and strategies to other situations.

The people we encounter in our classes, workshops, and meetings are often starting from different places in the educational process. They come with varying knowledge, attitudes, experiences, predispositions, prejudices, and expectations about diversity and social justice issues. On one end of this continuum may be people who are highly resistant to exploring multicultural issues. They may be very defensive and close-minded. Others may be cautiously open to new information and perspectives. They are guarded but willing to consider some alternative views. Some may be eager to explore these issues and are looking for ways to make change. They embrace the opportunity to grapple with diversity issues and to expand their awareness. Occasionally, on the other end of the continuum, we get people who are already committed to social justice and are anxious to further their growth and take positive action. Ultimately, I would like people from privileged groups to be committed to being allies and able to act in solidarity with people from oppressed groups (and others from privileged groups) to promote equity. Social justice education is about facilitating movement along this continuum.

As I will discuss at length, when people are resistant, they are unwilling to learn. Our first step is to reduce resistance and create an openness to the educational process. Once people are in a more neutral state, we can consider how to challenge apathy and spark interest. As concern and commitment grow, we need to nurture this development and foster ways to act on their convictions. In this book, I focus on a few places on this continuum from resistance to alliance. The first is on resistance—how to understand the reasons for resistance, and ways to prevent and address it. The second is on motivating support for social justice—exploring why people from privileged groups support equity and developing ways to appeal to and encourage this in our educational work. The third is on allies and action. This offers options for people from privileged groups who have developed a desire to foster change and need ways to consider how to do so effectively.

People from Privileged Groups

The term *people from privileged groups* implies that there are people from non-privileged groups. Systems of oppression are characterized by dominant–subordinate relations. There are unequal power relationships that allow one group to benefit at the expense of another group. The various ways people name the two sides of this dynamic reflect these qualities: oppressor and oppressed; advantaged and disadvantaged; dominant and subordinated; agent and target; privileged and marginalized; dominator and dominated; majority and minority. While I am not fully comfortable with any of the existing language, I will use a variety of terms to refer to groups in the more and less powerful roles. I chose the term "privileged group" for the title since it is the term that people seem most familiar with. Yet, I also use the term "dominant group" since it reflects the fact that this group not only gets unearned privileges and has greater social power, but also sets the social norms. Its values, images, and experiences are most pervasive in and representative of the culture—in other words, dominant. In using such language, I in no way imply that there are any inherent qualities that make either group deserving of their status. These are socially constructed and reproduced social dynamics; people in power decide which characteristics to use to categorize and rank people.

The categories and language to refer to different groups of individuals are imperfect and problematic for a variety of reasons. The power elite have used the categorizing and naming of groups for the purposes of control and domination. The Colonists used the racial category "White" as a way to consolidate their power and continue to enslave Africans and Native Americans. Furthermore, the ways identities are socially constructed and valued changes. When the Irish, and later Jews, first came to this country, they were not considered White by the dominant group (White Anglo-Saxon Protestants), but were granted that status in order to prevent them from aligning with African Americans (Ignatiev, 1995; Sacks, 2010). With the American with Disabilities Act (1990), we are continually redefining who is considered to have a "disability". We are ascribed membership in a dominant or subordinated group simply based on our social identity. Oppression operates based on how society (the privileged group) views and names individuals, not necessarily how people define themselves.

In addition, people often do not fit neatly into these "boxes". Dividing people into dominant and subordinated groups reflects and promotes dualistic and dichotomous thinking. It implies that people can easily be classified into one group or the other (i.e., White *or* a person of color, able-bodied *or* disabled) (Rosenblum & Travis, 1996, pp. 14–25). Yet, there are degrees, gradations, and variations within and between social groups. Theorists and activists working on issues related to sex, sexual identity, and gender identity/expression have been in the forefront of challenging this binary system (cf. Butler, 1990, 2004; Califa, 1997; Nestle, Howell, & Wilchins, 2002, Wilchins, 1997). The recognition of people who are intersex, transgender or queer, challenge and complicate simplistic and limiting ways of categorizing people.

Even though there are numerous problems with trying to organize people into dominant or subordinated groups, I think it is helpful in order to discuss power relationships and dynamics of oppression. Even though these categories are socially constructed, they have real implications for people's lives. The following chart (Figure 1.1) outlines some of the most common types of oppression in the United States and some of the corresponding dominant and subordinated groups. I have chosen to use a continuum since people experience varying degrees of advantage or disadvantage within the same category of oppression. People to the left of the dividing line are privileged while people to the right of the dividing line are oppressed but the extent of their access to power or their experience of marginalization may differ. For example, people who are middle class are considered privileged yet they could be placed closer to the center line since they have relatively less class privilege than someone who is upper class, who would be at the far left of the continuum. Two people may identify as African American, but depending on their skin color, their treatment and opportunities might be different. In addition, the names used to depict people on either side of the continuum do not necessarily reflect all the groups that could be included as part of the dominant or subordinated group but are examples (such as in religious oppression which does not list all the marginalized religious groups) or an umbrella term (like "transgender", which includes people who are transsexuals, genderqueer, transmasculine, transfeminine, gender non-conforming, and others). Given that the forms of systemic inequality and names of social identities continually evolve, it is essential that educators regularly update the categories and language we use. Also, there is not necessarily consensus on how "isms" and groups should be named. This is not an exhaustive

DOMINANT	SUBORDINATED
RACISM (race)	
People of European Descent (Whites)	People of African, Asian, Latin, Native American, and Middle Eastern Descent (People of Color and Multi-Racial People)
SEXISM (biological sex)	
Males	Females Intersex People
HETEROSEXISM (sexual identity)	
Heterosexuals	People who are Lesbian, Gay, Bisexual, Queer, Asexual
TRANSGENDER OPPRESSION (gender identity/expression)	
Gender Conforming Biological Males and Females	Transgender People
CLASSISM (socio-economic status)	
Upper-class People Middle-class People	Working-class People Poor People
ABLEISM (ability)	
Temporarily Able-Bodied People	People with Disabilities
AGEISM (age)	
Youth and Middle Adults	Elders
RELIGIOUS OPPRESSION (religion)	
Christians	Jews, Muslims, Hindus, Atheists, and other religious minorities
XENOPHOBIA (nationality)	
Native Born People	Non-Native Born People

FIGURE 1.1 Oppression Chart

list; I could include several others as well, such as oppression based on ethnicity, language, size/appearance, and age (children). Their lack of inclusion in the chart does not imply that these types of oppression are less important or less harmful. I encourage readers to apply what is relevant to other forms of social injustice.

Although these forms of oppression occur globally, my focus will be on how they operate within the United States.

Moreover, we all have multiple social identities which, depending on the social category, may place us in either a dominant or subordinated group, on different sides of the power dynamic. I, like most others, am part of both advantaged and disadvantaged groups. For example, I am a woman and a Jew, and therefore part of the subordinated group in sexism and anti-Semitism or religious oppression. Yet, I am also White, heterosexual, able-bodied, middle-class, U.S. born and in my middle adult years, which makes me a member of several privileged groups as well. Our particular constellation of social identities shapes our experiences and our sense of self. When we're part of an advantaged group, our subordinated identities may mitigate but not eliminate our access to power and privilege just as additional privileged identities may enhance it.

Throughout the book, I refer to individuals from privileged groups and, in doing so, imply that there are some shared experiences for members from different privileged groups as well as for people from the same privileged group. However, I recognize that people have other identities that make up who they are and affect their experience and identity as a dominant group member. Our individual social identities are distinct but interrelated. Even as I focus on a single privileged identity, it is important to remember that all aspects of our social identities simultaneously interact (e.g. being middle class, female, and Jewish impacts my experience of being White). An intersectional paradigm is increasingly being utilized to understand experiences of identity, privilege, and oppression (Anderson & Collins, 2010; Berger & Guidroz, 2009; Dill & Zambrana, 2009; Luft & Ward, 2009).

Obviously, in reality, one's dominant group identity cannot be isolated from his/her other social identities. Yet, in order to explore the meaning of being part of a privileged group, I have found it helpful to temporarily narrow the lens to focus on this dimension of one's experience. Others who advocate an intersectional perspective (cf. Luft & Ward, 2009) recognize that at times, especially at an introductory level, it may be more useful to have a single identity focus. Without first understanding how systems of privilege and oppression function, it can be difficult to grasp how these occur in more complex combinations. In addition, people from a privileged group can too easily shift the focus to their subordinated identity(ies) and avoid acknowledging their experience of privilege. However, once a foundation has been established, people can more readily explore how their own and other people's experiences of privilege are affected by their other intersecting identities.

Even though I continually try to keep present the fact that other social positions do make a difference and that all dominant groups are not the same, for the purpose of clarity and simplicity, I speak in more general terms. Frameworks that seek to simplify and make accessible complicated dynamics never capture the full complexity of the situation or issue. These models, concepts, and language can be useful as *pedagogical* tools, ways to help people recognize social dynamics, and their role in them. Please keep in mind that the map is not the territory. I hope educators will be able to highlight the variations and intricacies as they work with these topics in their particular settings.

As I wrote about people from privileged groups I struggled with whether to use the term "they" or "we", since depending on what identity I thought of, I could be one of "them" or not. For the most part, I refer to people from privileged groups with the less personal term "they," since I am not part of the dominant group in all cases. (I use the term "we" to refer to other educators.) When I refer to people from dominant groups, I am not referring to people who are part of the privileged group in all forms of oppression—White, heterosexual, Christian, middle-aged, able-bodied, native-born, middle/upper class men. I am only referring to people who, within a particular type of oppression, are part of the advantaged group.

Benefits and Limitations of Discussing Privileged Groups in General

Instead of choosing to focus on educating Whites about racism, or men about sexism, or heterosexuals about heterosexism, I have chosen to focus on educating people from privileged groups, in general. In utilizing this approach, I hope to highlight the common roots and the interlocking nature of systems of domination. There are many similar dynamics, patterns, and themes across different forms of oppression (Adair & Howell, 1988). Many of the same issues are encountered when working with people from privileged groups, regardless of the particular "ism". Because I, along with many others, educate about multiple forms of oppression, I thought this book would be more useful if it was kept broader, instead of narrowing it to only one type of oppression.

However, this does not mean that I think all forms of oppression are the same or that there are no differences in educating people from different dominant groups. Each type of oppression has particular characteristics and dynamics. For example, with sexism and racism, one's identity and dominant or subordinated status is usually fairly fixed. However, with ageism it is natural that it changes, and with classism and ableism, it is possible that it will. With sexism and ageism, there are usually close, even intimate relationships, between members of the dominant and subordinated groups, whereas with racism and heterosexism it is often possible for people from the dominant groups to avoid close relationships with members of the subordinated groups. There are also different attitudes toward the disadvantaged group. In racism, there is often fear; in ableism, pity; in heterosexism and trans-gender oppression, revulsion; in xenophobia, anger and in ageism, condescension. With some forms of oppression it is easier for some members of the oppressed group to "pass", such as with heterosexism, anti-Semitism, and classism, yet more difficult or nearly impossible for other people from subordinated groups, such as with sexism, racism, or ableism (if the person has an obvious disability). There are also different histories and social functions of the oppression (i.e., the particular use and treatment of African Americans in this country, the rise of Islamophobia since 9/11, etc). Young (1990) identifies five "faces of oppression" which include exploitation, marginalization, powerlessness, cultural imperialism, and violence. A social group may be considered oppressed if it experiences one or more of these conditions. Therefore, the type and degree of oppressive actions enacted and experienced may vary as well.

All of these differences warrant attention when educating about social justice. They also have implications for educating privileged group members about different forms of oppression. Even though there are many common responses and generally effective strategies, we are likely to encounter specific types of reactions when educating about certain types of oppression. For example, when addressing heterosexism, we are likely to find resistance based on moral and religious beliefs, which is unlikely to occur with other "isms". With classism, I have found that critiques of capitalism and our classist system can quickly evoke defensiveness and distorted views of other economic systems. People feel that their desire for upward mobility is being threatened or criticized, and that the only alternative is some version of repressive communism. Red-baiting may also occur.

There are clearly some limitations or dangers in choosing this broad, inclusive approach. Some of the nuances and distinctiveness of particular forms of oppression are sacrificed. What is gained in generalizability is lost in specificity. My intention is not to deny or obscure differences among various forms of oppression, though some of this occurs when speaking more generally. Using an inclusive framework does not eliminate the need to provide a more in-depth treatment of particular topics and "isms". This broader approach also means that I will not be able to adequately deal with issues that are unique to educating about specific forms of oppression. Given these various constraints, I strongly urge readers to utilize the resources listed in the appendix and available elsewhere, to gain the needed information to address these concerns.

Overview of the Book

In this chapter, I lay out the purpose, rationale, and parameters of the book. The concepts of privileged groups and social identities are clarified. Chapter 2 focuses on describing privileged groups in order to develop a better understanding of the people with whom we are working. I highlight key characteristics of dominant groups and dominant group members, discuss how multiple identities affect the experience of privilege, and explore the resistance to seeing oneself as privileged. Chapter 3 reviews several theories of individual development and change. These perspectives aid in creating environments and approaches that meet the needs of different individuals and that facilitate the learning process. In Chapter 4, I define and explore the various socio-political and psychological reasons for resistance from people of privileged groups. By understanding some of the sources of the resistance, we can better address it. This is the focus of Chapter 5 in which I discuss a range of strategies to prevent and address the resistance we may encounter when working with dominant group members. Chapter 6 presents a host of psychological, social, intellectual, moral/spiritual, and material costs of oppression to people from privileged groups. This challenges the win–lose framework that assumes that people from dominant groups solely receive benefits from injustice and would only lose out if there were greater equity. Chapter 7 describes the benefits people from privileged groups have gained by engaging in a process of unlearning privilege and oppression, and offers visions of healing and liberation. Chapter 8 then moves to why people from privileged groups would support social justice. I discuss how empathy, moral and spiritual values, and self-interest are key sources of motivation. Chapter 9 explores how to build on these elements to develop and enlist support for change. I demonstrate the importance of meeting people where they are, addressing their needs and concerns, and offering positive alternatives to our social, political, and economic systems. Chapter 10 focuses on allies and action. I describe how to be an effective ally, ways to sustain commitment, and avenues for working for social justice. The final chapter turns to issues for social justice educators. I consider how our own social identity development impacts our work, factors that affect our educational efficacy, and ways to enhance our effectiveness as educators and change agents.

Educating about diversity and social justice is a challenging yet rewarding endeavor. It is a never-ending process and an ongoing opportunity to learn. Many of the ideas in the book are works in progress and I offer them as contributions to the growing field of people struggling with how to best educate for social justice. I hope that they will advance our efforts to work with people from privileged groups and, as a result, strengthen our collective ability to make this world one that values and nourishes our full humanity. I welcome your thoughts and feedback. You can reach me through the publisher or at **drdianegoodman@gmail.com** and visit my website http://www.dianegoodman.com.

2

ABOUT PRIVILEGED GROUPS

In any educational context, it is helpful to know your audience, to understand with whom you're working. Being a member of a privileged group affects one's worldview, assumptions, and behavior. In this chapter, I'll explore what it means to be part of a privileged group and the significance of this for our educational efforts. Specifically, I'll discuss some common characteristics of dominant groups and dominant group members, multiple identities and the experience of privilege, and the resistance to acknowledging one's privilege.

Characteristics of Privileged Groups

There are several key attributes of privileged groups. In the first part of the discussion, I will focus on what characterizes a dominant group. I will then consider the implications of these qualities for members of privileged groups. While I will focus on what is generally true for dominant groups, it is important to keep in mind that there are also significant variations among forms of oppression and among individuals.

Normalcy

The dominant cultural and societal norms are based on the characteristics of the privileged group (Wildman, 1996). The dominant group becomes the point of reference against which other groups are judged. It becomes "normal". This standard of normalcy is also used to define what is good and right. These cultural norms become institutionalized and establish policy and practice. Catherine MacKinnon (1989) illustrates how this is true about males.

Men's physiology defines most sports, their health needs largely define insurance coverage, their socially designed biographies define workplace expectations and successful career patterns, their perspectives and concerns define quality in scholarship, their experiences and obsessions define merit, their military service defines citizenship, their presence defines family, their inability to get along with each other—their wars and rulerships—defines history, their image defines god, and their genitals define sex. (p. 224)

White, Christian, middle-class, heterosexual norms pervade our culture. Schools are one place where this is evident. The communication patterns and cultural styles used in most educational settings are more typical of White, upper-middle-class families. There is an emphasis on individualistic learning, competition, and quiet and controlled classrooms, as opposed to collectivist values, oral traditions, and more active behavior, which are more common in other cultural groups (Delpit, 1995; Greenfield & Cocking, 1996; Viadro, 1996). The structure and content of standardized tests have been based on White, middle-class males, giving rise to concerns about gender and racial bias (Sadker, Sadker, & Zittleman, 2009; Santelices & Wilson, 2010). The conformity, or lack thereof, to these norms has significant impact on educational success and achievement. For example, one study (Morns, 2007) found that teachers tend to view the behavior of Black girls as not "ladylike" and discourage behaviors and characteristics that lead to their class involvement and academic achievement.

This is also true in the workplace. Consider the style of speech and dress required for success in the business world. "Proper English", suits or other "professional attire", and a refined interpersonal style are the accepted standards. A study of the experiences of women, Jews, Blacks, Asians, Latinos, and gay men and lesbians in positions of corporate leadership found that while the faces may be more diverse, the behaviors and values remain the same (Domhoff & Zweigenhaft, 1998a). To be successful, these groups must conform to the norms and expectations of the domi- nant group. "Hedging against traditional stereotypes, Jewish and Black executives must be properly reserved, Asian executives properly assertive, gay executives tra- ditionally masculine, and lesbian executives traditionally feminine" (Domhoff & Zweighenhaft, 1998b, p. 44). People cannot be "too Jewish", "too Black", or "too gay".

The image of a "good family" (still) consists of a mother who is home raising children and a father who is earning the money. When I recently bought a house, I got a strong dose of these cultural norms. I made many calls about hiring someone to do work in the house, saying only that I recently bought it and my full name (first and last). With a few exceptions, people referred to me as Mrs Goodman, assumed that I had a "handy husband" and that I would be home during the day. The possibility that I might be single or a lesbian was not part of most people's thinking.

Other cultural norms are also widespread. I became painfully aware that I was not part of the norm when I attended a huge educational conference in a major hotel in San Francisco during the week of Passover and there was not a matzoh in sight. (Matzoh is unleavened cracker-like bread eaten by Jews during Passover as a substitute for leavened bread which is not allowed.) Look in most mainstream card stores and notice how often you see a person with a disability, a person of color or a gay couple on the front, unless the card is targeted for that particular population. Whiteness as the norm in skin tone was revealed in reports about the color of a gown worn by First Lady Michelle Obama which described it as "nude" or "flesh-tone" (later, revised to "champagne") (Critchell, 2010). It is particularly ironic since Mrs Obama is African American and the dress hardly matched her skin tone, clearly evident in all the pictures.

We often become aware of the norms when we are exposed to the reverse or an exception. Try switching to all female pronouns when reading something using the generic "he". When I visited Atlanta, I was struck the first time I saw brown mannequins throughout a department store, despite having lived around New York City and other urban areas of the Northeast. Guided fantasies which reverse the norms, such as ones where homosexuality is the most common and accepted form of sexual orientation also illustrate what we take for granted as standard and appropriate.

Moreover, we tend to indicate the identity of individuals only when they are not what we consider the norm, otherwise their social identity is assumed and unnamed. People are likely to refer to the "woman doctor", "Arab store-owner", "Latino businessman", "lesbian teacher" or "disabled lawyer", even when their social identity is not significant to the story. Yet how often would someone use the terms "male", "White", "able-bodied," or "heterosexual" to refer to individuals in similar positions? Sometimes, only through exposure to difference can we begin to see what we have become accustomed to and take to be "normal".

An example of how notions of normalcy get internalized is illustrated in a conversation I had with my daughter when she was eight. She was describing how a friend of hers who is bi-racial—Chinese and White, was being teased because of the shape of her eyes. In the course of this conversation, Halle said, "But my eyes are just. ... " She paused to search for the right word. She finished her sentence by hesitantly saying "normal." I used this teachable moment to offer her other language to describe her eyes (oval) and to discuss how what is "normal" depends on the context (in China, her friend's eyes would be considered "normal") and that things can be different without having to be considered "normal" or not.

When a group is part of the norm, they also get seen and see themselves as "objective" and "neutral". Other groups have biases and agendas. This was evident in the confirmation hearing of Judge Sonia Sotomayor to the Supreme Court. There was much discussion (and concern) about how her being a woman and Latina would shape her decisions, but virtually no discussion about how being male and White influences the decisions of the other Justices.

Superiority

This sense of normalcy also leads to a sense of superiority. Not only is it normal, it's better. Differences get converted into "better or worse" with the attributes of the dominant group the winners. For example, not only is "standard English" more socially accepted, it is considered "better" than other cultural dialects. Not only are heterosexual nuclear families considered more "common" than gay or lesbian families, they are considered the "best" family structure. White (European) culture, as expressed in music, art, dance, and literature is considered more sophisticated than and superior to the cultures of other racial/ethnic groups (which may be considered interesting but "primitive").

The conversion of differences into notions of superiority/inferiority, is seen in a study to assess children's attitudes, beliefs, and social preferences about children with different skin tones. (http://cnn.com, May 2010). Children in early childhood and middle school were asked various questions to see which skin tones (ranging from light to dark) they associated with positive and negative traits (e.g. smart, dumb, nice, mean, etc). The children, as a whole, revealed a "White bias", associating lighter skin with positive attributes and darker skin with negative attributes, though White children expressed a far greater bias.

Even the same traits may be named and valued differently depending on whether they are associated with a privileged or an oppressed group. Christians are "thrifty" while Jews are "cheap"; heterosexual men are "studs" while gay men are "promiscuous"; men are "leaders" while women are "bitches"; Whites are "shrewd" while Asians are "sneaky". Privileged groups uphold their own attributes as preferable while distorting and disparaging the qualities of others.

Superiority is not always conveyed in blatant and intentional ways. It is the expectation (often unconscious) that people of color should assimilate to White norms in order to be acceptable and accepted. A similar process occurs when women are expected to adopt "male" styles of leadership and communication in order to be viewed as competent and effective in the workplace (though, they can't be too "masculine" either). Trying to get people from disadvantaged groups to be "more like us" is usually a sign of supremacy at work, carrying the implicit message that "our way" is better.

This sense of superiority extends from the characteristics and culture of the dominant group to the individuals themselves. Oppression is commonly defined, in part, as the belief in the inherent superiority of one group over another. This influences how people are viewed and treated. People in professional positions are considered worthier of respect than people in working-class jobs. There is usually more public outcry when a White woman is raped or a White child is killed than when this occurs to a woman or child of color. People with developmental disabilities have been seen as appropriate guinea pigs for dangerous medical experiments. Even at the level of the Supreme Court, Judge Ruth Bader Ginsberg related an experience familiar to many women when she discussed how in conferences with the other Supreme Court judges, her points were often ignored until they were made by one of the male judges (Lewis, 2009).

People from disadvantaged groups are generally labeled as substandard or aberrant. They are assumed to be less capable due to innate defects or deficiencies (Miller, 1976). For example, women are too emotional, Blacks are less intelligent, gays are morally deviant, and people with disabilities are defective. Not only are people from subordinated groups somehow inferior, but by logical extension, people from dominant groups are superior. This reasoning allows privileged groups to rationalize the systematic unfair treatment of people from oppressed groups and to feel entitled to power and privilege.

Cultural and Institutional Power and Domination

Oppression involves unequal social power—access and control of resources, goods, and rewards/punishments that enhance one's capacity to get what one needs and influence others. This allows for domination, the ability for one social group to systematically subjugate, control, manipulate, and use other people for its own ends. Social power and domination is created and maintained through interpersonal, institutional, and cultural forces. The privileged group creates systems and structures that reflect its values, embodies its characteristics, and advances its interests. A structural perspective on inequality recognizes the role of public policies and institutional practices, not simply individual attitudes, in developing and perpetuating societal inequality. People are increasingly using the term "White supremacy", not to refer to racial extremists, but to describe how notions of White superiority are embedded in our institutions and ideology. Unequal power systems are sustained by shaping people's worldviews, controlling resources, and constraining opportunities.

Since social oppression has both ideological and structural dimensions, it can take many forms. At times, it is blatant and coercive and the advantages to the privileged group are clear, such as with Jim Crow laws or forced (uninformed) sterilization. Often, however, it is more subtle and insidious, with less obvious benefits to the privileged group, such as media images that portray women as sex objects, or economic policies that maintain some unemployment to ensure a pool of cheap, surplus labor.

Privileged groups define the mainstream culture—behavior patterns, symbols, institutions, values, and other human-made components of society (Banks, 1991). They determine what is acceptable and unacceptable, what is valued and ignored. Other groups are relegated as "subcultures". For example, the dominant cultural norms are reflected in our standards of beauty. The image of a beautiful woman is someone who is young, extremely thin, tall, light-skinned, with Anglo features, and finely textured hair, and often blond and blue-eyed. According to mainstream time norms, people should be ruled by the clock. People are expected to be prompt and to end meetings according to pre-arranged times. Other cultural groups are more relaxed about time, and begin and complete activities when they feel ready to do so. Often, this is seen as lazy and undisciplined.

Advantaged groups also establish the dominant ideology—a pervasive set of ideas and ways of looking at reality. The dominant ideology forms individual consciousness and both justifies and conceals domination (Kreisberg, 1992, p. 15). The concept of "hegemony" (Gramsci & Forgacs, 2000) describes the ways in which the privileged group imposes their conception of reality in a manner accepted as common sense, as "normal" and as universal. As Jean Baker Miller (1976) explains,

"A dominant group has the greatest influence in determining a culture's overall outlook—its philosophy, morality, social theory and even its science. The dominant group, thus, legitimizes the unequal relationship and incorporates it into society's guiding concepts"(p. 8). This dominant ideology, which I discuss in more depth in Chapter 4, is embedded in institutional structures and practices that shape our consciousness and experiences. What we learn (and don't learn) in school, what we see (and don't see) in the media, how we are expected to act at work, how our economy is structured, who are held up as role models, and what research gets funded and validated, reflects and reinforces the dominant ideology. This informs our sense of what is important, true, and real about ourselves, others, and the world. This power to define reality is labeled "true power" by Derald Sue (2010a). He explains, "When a clash of realities occur, mainstream groups have the tools—education, mass media, peer social groups and institutions to define and impose realities upon other groups" (p. 46).

When privileged groups have greater institutional power, it allows them to establish policies and procedures that can provide, deny or limit opportunities and access to resources and social power. In 2007, the top 1% of the population owned almost 35% of the privately held wealth in the US; the top 20% controlled approximately 85% of the wealth in this country (Wolff, 2010); in 2010, only about 3% of CEOs of the Fortune 500 companies were women (Catalyst, 2010); and women and people of color are still grossly underrepresented in Congress. They exercise control over access to health care, housing, education, employment, political representation, fair judicial treatment, and legal rights.

Privileged groups also define acceptable roles for people in subordinated groups. These roles usually involve providing services that people from advantaged groups do not want to do or do not highly value. This social manipulation impedes human dignity and self-determination. Conversely, people from privileged groups can provide benefits to others from their own social group—by sharing information, providing jobs, creating laws and policies, contributing money, making appointments to boards and committees, and facilitating social and political connections.

The control of the dominant belief system and major institutions results in psychological domination as well. People from both privileged and marginalized groups often begin to accept the messages from the dominant culture of dominant group superiority and subordinated group inferiority. When this is absorbed by people from the privileged group, it is sometimes called "internalized superiority/supremacy."

Sometimes it is conscious, but often "it is the unconscious, internalized values and attitudes that maintain domination, even when people do not support or display overt discrimination or prejudice" (hooks, 1989, p. 13). For people from oppressed groups, "internalized oppression" or "internalized inferiority" undermines their self-esteem, sense of empowerment, and intragroup solidarity. It encourages unhealthy, dysfunctional behavior. In addition, people from oppressed groups are encouraged to develop personal and psychological characteristics that are pleasing to the privileged group—being submissive, dependent, docile (Miller, 1976). As long as people believe that they are inferior or deserve their situation, consider their treatment fair or for their own benefit, or are constrained in their self-development, they will not effectively challenge the current system.

Since the dominant ideology is embedded in our institutional practices and individual consciousness, for oppression to continue, we just need to act "normally", to go along with the status quo. It does not require malice or bad intentions to perpetuate systems of domination. We have been conditioned to see our social systems as normal and natural, even if some societal inequities are recognized.

Since only privileged groups have institutional power and the ability to systematically enforce their views, only they may be "oppressive" (e.g. racist, sexist, ableist, etc). Certainly, people from *all* social groups (advantaged and disadvantaged) have prejudices and may act in discriminatory ways. Women may stereotype men, gays may deride heterosexuals, and Latinos may favor other Latinos for jobs. However, I, like many others, make the distinction between oppression and other terms such as prejudice, bigotry or bias. None of the oppressed groups has the societal power to systematically disadvantage the corresponding privileged group. Consequently, from this line of thinking, there is no "reverse racism" even though people of color can act in hurtful, unfair ways toward White people. The shorthand definition "prejudice + social power = oppression" is useful to capture this distinction.

Privilege

Oppression involves both systematic disadvantage *and* advantage. This "system of advantage" (Wellman, 1977) bestows on people from privileged groups greater access to power, resources, and opportunities that are denied to others and usually gained at their expense. Most discussions of social injustice focus on the subjugation of oppressed groups—the ways in which they are discriminated against, marginalized, exploited, manipulated, demeaned, and physically and emotionally attacked. Less attention is given to the other part of the dynamic—the privileging of the dominant group.

Social oppression creates privilege systems—benefits or unearned advantages systematically afforded people from dominant groups simply because of their social group membership. " ... What makes something a privilege is the unequal way in which it is distributed and the effect it has on elevating some people over others"

(Johnson, 2005, p. 175). It includes what we are able to take for granted or not have to think about simply because we are part of an advantaged group; people from disadvantaged groups cannot make the same assumptions. Peggy McIntosh (1988) describes White privilege as "an invisible weightless knapsack of special provisions, maps, passports, codebooks, visas, clothes, tools and blank checks" (p. 71). Privileges can be both material and psychological; they can include concrete benefits as well as psychological freedoms; often these are interrelated. McIntosh lists numerous privileges for Whites that reflect these two interconnected dimensions. She writes,

> I can go home from most meetings of the organizations I belong to feeling somewhat tied in, rather than isolated, out-of-place, outnumbered, unheard, feared or hated; I can arrange to protect my children most of the time from people who might not like them; I can go into a supermarket and find the food I grew up with, into a hairdresser's shop and find someone who can deal with my hair; I can be pretty sure that if I ask to talk to 'the person in charge' I will be facing a person of my race; I can be pretty sure that my children will be given curricular materials that testify to the existence of their race; I can take a job with an affirmative action employer without having co-workers on the job suspect that I got it because of my race; I can do well in a challenging situation without being called a credit to my race; I can swear, or dress in second hand clothes, or not answer letters, or be late to meetings without having people attribute these behaviors to the bad morals, the poverty, or the illiteracy of my race; I can think over many options, social, political, imaginative or professional, without asking whether a person of my race would be accepted or allowed to do what I want to do. (pp. 5–9)

(Using her work as a template, there are now lists of privileges for many other groups.)

Male privilege is evident in an exercise I do with groups of university men and women.[1] I ask them to describe what they do on a daily basis to ensure their safety. The men have a hard time coming up with a list. On the other hand, the women quickly cite numerous efforts: locking doors, walking with buddies, getting rides, avoiding certain areas, checking their cars, staying inside during late hours. Men have the privilege of being able to move about with less thought, worry, and constraint. (For men facing other forms of oppression—racism, classism, heterosexism, ableism—the privilege of safety may be significantly limited).

People with class privilege have access to the best medical care; to leisure and vacations; to good housing, food, and clothing; and to governmental financial advantages (e.g. tax breaks, write-offs for mortgages). They feel entitled to be treated respectfully, to be taken seriously, and to have opportunities to use their talents. They can choose work that may be meaningful, though not well-compensated, knowing they have a safety net—other marketable skills, opportunities for education, or financial resources. They can use connections to get jobs or to be admitted to college. It's interesting to note that when opportunities are gained due to connections, there is not the outcry about merit. On the other hand, affirmative action is constantly attacked (cf. Larew, 2010).

Able-bodied people do not have to think about access to buildings—for education, cultural events, employment, socializing; about travel—around one's own town, vacation areas, conference sites; or about needing assistance to do basic daily tasks. They do not fear that people will assume them to be less intelligent or less productive solely because of a (possibly irrelevant) disability. My privilege as a hearing person became starkly apparent at a conference I attended. One of the participants in a session I was facilitating was a woman who was deaf. The conference provided interpreters during the workshop. At one of the social events, she motioned me over to say hello to a colleague who was also deaf, but there was no interpreter. We were unable to communicate effectively since I didn't know sign language. Not only did I feel frustrated and disappointed that I was missing out on getting to know some interesting people, I realized how much I enjoyed and gained from being able to socialize and network with so many people at the conference while they sat by themselves, unable to interact with the rest of the participants.

People with Christian privilege do not have to take personal days to observe their religious holidays or worry whether institutional dining halls and cafeterias will have foods that meet their religious dietary needs. They can travel around the country and find churches they can attend and hear music on the radio or programs on TV that reflect their religion. Prayers at public occasions will usually be based on Christianity (even if they're intended to be non-denominational) and their holy day (Sunday) is taken into account when scheduling work, school, or public events (Blumenfeld, Joshi, & Fairchild, 2008; Schlosser, 2003; Seifert, 2007).

Heterosexuals can freely display public affection, talk openly about their partner, have their relationship publicly acknowledged and celebrated, and be protected from discrimination. They don't need to worry if it's all right to bring their partner to events (and then, if they can dance together); if they'll lose their job if they're "out"; if they'll be accepted by their neighbors, or if their partner will be considered "family" under hospital guidelines and thus be able to visit or make medical decisions.

I became aware of another aspect of heterosexual privilege when I worked on a committee against homophobia on a university campus. When I was hired to do human relations education, it was clear that few people on campus were willing to publicly deal with issues of heterosexism, despite the often stated need and some very active (though essentially closeted) gay and lesbian faculty and staff. I quickly formed a committee (open to everyone) to address gay, lesbian, and bisexual issues on campus (transgender issues weren't in people's consciousness then). There was a lot of interest and a strong representation of lesbians, gay men, and bisexuals. While we worked very collaboratively, I was the "chair" and "contact person"—regularly sending out notices of our meetings and events, being called by the student newspaper to report on our activities. On a campus that felt unsafe to most gays, I realized that as a heterosexual, I had more freedom to be public about working against homophobia than my lesbian and gay colleagues. I had the safety of not being "found out", despite assumptions that I was a lesbian. It felt like a privilege to be visible around this issue. (This is not to deny the fact that people from privileged groups do face risks when being allies.)

Promoting identification with superiority and privilege helps to prevent people from an advantaged group from allying with people from one of their disadvantaged groups. White poor and working class men have often used (and have been encouraged to use) their "whiteness" to feel privileged while rejecting an alliance with men of color in a similar class position (Roediger, 1991). They rely on racism and their sense of White privilege to create separation, instead of forging a common struggle against classism and economic exploitation.

Moreover, oppression is maintained not just by taking actions *against* disadvantaged groups but by increasing privileges *for* advantaged groups. "Inequality gets reproduced through advantages to Whites as much or more so than it does through discrimination against minorities" (DiTomaso, 2003). We need to examine both parts of the dynamic. For example, even when White women and people of color (and others from subordinated groups) are not actively denied jobs, unless they are included in the informal social network, mentored, encouraged to take on new responsibilities, and provided opportunities for professional development, the net effect will be that they will not advance at the same rate as White men. White men are being privileged even though White women and people of color may not be facing overt discrimination.

There is a growing recognition of how the history and cumulative effect of interlocking benefits for the dominant group affect current inequities, particularly related to race (California Newsreel, 2003; Katznelson, 2006; Lipsitz, 1998; Lui, Robles, Leondar-Wright, Brewer, & Adamson, 2006). There has been a legacy of institutional (including government) policies, as well as more informal practices, that have unfairly privileged people from dominant groups. "Histories of unearned advantages, unequal distribution of resources, the effects of housing segregation, access to job connections—these are the factors that reproduce the unequal outcomes that we see" (DiTomaso, 2003).

Moreover, people from dominant group receive privileges regardless of their individual attitudes. They neither have to be aware of the advantages nor want them to receive them.

> In the same way that men benefit from a patriarchal system by the way resources are distributed, even if they don't have antipathy toward women, white people are given the spoils of a racist system even if they're not personally racist. (Powell, 2003)

McIntosh also makes distinctions among privileges. She suggests that some are advantages that everyone is entitled to and should be a right; these need to be extended to all. Examples include having your neighbors be decent to you, not having your race work against you in employment, or not being followed or harassed in stores. Other privileges confer dominance and reinforce our present hierarchies, such as being able to ignore less powerful people, to manipulate our legal system to avoid punishment, to withhold information or resources, or to advance your interests to the detriment of others. These need to be rejected and eliminated. Therefore, as we examine privilege systems, we need to consider how privileges are constructed, how they are used to further systemic and structural inequality, and how to ensure that everyone has access to the privileges that should be human rights.

Individuals from Privileged Groups

Individuals are affected by being part of a privileged group and the dominant culture. Their experiences and perspectives are shaped by their social position. The effects of being dominant group members are reflected in people's attitudes, thinking, and behavior. I'll discuss several of the most common traits. Again, these vary according to the individual and their other social identities.

Lack of Consciousness

People from privileged groups tend to have little awareness of their own dominant identity, of the privileges it affords them, of the oppression suffered by the corresponding disadvantaged group, and of how they perpetuate it. In the first place, people from privileged groups generally do not think about their dominant group identity.

I conduct a couple of activities that highlight this point. At the beginning of a class or workshop, I'll ask people to introduce themselves by choosing words to describe who they are. People of color will virtually always refer to their racial/cultural identity, while someone who is White rarely will (Wildman, 1996 and Tatum, 1997 report similar findings).

In another activity, I list common social categories: race, sex, religion, sexual identity, ability/disability, class, age, and ethnicity, and ask people to choose the two or three that are most important to who they are, to their sense of identity. I later ask them to choose the three that feel least important. Again, most people include in their three most important identities subordinated ones (though depending on the group, people are less likely to reveal their sexual orientation if they are gay, lesbian, or bisexual). The three least important are dominant identities. The one consistent exception is sex; both females and males often include it in their top three. This is not surprising since sex is such a salient and referenced social category.

When these results are pointed out to people in the class, I ask them why they think this occurs and why they chose the identities they did. People who choose a subordinated identity as most important talk about feeling very aware of that identity—it makes them feel different, others make them aware of it, it has created obstacles to overcome, or it is where they get mistreated. On the other hand, they recognize that their dominant identity is something to which they generally do not need to pay attention.

Even though we are most exposed to information about privileged groups, people from these groups tend to have the least self-awareness about that aspect of their identity and its social significance. This absence of consciousness about their social identity, seems to, in part, reflect unequal power relationships. Miller (1976) maintains that people from dominant groups are deprived of feedback about their behavior from people from subordinated groups (since it's unsafe to tell), and therefore don't learn about their impact on others. Nor do mainstream institutions (media, schools) provide this kind of perspective. (I also think that most people from privileged groups are not interested in or are afraid of knowing anyway, a point discussed later.) Nonetheless, people from advantaged groups are allowed, in fact encouraged, to remain unaware. In contrast, people from disadvantaged groups become highly attuned to and knowledgeable about the dominant group since their survival depends on it.

This lack of awareness relates to being the norm, and therefore not needing to think about one's social identity. It's like being a fish in water—when you're surrounded by water as part of your natural environment, it's hard to be aware of it. And, this water has been filtered through the dominant ideology. People from privileged groups are surrounded by their culture and therefore don't notice it. This allows them to see themselves as individuals, not as part of a group that has social power and privilege. While members of other social groups may be lumped together, obliterating individual and intragroup differences, people from privileged groups tend to see themselves as unique individuals who succeed or fail based on their own merit.

Moreover, this "fish in water" phenomenon contributes to the lack of awareness people from dominant groups have about their privileges. Because the norm or reality is perceived as including these benefits, the privileges are not visible to the dominant group (Wildman, 1996). As I stated earlier, since privileges are things we usually take for granted and assume to exist, they therefore tend to be invisible. Frequently, we do not realize that something is a privilege until we compare it with the experience of the disadvantaged group. Several examples illustrate this occurrence.

One Sunday morning I was in New York City saying goodby to my then boyfriend. As we stood on the curb next to my car kissing, I heard some people down the block behind me clapping. We stopped, and as I slowly turned around, I saw four men sitting on the back of a truck laughing and applauding. I felt mortified. As I was recounting this episode to a lesbian friend of mine, it suddenly occurred to me how this was about heterosexual privilege. I could blithely and obliviously kiss on the street, and then be applauded for my action. I doubt that my gay or lesbian friends would so unconsciously kiss their lover in public, or that they would likely get such a positive reaction. I had the luxury of just worrying about being embarrassed.

I am usually unaware of my privilege as an able-bodied person until I am with a person who has a disability. For several days of a conference I was attending, I wandered about the large hotels looking for the sessions, joined friends for meals, and explored the city. I then met a colleague who used a wheelchair. She generally limited herself to the sessions that were being held in one hotel since navigating it was difficult enough. Trying to get out of the hotel, cross the streets, and move about other hotels was too time-consuming and exhausting. Finding an accessible place to have dinner became another issue. After spending most of the day together, we arrived back at our hotel and found that the elevator in the lobby that stopped at our floor was closed for the evening. Since the suggested alternative was up an escalator (which was impossible to do in a wheelchair), we ended up taking the freight elevator. Technically, the hotel and the conference were wheelchair accessible. However, it made me realize how much I take my mobility, and what it affords me, for granted.

In these previous examples, the privilege is clear if we try to become conscious of it. In other cases, the privilege is more hidden. In an effort to explore sex discrimination, the television show *Prime Time* matched a White man and a White woman on all variables except sex (e.g. overall appearance, education). (*The Fairer Sex*, 1993). They went out separately to look for jobs, buy a car, etc. Both applied for a job as a territory manager for a landscape business that was advertised in the newspaper. Even though based on their resumes she was better qualified for the job, when the man was interviewed he took an aptitude test and was told about managerial possibilities; when the woman was interviewed, she took a typing test and was asked about her secretarial skills.

They conducted a similar experiment with a White man and a Black man to examine racism (*True Colors*, 1992). In one situation, they both responded to an ad for an apartment to rent. The Black man was told that the apartment was rented, while the White man, who went in later, was told that the apartment was still available. In both of these situations, not only did the White man receive better treatment and more opportunities than the woman or Black man, but those options and advancements were gained at their expense. The White man had these chances because others were denied the same opportunity. If there weren't hidden cameras, the White man never would have known that the woman or Black man were not treated as he was. He was just being treated nicely. Unfortunately, this kind of treatment becomes a privilege, an unearned advantage.

While these segments are becoming dated, personal stories and more recent research indicate that these same dynamics continue to exist (cf. Bertrand and Mullainathan, 2004; U.S. Housing Scholars and Research and Advocacy

Organizations, 2008). Dominant group members may be unaware that they are the recipients of privileged treatment and that it is at the expense of others. They therefore believe that their achievements are based on their own merit, not on systematic advantage. (See Hawkesworth, 1993, Chapter 2, for a review of the research that documents how sexist bias privileges men at women's expense.) They are less likely to realize how "business as usual" could still cause injustice.

Lastly, because the privileges are sometimes hidden and the discrimination subtle, people from privileged groups don't realize the pervasiveness of oppression. They assume their experiences and treatment are "normal". This assumption, coupled with little knowledge of the injustices that people from disadvantaged groups face, allows them to remain unconscious. People from advantaged groups are taught to notice neither inequalities nor privileges. They are "privileged to remain innocent" (Lazarre, 1996).

This lack of consciousness allows for the unintentional perpetuation of injustice. People do not realize that what they are doing is biased or discriminatory. Gaertner and Dovidio (1986) coined the term *aversive racism* to refer to when White people espouse egalitarian values but unconsciously hold negative feelings and beliefs about people of color. This leads them to engage in racist acts without being aware of it and to deny that racism is affecting their behavior (Dovidio & Gaertner, 2005). More broadly, the unconscious and unintentional expressions of bias and prejudice toward socially devalued groups are often called microaggressions (Sue, 2010a, 2010b). There are innumerable examples of these, yet one situation captures this well. A photo in a local newspaper featured a White boy and an African American boy, with the White boy in the foreground. The title was announcing the winner of the "geography bee". The caption began with the name of the White boy and the fact that he finished in second place. It then explained that the other boy was the winner, and gave his name. Even when the African American deserved the spotlight, from looking at the photo (and the order of the information in the caption), it appeared that the White boy was the winner. A positive image of an African American male was diminished, yet newspapers have no difficulty highlighting African American males when they are involved in illegal activity. While some people may intentionally promote racist or other oppressive images, I doubt whether the photographer of the picture or the editor of the newspaper intended to convey such a distorted and implicitly racist message. Yet, they colluded with institutional racism. Since people do not have to act in overtly discriminatory ways, but just behave "normally" or "unconsciously" to perpetuate oppression, it is easy to remain unaware of the impact of their own actions or of their institution's practices.

Denial and Avoidance of Oppression

There is a fine line between recognizing that some privileges may be less obvious and therefore easy to overlook, and choosing not to see or look for them. Similarly, there is a difference between lacking an awareness of the extent of social injustice and deciding not to acknowledge it. People from privileged groups have the options to deny the existence of oppression and to avoid dealing with it. Lazarre (1996) refers to this as "willful innocence." (See Kivel, 2002 for a discussion of the tactics people from privileged group use to retain their benefits and avoid their responsibility.)

For the reasons cited earlier, people from privileged groups tend to be less conscious of oppression and more likely to deny that it exists. In their reality, they are generally unhampered by their social identity and ignorant of the mistreatment of others. Along with a sense of superiority, it becomes easy to proclaim that if it is not an issue from their perspective, then it's not an issue. Since their life can proceed rather well under the current circumstances, they do not need to bother to explore or listen to the complaints of others. They can ignore claims of discrimination and label those who raise issues as oversensitive or troublemakers. Denying that there is oppression also allows the system of domination to remain in place *and* to be justified.

This is exacerbated by the fact that people from advantaged and disadvantaged groups tend to define oppression differently. In the case of racism, Whites are more likely to see racism as "individual acts of meanness" (McIntosh, 1988. p. 5), individual acts of prejudice and discrimination, or as extreme actions that are the exception rather than the norm. Blacks are more likely to see it as daily indignities and as a system of institutionalized practices and policies that work to their disadvantage (Duke, 1992; Shipler, 1997). Therefore, if people only recognize injustice when it is blatantly expressed by individuals, they will never understand the depth and breadth of social oppression.

Admitting that there is oppression and that one participates in it opens up the possibility of personal discomfort. As Allan Johnson (2005) explains, people from privileged groups feel they should be exempt from such an experience.

> Dominant groups typically show the least tolerance for allowing themselves to feel guilt and shame. Privilege, after all, should exempt one from having to feel such things. They experience reminders of their potential for feeling guilt as an affront that infringes on their sense of entitlement to a life unplagued by concern for how their privilege affects other people. The right to deny that privilege exists is an integral part of privilege itself. So men can be quick to complain about "being made to feel guilty" without actually *feeling* guilty. (p. 62, italics in the original)

This privilege is sometimes referred to as "the right to comfort". This was expressed very directly at a training I conducted with a group of university students. The first several activities highlighted the groups' diversity and clearly made the point that we need to value our differences and create equality for all groups. After participating in an exercise that physically demonstrated White privilege and institutional racism, a White male said that he didn't like the activity because it made him feel uncomfortable and bad about being White. He understood that the point of the activity was to demonstrate inequities and knew that the purpose was not to make White people feel guilty. Nevertheless, he still insisted that his discomfort made him not want to engage, and therefore the activity was counterproductive. He felt entitled to the privilege of not having to be uncomfortable, and therefore had the privilege of choosing not to confront issues of racism.

People from privileged groups can also choose to remain silent when they are aware of injustice. The impact on people from disadvantaged groups in usually more profound and immediate, and thus more likely to elicit a greater need to respond. Since people from privileged groups are usually less directly affected, they can decide not to take action. In fact, there is incentive not to do so. First, people from advantaged groups who point out inequities and challenge the status quo often put themselves at risk. They may face retaliation at work or school, ostracism, harassment, or violence. Second, it disrupts a system that largely works to their benefit. People from privileged groups tend to have more to lose, at least in the short run, if they make waves. (However, in Chapter 5, I'll discuss the extensive costs of oppression to people from dominant groups as well.)

Sense of Superiority and Entitlement

Being part of the norm, a member of the dominant group, and the beneficiary of (invisible) privileges often leads to a sense of superiority and entitlement or internalized superiority/supremacy. Even though this sense of identity is false and unearned, people from dominant groups come to expect certain treatment and opportunities. They feel they *deserve* the privileges they have come to assume will be theirs. This attitude is beyond a healthy sense of self-respect or pride in one's cultural group; it can be arrogance and snobbery. They not only expect their needs to get met, but often believe that their needs should supersede others' needs.

People with class privilege (money or status) expect their phone calls to be returned promptly and their work to receive priority. I notice that students who are upper middle class, especially males, feel more entitled to my time and attention as a professor. They expect individual attention and accommodations to meet their needs. In general, men expect their wants and desires to take precedence over a woman's. Sometimes, people have a clear sense of entitlement and consciously believe that they deserve special treatment. Many times, people who are acting entitled rarely see their behavior in this light. They are just doing what they think anyone would or should do.

This sense of superiority often becomes evident when people from an advantaged group encounter someone from a disadvantaged group in a position of expertise or authority over them. Men may balk at having a woman boss or Whites may be uncomfortable with a person of color as the doctor or consultant. People from privileged groups are often suspect of the ability, knowledge, or right to such status of people from oppressed groups. This may reflect more than just stereotypes and bias. This arrangement calls into question the implicit superiority of people from the dominant group and what they assume is the appropriate social order. Some of the personal and political attacks on President Obama could be viewed in this way.

Multiple Identities and Experiences of Privilege

In my description of common characteristics of people from privileged groups, I have narrowly focused on a single aspect of one's identity. However, that is only one strand of a whole tapestry. Individuals' other social identities color their experience of that dominant identity, and more broadly, affect one's overall experience of both privilege and oppression. Not everyone benefits equally; privileges are mediated by one's other social positions. Other social statuses affect the degree to which an individual experiences the advantages of privilege.

Privileges gained through a dominant identity may be mitigated or reduced because of a subordinated identity. Class privilege certainly provides many advantages, yet it may be limited by racism, sexism or heterosexism. Even middle and upper class Black men get stopped by police and suspected for criminal activity; in fact, being in a "nice neighborhood" or driving an expensive car will often bring on this suspicion. Women in high-level positions still do not command the same respect or influence as men in similar positions. Openly gay men do not have the same access to corporate or political power (or membership in the "Old Boys Network") as heterosexual men. (As described earlier in this chapter, people from various oppressed groups rarely have the same access to high-level institutional power, and when they do, it is at a cost.)

Nor does privilege in one area prevent subordination in another. Wealthy women are still subject to sexual violence even though they have greater opportunities to protect their safety. Being able-bodied, heterosexual, and White does not exempt a working class person from class oppression. A White man in his 30s who has the benefits of race, sex, and age may still face employment discrimination because he has a disability. In extreme cases, other dominant identities or privileges are irrelevant. No aspect of privilege could protect the Japanese from internment, Native Americans from removal, or Jews from extermination.

On the other hand, the experience of oppression in one aspect generally does not eradicate the experience of privilege in another. Some feminists feel that because they are all women and experience sexism their experiences are similar. White women, able-bodied women or heterosexual women may ignore the way they have privileges in other parts of their lives. Some Jews may be subject to anti-Semitism, yet still have white-skin privilege. Men of color confront racism, yet still benefit from sexism and patriarchy.

Moreover, one's other intersecting identities not only affect one's degree of privilege but also shape that privileged identity. For example, a Black man's experience and identity as a man is different than a White man's; a Jewish person's experience and identity as a White person is different than a White Anglo-Saxon Protestant's.

Though not absolute, our particular mix of identities does shape our experiences. Privilege can help alleviate experiences of oppression. The more dominant identities one has, the more one can draw on those privileges to deal with the discrimination and disempowerment faced in his/her subordinated roles. The more subordinated identities one has, the more likely the privilege one does have is eroded. However, this is not simply an additive game; our social identities are not a balance sheet where one can just compare the number of identities on the dominant side and the number on the subordinated side and know how much power, privilege, or freedom one has. Individuals and the dynamics of oppression are much more complicated than that. Some people argue that certain oppressions are worse than others or have greater impact. As noted in the previous chapter, Young (1990) points out there may be different "faces" or manifestations of oppression which are experienced to greater or lesser degrees by different oppressed groups. Oppressions may be linked but not comparable. As Audre Lorde (1983) asserts, "there is no hierarchy of oppressions".

Resistance to Seeing Oneself as Privileged

Many people have reactions to considering themselves privileged or dominant. Some people have difficulty thinking in those terms about themselves; others can do it, but just don't like the idea. There are several reasons for these types of responses.

First, being "privileged", "dominant", or an "oppressor" has negative connotations. Many people assume it means that individuals willfully discriminate against or mistreat others. It seems to refer to the "bad guys". Most people don't see themselves, or want to see themselves, in that light. They consider themselves nice people who try to treat people fairly.

Second, most people do not even realize that they are privileged or part of groups with greater social power. As I have described, most people from dominant groups don't think about that identity; they are simply "normal". They also do not realize the extent of systemic inequalities and the ways they are advantaged. It is hard to accept being privileged when you are unaware of your privileges or feel you have earned them.

Even if people from dominant groups are aware of their social status, they don't *feel* privileged or powerful. Most people are struggling to live their lives. They worry about their jobs, their families, and their health. They personally do not have access to great amounts of resources or make decisions that affect the nation. More people feel controlled rather than in control. Given the individualistic and competitive nature of our society, few people feel secure. The fact that most people think of themselves as individuals, rather than as members of a social group exacerbates the difficulty of seeing themselves as privileged. Since individuals themselves do not alone create and maintain dominant ideologies and oppressive structures, it is understandable that an individual would not feel that they have had much of a role in societal oppression. Since they *personally* don't feel advantaged, it is difficult to acknowledge that they are part of a group that is. A White woman expresses this realization:

> I never thought about it before, but there are many privileges to being White. In my personal life, I cannot say that I have ever felt that I had the advantage over a Black person, but I am aware that my race has the advantage. (Tatum, 1997, p. 102)

Alternatively, some people from dominant groups feel that they are the ones at a disadvantage. This is particularly true for Whites who feel that people of color are now the ones getting the benefits, especially in the job market. However, when conducting exercises where White people are asked if they would rather be a person of color, virtually no Whites indicate that they would like to switch.

Moreover, the sense of privilege is relative. First, Johnson (2005) contends that people tend to assess their relative standing in comparison to people like themselves (looking sideways) or to people more advantaged than themselves (looking up). Rarely do we judge ourselves in relation to people worse off than ourselves (downwards). Therefore, if our "peers" or those "above" us seem better off than we do, it is of little comfort or consequence that others are in worse positions. Therefore, people are usually quite aware of their relative deprivation but refuse to acknowledge their relative privilege.

Second, not all people in a particular advantaged group are similarly situated. Certainly the experience of class privilege of someone in the top 1% of wealth in this country is quite different from someone who is comfortably middle class. Third, other subordinated identities erode one's sense of privilege. Some people from a targeted group claim that their oppression undermines any privileges they may receive from their dominant identity. Rather, I would say that other social positions affect the *degree* to which someone is advantaged in one's dominant identity. An individual can recognize privileges due to one's dominant identities while also acknowledging how those identities are affected by one's other targeted identities. Privilege and oppression are not mutually exclusive, even if there is a dynamic between them.

As noted before, people tend to focus on their subordinated identities. For people who are part of a privileged group, their targeted identity(ies) will usually have greater significance than their dominant identity(ies). This makes it more difficult for them to identify as someone from a privileged group and to acknowledge that status. Most people will tend to see themselves as someone from a disadvantaged group, ignoring their privileges in other aspects of their lives. In the models of social identity development I will describe in the following chapter, there is a stage where people are very invested in their subordinated identity. At this point, it is particularly challenging for individuals to examine their privilege from a dominant identity.

Conclusion

This chapter broadly describes privileged groups and offers perspectives to appreciate how they might see themselves and the world. The dominant culture, both overtly and covertly, promotes the normalcy and superiority of the advantaged group, and their right to power and privilege. People from advantaged groups therefore tend to be less aware and less sensitive to oppression and feel entitled to privileges (which they don't see and believe are deserved). There is generally little opportunity, support or incentive for people from privileged groups to explore their identity and examine its social implications. Thus, this provides a social imperative and challenge for social justice educators. In the following chapter, I will discuss ways to approach facilitating an educational process toward awareness and change.

3

PERSPECTIVES ON INDIVIDUAL CHANGE AND DEVELOPMENT

Education, especially social justice education, is about change. The hope is to transform or broaden attitudes, beliefs, and behaviors. We may use a variety of strategies: cognitive strategies that offer new information or analyses; behavioral strategies that foster interpersonal contact or participation in new experiences; or emotional strategies that encourage empathy and personal insight. However, an educator cannot *make* someone change. Rather, we can provide the context, content, and process that allow an individual to grow.

There are many things that affect whether there will be shifts in someone's views or actions, including one's psychological state, personality structure, previous experiences, time in one's life, and relationship with the educator and colleagues/ classmates. These aspects all have an impact on a person's openness to learning and change. Just as we cannot control the experience of each individual, we cannot control many of the other factors that influence one's growth. In the time that we work with someone, they may not be able or willing to engage in a process of reflection and change. We can just do our best to understand the people we are working with, and to provide the ingredients that we believe will most facilitate their education.

In this chapter, I will discuss several theoretical frameworks that I find helpful in designing and facilitating educational experiences, and in understanding the perspectives and behaviors of people from privileged groups. They will be addressed in relation to diversity and social justice education, though their relevance extends to other contexts. I will primarily focus on developmental perspectives as related to personal growth in general, and to intellectual development and social identity development in particular.

Addresing the Emotions and the Intellect

Good education involves addressing its emotional (affective) and intellectual (cognitive) dimensions (Rogers, 1980). Learning is more stimulating and meaningful when both the intellect and feelings are attended to. To effectively educate about diversity and social justice, we must deal with both.

Anyone who has done social justice education knows that it is more than an intellectual activity. Of course, we need to expose people to new perspectives, facts, theories, and analyses. Students need to acquire more accurate and complex information about issues which the mainstream media often ignore, simplify or distort. Yet, even when enlightening facts and theories are provided, people may still be unmoved and remain uninvolved.

Addressing the affective aspect is important in two respects. First, it is a key component of the learning process and central to a sound social justice pedagogy. Fostering self-awareness and the concern for others, two aspects of social justice education, require dealing in the realm of feelings. People need to emotionally connect with and care about other people and situations. The promotion of empathy, an important educational approach, requires that people can relate to the feelings of another. (See Chapters 7 and 8 for more about empathy.) Considering one's own feelings in various circumstances provides helpful bridges to understanding the experiences of others. Without an emotional investment, there is less incentive to explore social justice issues or to engage in personal or social change.

Second, feelings arise in the process of learning about diversity and justice. Participants are more likely to stay engaged with the material and the process when we help them deal with their feelings. In educating for social justice, we ask people to question their fundamental belief systems and assumptions about how the world operates. Challenging people's self-concepts and worldviews is threatening, leading them to feel anxious, fearful, confused, angry, guilty, and resentful. Different stages of social identity development, described later, are often accompanied by particular emotions. Thus, as people examine deeply rooted beliefs, we can expect emotional reactions. In addition, conflicts, with corresponding emotions, often occur among participants as issues are discussed. The learning and growth process will be impeded unless these feelings and dynamics are addressed. (This will be discussed in more detail in Chapters 4 and 5 on Resistance.)

Rose (1996) describes why dealing with emotions is critical for people from dominant groups if we expect them to be allies. In reference to racism, she explains,

> If White people only confront these issues [feelings of guilt and betrayal] on a cognitive basis, they will wind up as hostages to political correctness. They will be careful about what they say, but their actions will be rigid and self-conscious. When the process is emotional as well as cognitive, the state of being an ally becomes a matter of reclaiming one's own humanity. (pp. 41–42)

As people work through limiting and oppressive attitudes and behaviors, they can experience feelings of joy, liberation, release, and excitement.

Many educators are more comfortable staying at an intellectual level. However, students often do not allow this to occur. Whether wanted or not, invited or not, their feelings intrude. Meaningful social justice education is inherently an emotion-laden process. In order for students to be connected to the content, there needs to be an emotional link. Likewise, in order to help them remain involved in a process of growth and change, we need to help them work through their feelings. We can intentionally structure into the class/workshop opportunities for people to appropriately deal with their emotions (e.g. journaling, sharing with peers, support groups, etc). In any case, dealing with both the cognitive and affective is part of the educational agenda.

Developmental Perspectives

A developmental perspective suggests that change occurs through particular sequences. As one's current perspective or way of being becomes inadequate, this creates a sense of disequilibrum, and the impetus to move to new ways of seeing and being. There are common, though individual, patterns and processes to one's growth.

I have found psychosocial and cognitive developmental theories helpful in assessing people's frames of reference or ways of understanding. It is an educational truism that we need to meet people where they are. And even though we would often like our students to be somewhere else, we are ineffective when we appeal to the wrong level. As Paulo Freire says, "You never get *there* by starting *there*, you get *there* from starting from some *here*" (1994, p. 58, italics in the original). But how do we know where "here" is?

Developmental theories are one way that we can figure out how best to approach particular students. Like other theories, they provide a framework from which to understand people, and to develop ways to respond that can facilitate their learning and growth. I can better sense where they've been, where they are, and where they may be headed. It makes it easier to anticipate certain types of reactions and interactions. Instead of the educational process feeling like random events, in which we hope for the best, developmental theories can help it seem more coherent and help us be more proactive.

Some developmental "stage" theories may sound overdetermined and hierarchical. I find it most helpful to think about "stages" as the predominant lenses or perspectives people use, which guide their way of perceiving and acting. Although people may exhibit thinking and behavior from various stages, they will usually have a predominant stage and are unable to fully understand or consistently act from higher stages (especially, if it is more than one stage beyond their predominant stage). Likewise, even though some stage theories suggest linear, one-directional movement, I find it more useful to consider that some people may move back and forth between stages and that their development may be more like a spiral—they continue to grow but revisit similar issues in new ways. I offer these theories as I use them—as guides, not absolute truths for each individual. They are not intended as a way to label people, but as an aid in understanding different perspectives and in developing educational strategies.

Confirmation, Contradiction, Continuity

Robert Kegan (1982) has suggested a theory of human development that describes the changing ways people make meaning of themselves, others, and the world. He describes a process that facilitates growth to new stages of development. This process can be applied to social justice education as well. He maintains that growth unfolds through alternating periods of dynamic stability, instability, and temporary rebalance. Individuals need a sense of "confirmation", an environment of support, before moving on to situations of "contradiction", conditions that challenge current meaning-making systems. They then need a context for "continuity" which allows for transformation and re-equilibration. A sequence of confirmation, contradiction, and continuity can provide a framework for designing and responding to issues in social justice education. I will explore each of these phases in more depth.

Confirmation

By its very nature, social justice education creates discomfort. As noted previously, we are asking people to do something quite difficult—to question core values and beliefs about themselves and the world. We therefore need to offer enough safety so that people can engage, but enough challenge so that people can change. Some people take issue with the concept of "safety". One reason is that they maintain that people from dominant groups should not expect the "privilege of safety" before being willing to examine privilege and oppression, especially since people from subordinated groups virtually never get to feel "safe" when in a group with dominant group members. I do not use "safety" in an absolute sense but do believe that people need a sufficient sense of security to engage in open ways. Confirmation is concerned with providing a context that creates enough safety and support for people to take emotional, social, psychological, and intellectual risks. When people feel too threatened, the fight or flight response is activated and the likelihood of learning is diminished. Even though this is the first step, it continually needs to be revisited as people get scared or defensive so that sufficient safety can be reestablished. At this point, some key aspects of the confirmation phase will be reviewed. Creating a "confirming" environment in the context of preventing and addressing resistance is discussed in Chapter 5.

One aspect of confirmation is establishing trust and rapport between the educator and the student. Other psychological and educational theorists have highlighted the importance of establishing this relationship. In counseling and family therapy, psychologists refer to this as "joining." The therapist must be able to form a partnership with the client or family, creating a bond of trust and common purpose.

> Joining a family is more an attitude than a technique and it is the umbrella under which all therapeutic transactions occur. Joining is letting the family know that the therapist understands them and is working with and for them. Only under his [sic] protection can the family have the security to explore alternatives, try the unusual, and change. (Minuchen & Fishman, 1981, p. 32)

As this brief quote highlights, it is the stance and expression of acceptance that is central, not the particular behaviors or techniques an individual teacher uses. This is echoed by Rogers (1980) who identifies acceptance (or unconditional positive regard), genuineness, and empathic understanding as the critical conditions of any growth-promoting relationship, including those in the classroom. Educators need to respect and value people and to affirm their fundamental integrity, dignity, and self-worth. Students must be able to trust the educator before they will be willing to allow themselves to be vulnerable. The need for students to feel heard, understood, and cared about is paramount.

There are numerous ways educators can create a safe environment that communicates care and respect to students. It is critical to listen attentively, both verbally and non-verbally, and acknowledge students' experiences and feelings. Develop class/workshop guidelines with the participants for classroom interactions and ensure that these agreements are upheld. Self-disclose about our own backgrounds, our experiences with different forms of injustice, and our efforts to unlearn oppression. Name or have students share the fears and concerns people often have when dealing with these issues. Reassure students that this is a learning environment by encouraging "stupid" questions and stressing that critical thinking, not the presumed party line, is what is expected. (In some contexts, we may need to acknowledge that even when people have differences of opinion, they may be expected to uphold certain standards of behavior.) We can build on what they already know, validating their current expertise and experience. Soliciting students' input about class rules, topics to be covered, assignments or class activities also communicates respect. Creating comfort among students or participants is also important. Ice-breakers and work in pairs or small groups which allow people to get to know each other are helpful. Low-risk personal sharing and self-disclosure activities help to build trust. Encouraging people to notice their commonalties—similar experiences, likes, interests—also increases rapport. In order for people to feel able to let down their guards and grapple with challenges to their belief systems, there needs to be a safe and supportive enough environment that includes trust of the educator as well as peers.

Contradiction

Once a sense of confirmation has been established, the goal is not to overprotect students or to have them avoid uncomfortable feelings. Sufficient safety does not equal comfort. The aim is not to allow people to remain in their often limited worldview but to help them construct new and more complex understandings of themselves and society. Significant growth often occurs when people are out of their "comfort zone" or at their "learning edge". During contradiction, by creating disequilibrium, we foster the conditions that promote growth. The bulk of diversity education tends to focus on this phase. However, without first establishing enough trust and safety, we are less likely to be successful.

In social justice education, the phase of contradiction corresponds with what is considered developing critical consciousness (Freire, 1970). According to Freire, *conscientization* is critical social and political awareness. It is "learning to perceive social, political and economic contradictions, and to take action against oppressive elements of reality" (1970, p. 19). It places the status quo in question and supports the transformation of individual and social consciousness.

Although critical thinking, in general, does not always encompass such social and political critiques, it can have elements in common with developing critical consciousness. In describing the components of critical thinking, Brookfield (1987) includes: identifying and challenging assumptions; becoming aware of how context shapes what is considered normal and natural ways of thinking and living; and imagining and exploring alternative ways of thinking and living (pp. 7–8). He also warns educators about this process.

> Trying to force people to analyze critically the assumptions under which they have been thinking and living is likely to serve no function other than intimidating them to the point where resistance builds up against this process. We can however, try to awaken, prompt, nurture and encourage this process without making people feel threatened or patronized. (Brookfield, 1987, p. 11)

Overall, the contradiction phase engages people in reflection and analysis. As educators, we can provide opportunities to people to become aware of their unquestioned beliefs and attitudes, and then evaluate their validity. Ask them to compare their currently held views with other versions of reality. Present various analyses of how and why oppression operates. Help students move from basing opinions on emotional reactions to utilizing critical analysis. Have them consider how the dominant ideology shapes individual consciousness, institutional structures and practices, and cultural norms. Assist them in understanding how our ideas and behaviors are culturally and historically specific and socially constructed. Encourage people to explore how the personal is political, how individual problems often are reflective of larger social issues. Help them to examine their privilege and to consider how oppression hurts the dominant group. Finally, suggest alternatives to our current system and to their present behaviors. For example, some people look at a woman in an abusive relationship with a man as an isolated occurrence. They may see her behavior simply as a personal weakness or an individual psychological problem. They do not consider how sexism has contributed to this relationship: how women are socialized to be submissive to men, to take care of others before themselves, and to feel incomplete without a relationship. There are cultural messages that the woman is somehow to blame for the abuse and economic realities that make it hard for women to be financially independent, especially if they have children to support. Men also have been conditioned to be dominant, aggressive, and in control, and to see women as possessions. We can help students to consider a broader social analysis which then leads to different ways of thinking about how to address the issue of violence in relationships.

Educators engage people in these tasks in many ways. The specific content and activities in the contradiction phase will vary greatly depending on the group, the context, and the goals. People can be exposed to new information and analyses through readings, videos, speakers, and sharing among participants. They can actively investigate issues through research, interviews, observations, fieldwork, and participation in events. Case studies, role plays, debates, simulations, and guided imageries promote the consideration of other perspectives and alternative possibilities. In general, experiential activities are particularly effective in helping people gain new insights in fun and unexpected ways. There needs to be opportunities for self-reflection and adequate processing (discussion and debriefing) of activities and experiences, so participants can gain the most from them.

The contradiction phase is also the time to expand on data generated during the confirmation phase. By building on what people have said about their own feelings and experiences, we can help them to understand their experiences in a larger social, political, and historical context. Participants need to expand their individualistic framework to include a more structural analysis. They often want to see everything on an individual basis and ignore the treatment of *groups* of people and institutionalized practices. When a person of color is denied a promotion, it may be attributed to that individual's qualifications. Yet if they review the data on the hiring and promotion of people of color, they may see a pattern of racial discrimination in that company, and other organizations. In addition, people from privileged groups may use their own personal experiences to generalize or incorrectly assume that there is pervasive discrimination of people from their group, while minimizing the discrimination faced by people from oppressed groups. A White person may also feel that they have been unfairly denied a job. It is necessary to help people make the distinction between behavior directed at an individual in a specific situation and actions taken systematically against groups of people over time.

Participants need to understand the differences in access to social power as well as the extent to which people may face discrimination or unfair treatment. In systems of oppression, despite the stereotypes and mistreatment some people may face, privileged groups still have greater opportunities, choices, access to resources, and power to define normalcy than dominated groups. A range of information (including statistics, historical perspective, and data about institutional and cultural oppression) can help people broaden their understanding of their own and others' experiences, and gain a clearer picture of social reality. People need accurate information to correct misperceptions, to challenge faulty assumptions, and to fill in gaps in knowledge. They need a basis from which to question the myth of meritocracy and recognize that the playing field is still unequally sloped and rocky.

During contradiction, we try to promote questioning, generate discussion, offer alternative viewpoints, encourage risk-taking, and provide resources. As disequilibrium is created, we need to be mindful of students' reactions. If too much dissonance is created, they may become fearful and defensive. If it feels too scary and overwhelming, they may retreat from the educational process. We have to respect people's pace and ability to handle threatening material. Re-emphasizing some of the aspects of confirmation—ensuring a safe and supportive environment, and reaffirming a sense of trust and rapport—helps keep students engaged.

As participants begin to reevaluate their beliefs and develop new understandings of themselves, others, and social reality, they need ways to integrate these new perspectives. After experiencing a sense of disequilibrium, they seek to reestablish a sense of balance, incorporating their new consciousness. This leads to the next phase that assists them with this transition.

Continuity

In the continuity phase, our goal is to help students integrate and apply their new knowledge and awareness. They are seeking to recreate a sense of equilibrium. If a class or training is ending, it is also the time to establish closure. In the natural course of human development, this process of confirmation, contradiction, and continuity proceeds according to its own timing. In the context of a course, people may still feel in the midst of contradiction as the class is ending. Therefore, students may need to consider how to use the awareness gained so far and how to continue this process outside of the class setting.

During the continuity phase, it is useful for people to develop plans for taking action and applying what they have learned. Discuss where they can have an impact and a range of actions they can take (including those of lower and higher risk, and those that target individual, institutional, and cultural oppression). Encourage people to develop a sense of empowerment and possibility as opposed to feeling overwhelmed with the magnitude of the problems. It is especially important for people to identify ways they can get support for their newfound consciousness and commitment. Since their friends and family most likely have not shared this experience, they often do not provide the kind of support or understanding people need at this point. In addition to support, help people explore how they can continue their own education through workshops, classes, groups, or community/ campus activities. (See Chapter 8 for more discussion of actions for allies.)

The model of confirmation, contradiction, and continuity provides an overarching framework from which to design educational experiences. As I'll discuss further in Chapter 5, the importance of confirmation cannot be underestimated and often is shortchanged. Establishing and reestablishing a supportive climate allows for disequilibrium and reequilibrium to occur. This framework, which is applicable to both individuals and the class overall, provides a broad understanding of the process of change. In the next sections, I will describe two models that illustrate specific aspects of individual development—intellectual and social identity development.

Intellectual Development

During the contradiction phase, we expect people to engage in critical thinking by examining assumptions, exploring various viewpoints, analyzing positions, engaging in self-reflection, and developing their own perspectives. Their stage of intellectual development greatly impacts both their competence in and their approach to these activities. It affects people's epistemological beliefs—their assumptions about knowledge and knowing. As educators, frameworks of intellectual development aid us in understanding the varied reactions to the structure and content of the class/ training. These perspectives help us to create learning experiences that more effectively match the intellectual needs and abilities of our students. Moreover, they allow us to see that students' responses are often developmentally related, that they are not just being stubborn or narrow. This, in turn, helps us to be more empathic and less judgmental.

I will briefly describe the model of intellectual development developed by William Perry (1968) and expanded upon by Belenky, Clinchy, Goldberger, & Tarule (1986). Perry's research focused on White, elite, college men, while Belenky, et al.'s included women from various backgrounds and settings. Integrating the findings from these two studies, I will review the fundamental characteristics of each stage, and then consider their educational implications. For a more complete and thorough discussion of these theories, I encourage readers to explore the original works as well as the many other writings that have been sparked by their research that address both theory and practice. (See, for example, Baxter, 1992; Capossela, 1993; Goldberger, et al., 1998; Kloss, 1994; Kurfiss, 1988. Also, see King & Kitchener, 1994 for a related model of the development of reflective judgment.)

Belenky, et al. identified a position before the first stage in Perry's scheme. They labeled this *Silence*. These women felt mindless and voiceless, passive and powerless. These women were dependent on external sources for knowledge and often feared male authority. They were the youngest and the most socially, economically, and educationally disadvantaged of all the women they interviewed; no college women were represented in this group.

In *Dualism/Received Knowledge* (the first stage in Perry's scheme), people see knowledge as a collection of facts and look to the authority as the source of all knowledge. Knowledge is received, not created (for women, especially, it is gained through listening). This phase is characterized by dualistic or dichotomous thinking—right/wrong, good/bad, either/or, us/them, etc. People in this stage are intolerant of ambiguity, whether in the content or the structure of the class. As a result, they often feel confused, angry, or frustrated when the educator does not give them the "right" answer. Individuals frequently strive to figure out what the teacher "really wants." Teachers may feel frustrated when students take simplistic or narrow views on complex issues.

Students in this Dualism/Received Knowledge stage struggle with considering multiple perspectives or analyses. They are unable to see more than one view as legitimate and often have difficulty empathizing with others, especially when they don't agree. For example, suppose students were asked to consider the immigration policy in the United States—whether or not there should be more restrictions on immigrants. People in the dualism stage would likely hold a clear position, often based on what they have heard from a respected authority, such as a parent, politician, professor, or social scientist. They might insist that immigrants unfairly take jobs way from US citizens, put undo strain on public schools, and are a burden on our economic system, though they lack a full understanding of the issue. They would likely dismiss or be confused by someone who makes a contradictory argument, outlining ways immigrants contribute to our economy and quality of life.

Ongoing exposure to multiple interpretations, different experiences, and varied opinions helps challenge their faith in authorities and in finding the "right" answer. In *Multiplicity/Subjective Knowledge*, people begin to recognize that some things are unknown and that there is no definitive "truth". Knowledge is seen as a matter of opinion and is gained through first-hand experience. All opinions are valued and seen as equally valid. They begin to trust their inner voice as a source of knowledge. There is little interest in or respect for "authority"; women particularly tend to turn inward away from external (male) authorities.

Even though they now recognize some level of complexity, people in Multiplicity/Subjective Knowledge lack the ability to assess different viewpoints. Instead, they rely on intuition, feelings, or "common sense". In the immigration example provided previously, people in this stage would come to an opinion based on their gut feeling or what they personally have seen, heard about, or experienced. They would respect each person's opinion and claim that people are entitled to feel as they do, without thinking that there is a generally "right" answer. However, they would tend to align with those who shared their view.

Educators' expectations and challenges to support their opinions (verbally or in written assignments) will often be experienced as a personal attack or a result of unclear criteria for judgment. They may feel that they were graded unfairly because they didn't agree with the teacher. However, as they repeatedly experience the need to provide evidence, and encounter that in the materials they read, they may begin to move into the next stage.

With *Relativism/Procedural Knowledge* comes the ability to evaluate knowledge. People realize that opinions differ in quality and need to be supported with reasons. This stage is sometimes referred to as "contextualism" or "contextual relativism" since people begin to understand that knowledge is relative and contextual, that what one considers to be true depends on their experience, perspective, and methods of reasoning—on their "standpoint". Authorities are now valued for their expertise, but are not seen as the arbiters of truth.

People begin to learn and to apply the methods (procedures) within a discipline to evaluate different positions. They use a systematic approach for answering questions and finding solutions. Belenky et al. identified two types of procedural knowers: separate knowers and connected knowers. Separate knowers tend to use objective analysis and argument to support and justify opinions. Connected knowers actively try to understand divergent views by putting themselves in the others' heads to explain and clarify their positions. Relativists/Procedural knowers might approach the immigration situation by systematically examining studies that explore the impact of immigrants on different sectors of our society. They would be concerned with the quality of the studies—the methodologies used and who did them. They might consider how one's social position and history informs one's view. Connected knowers would be particularly interested in understanding, *from the other person's perspective*, why that person held a specific opinion—what has led them to this belief. They might now understand that immigration issues are not clear-cut, articulate the various benefits and challenges immigrants bring, and be able to make a reasonable case for a particular position. However, they may be reluctant to take a *personal* stand on immigration policy yet, as people more fully understand complexities, they recognize that they must make choices and commitments, thus ushering them into the next phase.

In the stage of *Commitment in Relativism/Constructed Knowledge* people integrate both inner and outer knowledge, blending one's inner truth with knowledge gained from others. In the process, they construct a personal worldview. Despite disparities and the lack of absolute surety, they make a stand or take a position. They appreciate historical and cultural contexts, and recognize that the knower and the known are intertwined—that there is no "objective truth". They engage in abstract thinking and meta-analysis. Constructed knowers have gained moral depth and sensitivity which guides their reasoning and action. In the immigration situation, people at this stage would decide what immigration policies to support based on their sense of empathy, morality, and thoughtful reasoning about the information gathered.

Educational Implications

The two most challenging stages for educators tend to be Dualism/Received Knowledge and Multiplicity/Subjective Knowledge. In these stages, it is most difficult for people to engage in critical thinking and a systematic evaluation of knowledge. Critical thinking challenges these students' fundamental epistemological beliefs—that things are right or wrong, and that everyone is entitled to their own opinion which are equally accurate and valid. What may be seen as resistance may, in fact, be a reflection of the level of cognitive development.

People in Dualism/Received Knowledge are attached to their views and don't know how to deal with the complexity of issues. We can introduce a moderate degree of diversity (two or three different perspectives on the issue) as we try to challenge simplistic conceptions and open up alternatives. We can help them to develop basic analytic and critical thinking skills in order to make this task less overwhelming, and encourage personal reflection and empathy. They need lots of opportunities to practice these skills. People in Dualism/Received Knowledge benefit from concrete (not abstract), experiential learning where the concepts or issues are made "real"— through examples, role plays, simulations, debates, case studies, etc. Activities, requirements, and assignments should be highly structured (this creates safety and eliminates some ambiguity). As people struggle with complexity, they need validation and support for their efforts from the instructor and their peers. It is unsettling to be shaken from feeling certain about an issue and to be asked to think in a way in which one is unaccustomed. Even though they may resist valuing other students as legitimate sources of knowledge, discussion with peers helps create the safety to explore new ideas and exposes them to varied experiences and opinions.

People in Multiplicity/Subjective Knowledge appreciate cooperative, peer-oriented classrooms where they get to share their perspectives and experiences. They also need tools that help them to evaluate different views, weigh evidence, distinguish between strong and weak support, and consider counter-arguments. People can be expected to provide evidence for opinions and substantiate how they reached their conclusions. Clear criteria for assessment are helpful, as are models of what a good argument looks like. To help students understand that requirements for support are not personal criticism, we can explain that in order to be credible to others, they need to be able to defend their views in a convincing way. In graded classes, it is helpful for students at all levels if we provide clear (and appropriate) criteria for how they will be evaluated, review examples of sample papers or answers that meet different levels of the criteria, and provide students with ample opportunity and support to meet our standards.

People in Relativism/Procedural Knowledge need to be taught various reasoning strategies that value both separate and connected knowing. Not only can people be expected to critique a position according to particular methods, but also to "feel into" a position to understand why someone reached a particular conclusion. Since they view knowledge as contextual and relative, they may find it difficult to commit to a position. We can help people to see that disciplinary methods can complement one's inner voice, rather than supplant it. We can encourage them to use both these sources of knowledge to make a personal commitment to a perspective, to develop courage and integrity.

Most students enter college in Dualism/Received Knowledge and move into Multiplicity/Subjective Knowledge or Relativism/Procedural Knowledge by the end of their college years. I frequently have adult students in graduate school who are still in the early stages. If a group is predominately in one stage, then the class can be geared toward helping people progress through that stage and into the next. Often in classes, and especially in doing training in organizations, we can expect to find a range of developmental perspectives. As always, it is a challenge to accommodate the varying levels and needs. Here, as elsewhere, providing a variety of experiences and opportunities is most useful. I have found that a mix of both presentation and experiential activities tends to span these differences. People appreciate hearing factual information and analyses, and participating in active learning. Individuals can engage in and process the activities in ways that fit their developmental level. Everyone can learn from reflecting on their own experiences, hearing different reactions, and being exposed to various connections and conclusions.

For example, I do an activity that addresses stereotypes and assumptions that tends to be effective with a range of people. Students are asked to anonymously write down two things they have felt, heard, or believed about a particular group (I'll ask them to consider several groups). They switch papers and read out what is written. When the responses are recorded on newsprint for all to view, they consider which ones they personally feel are true or have questions about. In processing this activity we explore stereotypes, compare similarities and differences among groups, look for patterns within groups, and consider the historical and cultural context. This activity tends to be concrete enough for dualistic thinkers, but complex enough to allow for varying levels of self-examination and social analysis.

As people struggle with the process of developmental change, it is helpful to remember that what is at stake is generally more than just an intellectual perspective. As Belenky et. al. well demonstrate, epistemological assumptions are usually related to one's sense of self and morality. One's way of being is often intertwined with one's way of knowing. Therefore, this process can be quite emotional as well as cognitive. This can explain some of the intensity we encounter, such as the strong investment in a particular view in Dualism/Received Knowledge, or the hurt or anger as one's opinion is challenged in Multiplicity/Subjective Knowledge. As people shift from one cognitive developmental stage to the next, they also shift how they see themselves—from a person incapable of creating knowledge, to someone who has inner wisdom and/or their own opinion, to someone who can think reflectively and analytically, to someone who can construct their own sense of truth. This impacts how they relate to others and how they see the world. This process can be both scary and exciting, disconcerting and empowering.

Moreover, intellectual development is occurring within a social and political context. Our culture supports simplistic, dualistic thinking. Rarely are people exposed to complex, analytical perspectives on issues, especially as news continues to get reduced to soundbites and political slogans. A real range of viewpoints and alternative perspectives are hard to obtain in the mainstream media. Hierarchical structures reinforce received knowledge. They encourage people to listen to what the authorities say and to figure out what they want. This constrains opportunities to critical thinking. Furthermore, since inner knowing is not publicly valued, it is harder for people to develop this aspect of knowing and then to integrate it with external sources of knowledge. This presumably individual intellectual process is emotionally and culturally charged.

Social Identity Development

While theories of intellectual development help us understand how people approach knowledge and knowing, models of social identity development give us insight into how people make meaning of their social identities and social reality. Social identity development theory describes a psychosocial process of change in the ways that people think about their own social group membership, other social groups, and social oppression. It allows us to anticipate and make sense of students' responses and classroom interactions, and to formulate educational approaches.

I will first discuss the theory developed by Hardiman and Jackson (1997) that grew out of their research on Black and White racial identity development. They have expanded it to include social identity development in general, for people in dominant as well as subordinated groups. In this chapter, I will just describe the process for people from privileged groups (in Chapter 9, I review the stages for people in subordinate groups as well). I will also present a model of White racial identity development developed by Janet Helms (1990, 1995, 2008) that is particularly useful in understanding the process of racial awareness for White people.

Both of these models suggest that people from privileged groups begin with an acceptance (conscious or unconscious) of the dominant culture's ideology which justifies the dominance of their own group. They tend to be ignorant about institutionalized oppression and privilege. Some individuals then move to questioning and resisting this worldview and structure of social relations. They begin to explore and act against oppressive attitudes and practices. Some people develop the need to create a new sense of their dominant identity that affirms their own as well as others' cultural group. Finally, this new sense of self and social reality is internalized.

The social identity development model created by Hardiman and Jackson suggests five stages that people in the advantaged groups go through in sequential order. Each stage reflects a particular way of viewing the world and oneself as a member of a social group. While people can act from more than one stage, they will have a predominant worldview. Moreover, for some of the stages there are active (conscious) and passive (unconscious) manifestations. This model applies to different forms of oppression and social identities, though there are differences and variations depending on the social group. In addition, people may be at very different places in their identity development depending on which aspect of their identity is being considered (i.e., my White identity and racism or my middle-class identity and classism).

In the first stage, *Naive*, there is little or no awareness of social identities and systematic inequality. This is usually the case only for young children. While young children may be aware of differences, they do not initially attribute meaning or judgment to them as they will as they get older. Yet, children are very receptive to messages from their parents and their environment, and move fairly quickly into stage two.

The second stage, *Acceptance*, is characterized by the acceptance of and participation in the value system and social arrangements of an unjust society. People have internalized the dominant belief system. This includes the stereotypes and messages about the superiority of their own group and the inferiority of the disadvantaged group. People in privileged groups commonly deny that there is a problem and are angry at having to deal with it or be implicated in it. They are unaware of their privileges and tend to see assimilation as the way for people from the oppressed group to behave and be successful. They often blame the victim.

In Active Acceptance, people consciously and overtly express an oppressive perspective. They tend to rationalize inequalities, attributing them to innate deficiencies. They may claim that people on welfare are just lazy and could find good work if they wanted to, or that African Americans don't do as well in school because they're genetically less intelligent. In the most extreme, people in Active Acceptance may join supremacist organizations.

People from privileged groups who are in in Passive Acceptance unintentionally and covertly perpetuate systems of inequality. From the passive (unconscious) perspective, people often deny differences, injustices, or their own collusion. "Color blindness" is one way to avoid acknowledging systematic inequities in power and privilege. They may insist on treating everyone the same, regardless of background (ignoring cultural differences or experiences with oppression) or wonder why someone can't just act more "White" or "less gay" so they could fit in better. They will also maintain a sense of superiority, assuming that they need to help the disadvantaged group because they are unable to take care of themselves or cannot make appropriate decisions. By simply accepting the dominant ideology, people in passive acceptance unconsciously maintain injustice.

After people have been confronted with some experiences and information that contradict and challenge their worldview and beliefs, they may move into the third stage, *Resistance*. (The term *resistance* in this model is used differently from the way I am using it in other parts of this book to refer to the unwillingness to engage in critical thinking about social justice.) They begin to question the oppressive ideology and seek to uncover the ways in which inequality is manifested individually, institutionally, and culturally. People in the dominant group begin to acknowledge their own discriminatory behaviors and examine ways that have been complicit in supporting and perpetuating inequality. They shift from blaming the victim to realizing the role of privileged groups in maintaining oppression. They gain an understanding of privilege systems and structural inequality. This is often accompanied by feelings of shame, guilt, and anger. Sometimes, they will want to disassociate themselves from other "oppressors", to be the special or "good" one, and to try to over-identify and affiliate with people in the disadvantaged group. (i.e., Whites associating only with people of color, or middle/upper class people hanging out only with poor or working-class people.) People in Active Resistance will confront discriminatory attitudes and practices, often in vocal and visible ways, such as writing letters, interrupting stereotypical comments, and changing organizational policy. People in Passive Resistance may be aware of injustice but engage in little behavioral change, avoid taking public stands or actions that entail risk, or decide to distance themselves from mainstream society.

The Resistance stage is primarily concerned with "Who I am not", and reacting to the unjust society. The focus has been on the injustice faced by the disadvantaged group, not on their own identity or culture. With this new consciousness, people from the dominant group may need to begin to answer the question, "Who am I?" After feeling guilty or ashamed of their dominant identity, they may need to develop a social identity that is positive and affirming. For example, they need to consider what it means to be an anti-racist White or a pro-feminist man. This may move them to develop a new sense of identity that characterizes the next stage.

The fourth stage is *Redefinition*, when people try to find new ways of defining themselves and their social group. In conjunction with others in the same social group, this process of identification leads to new ways of naming themselves. Their awareness of this one form of oppression also allows them to reconsider their other social identities and forms of inequality. This can result in a more complex sense of themselves and a better understanding of the interrelatedness of different oppressions.

The final stage is *Internalization*. Once people become comfortable with their new sense of identity, they are able to internalize it and apply it in different parts of their lives. In order to sustain this new identity in a hostile world that socializes and pressures people to maintain the current social order, it must be nurtured and supported by others. People at this stage need peers or organizations where there are people who share their perspective and can affirm this sense of identity.

The model by Janet Helms is similar to the Hardiman and Jackson model but focuses specifically on White racial identity development. Her model further elaborates the transition from racist to anti-racist consciousness. In her six-stage theory, the first three perspectives or "statuses" are racist identities, while the last three are anti-racist. Using the works of Carter (1997), Helms (1990, 1995, 2008), Jones & Carter (1996), and Tatum (1997), I will briefly describe this model.

The first status is *Contact*. It is characterized by innocence and ignorance about race and racial issues. Little attention or significance is given to race. Attitudes and stereotypes about people of color are uncritically absorbed from the dominant culture. People may acknowledge individual acts of prejudice but not institutionalized racism and White privilege. As far as they are concerned, White is just normal. Although individuals may be racist without knowing it, they do not see themselves as prejudiced.

In the next level, *Disintegration*, people start to notice the social significance of race and develop an awareness of racism and White privilege. They become conscious of their own prejudices. This gives rise to anxiety, guilt, shame, and anger. They experience some confusion and conflict about what to do with this new perspective which causes them discomfort.

This leads to *Reintegration*. Their feelings of guilt or denial are transformed into fear and anger at people of color. As a self-protection strategy, they will blame the victim. They seek to justify Whites' positions of advantage and superiority by devaluing people of color and idealizing Whites. People may do this in active and conscious ways or passive and subconscious ways. It is their attempt to regain some psychological equilibrium.

During the next phase of development, Whites begin to achieve an anti-racist identity. As people gain a more complex understanding of the dynamics of racism or have experiences that sufficiently challenge their ability to rationalize racial inequality, they may move to *Pseudo-Independence*. This stage is characterized by the guilty White liberal. People may be self-conscious and ashamed of their Whiteness, and prefer to associate with people of color. They may focus on helping people of color become equal to Whites by encouraging assimilation. Individuals may have an intellectual awareness of race and racism, but have not consciously dealt with Whites' (and their own) responsibility for maintaining a system of racial injustice.

In *Immersion/Emersion*, people begin to assume personal responsibility for racism and actively explore racial inequality and White culture. As they seek to understand Whiteness and develop a more positive White identity, they seek out other Whites engaged in a similar struggle for support or who can be role models. People in Immersion/Emersion also actively confront racism and look for both same-race and cross-race experiences.

Finally, in *Autonomy*, people internalize a new meaning of Whiteness, in which race is a valued part of their identity though not based on superiority. Since they have a complex, respectful, and sophisticated racial worldview, they are comfortable and effective cross-racially. Confronting racism and oppression is part of their daily life. Even though they have achieved this level of racial identity, they continue to be open to new information, new ways of thinking, and increase self-awareness.

Educational Implications

These theories of social identity development help us appreciate the different and changing worldviews of our students. These stages can help explain individual responses as well as interpersonal dynamics. In the Hardiman and Jackson model, individuals in Acceptance, particularly Active Acceptance, are most likely to be resistant to social justice issues since they are most entrenched in a worldview that supports the status quo. People in Resistance will likely be receptive, though they may be prone to avoidance if they begin to feel too guilty and uncomfortable.

People will tend to align with others at a similar stage. Tensions often arise between and among students at different points in the process. For example, people in Resistance will usually have little tolerance for someone in Acceptance. People in Redefinition or Internalization may find it easier to be an educator or coalition builder. However, they may be seen by some people in Resistance as too mainstream and by others as a role model. The aforementioned framework can also be useful in understanding our own responses to particular issues and people as well. I will address this in Chapter 8.

We can also use these models to provide educational experiences that would be most appropriate. Obviously, students can be at various levels, though most people tend to be in the Acceptance or Resistance (and occasionally, at the Redefinition) stages. Individuals in Acceptance particularly need to be exposed to material that challenges the dominant ideology and their stereotypes about different groups. They especially gain from opportunities to learn about the experiences of people from disadvantaged groups and how oppression is institutionalized. Often first-hand encounters with real people and situations, and information that they uncover themselves will be most powerful. People in Resistance need the chance to delve more deeply into issues of injustice, find support for their growing consciousness, and develop ways to effectively channel their energy and feelings about social injustice. Those in Redefinition benefit by being able to explore their cultural background, and learn about or talk with others who are social change activists with a positive sense of their identity. By offering a range of information, experiences, and choices, we can most likely meet the needs of our different students.

Conclusion

For those unfamiliar with developmental theories, it can seem overwhelming to try to apply them all at once. I suggest that readers choose one they find most interesting and begin there. I have found over time that the more lenses I have to view a situation, the more ways I have to think about it, and to develop strategies to address it. Various developmental frameworks help us to appreciate the behaviors of our students and to improve our educational effectiveness. These perspectives may also enhance our empathy and improve our attitudes toward students. Upon learning the Perry scheme, Robert Kloss (1994) notes, " ... I then both understood them and judged them less harshly as a result" (p. 152). This can move us away from blame or frustration and toward more constructive engagement. Learning about diversity and social justice presents tremendous emotional and cognitive challenges for our students. The process of growth and change in these areas is especially profound. For educators, managing not only individual but intragroup dynamics is a formidable task. Fortunately, developmental theories provide us with maps and guides for meeting and leading our students through this rocky terrain.

4

UNDERSTANDING RESISTANCE

In the previous chapter, I described the phase of contradiction where the intention is to help people engage in critical thinking and the development of critical consciousness. People are encouraged to question assumptions, explore new ideas, and consider alternative perspectives. In diversity and social justice education, this process involves examining power relationships, structural inequalities, and ideology. It includes personal reflection and critical analysis that usually challenge how people view the world and see themselves. While some individuals may embrace this exploration, others resist. Consider the following situations:

- Whenever stories are shared which illustrate how racism affects people of color, a White male asserts that he is really the one being discriminated against.
- A student sits in class with arms crossed, does not participate and appears inattentive. She then turns in well-written papers that echo progressive perspectives on diversity issues.
- A lesbian teacher who discusses heterosexism, along with racism, sexism, and classism, is accused of always talking about gay issues and imposing "her" cause.
- While rejecting any information describing institutional barriers to overcoming poverty, a middle-class person insists that if people just worked harder they could succeed, and that most people on welfare are just enjoying a life where they don't have to work.
- Any discussion of patriarchy or male privilege is immediately labeled "male bashing" by the men in the group.

These examples illustrate some of the ways people express resistance to social justice issues. Many educators have written about their experiences with resistance. Often, it is overt—discrediting people, discounting information, challenging every fact, changing the focus, avoiding assignments, or disrupting the class/meeting. Other times, it is subtle—conforming to assumed expectations or non-participation. In any case, people resist learning and change.

Resistance grows out of social realities and reflects psychological issues. In this chapter, I will explore how societal and psychological factors underlie resistance. Since the social and psychological are so intertwined, and their interplay so powerful, the factors can be hard to isolate. Some of the distinctions seem blurred and, at times, somewhat arbitrary. Nonetheless, my intention is to try to identify the various forces that create resistance. While many of these dynamics are true for people from disadvantaged groups, my focus is on people from advantaged groups. I will discuss reasons for resistance that are applicable to different forms of oppression and to social justice in general. In the next chapter, I will suggest ways to prevent and address it.

Just as there are differences among different types of oppression, there can be particular kinds of resistance to specific "isms". For example, I have found that people become defensive during discussions of classism when there are challenges to the class system. People immediately interpret this as advocacy for socialism or communism (which are considered dirty words and of which they usually have distorted views). They also perceive it as a threat to their desire for upward mobility and "making it". In addition, there is frequently resistance to issues related to heterosexism due to religious beliefs. Resistance to exploring ableism often involves the fear of facing one's own vulnerability to becoming disabled. I will not address resistance to specific forms of oppression. Even though some of these topics require particular insight and strategies, the perspectives and approaches I am presenting can be helpful in most circumstances.

What is Resistance?

When people are resistant, they are unable to seriously engage with the material. They refuse to consider alternative perspectives that challenge the dominant ideology that maintains the status quo. They resist information or experiences that may cause them to question their worldview. They may dismiss the idea that oppression or systemic inequalities are real.

Resistance stems from fear and discomfort. Since we are asking people to question their fundamental belief systems, it makes sense that people feel threatened and act resistant. Defensiveness, specifically, is a way to mitigate anxiety, assuage guilt, or protect against other painful feelings. It is irrational, an automatic reaction rather than a considered choice (Clark, 1991, p. 231). When people's needs for safety and stability are not met, they turn off, shut down, and avoid new information—hardly conditions for education to occur.

In some educational literature, "resistance" is used in a different way (Giroux, 1983; Apple, 1982). "Resistance theory" refers to a student's unwillingness to learn as a political act. Students from oppressed groups may refuse to participate in their education when they perceive the school and the curriculum to be culturally inappropriate or oppressive. This is not the type of resistance I am referring to. In this book, I specifically focus on resistance by people from dominant groups to learning about social justice.

Let me further clarify what I mean by resistance. Resistance is not the same as prejudice. Prejudices are pre-judgments—attitudes and beliefs about particular social groups. Resistance is not about people's specific views, but their openness to consider other perspectives. Prejudice reduction asks that people identify and reevaluate the messages they have received and the assumptions they make. The unwillingness to participate in that type of personal exploration is exactly what resistance is. Some people may not hold negative views about individuals from certain dominated groups, yet they deny the existence of social oppression. Needless to say, as we educate about social justice issues, we must help people examine their prejudices. But addressing resistance is the precursor to that endeavor.

I also do not consider questions and debate about the material done in the spirit of open inquiry to be resistance. Genuinely grappling with issues can reflect engagement. In fact, critical thinking can involve analyzing, questioning, and challenging ideas. My goal as an educator is not to have everyone think the same way or as I do. Rather, I want them to engage with the material in a critical and self-reflective way, to develop a more informed and thoughtful understanding of themselves and their world.

There is the danger of mislabeling certain behavior as resistance due to our own fears or cultural ignorance. Some educators are uncomfortable with strong emotions, conflict or challenges. Their own discomfort leads them to see these behaviors as resistance and unproductive. The communication styles of some cultural groups (i.e. Jews, African Americans) tend to be more emotional and confrontational (Kochman, 1981; Tannen, 1990). Challenge and debate can actually be a sign of engagement and learning. Trying to suppress these types of exchanges may unintentionally undermine educational goals. On the other hand, other cultural groups (e.g. Asians) may be more quiet and deferential to the teacher. This might be construed as a type of passive resistance; the educator might assume that the student is not engaged and is simply trying to please the teacher. We need to be careful not to misinterpret these various kinds of behaviors and presume resistance when there is none. Gaining knowledge of different cultural styles is one way we can help ensure we don't mislabel behavior. We can also see if people, despite their particular style, are willing to consider new perspectives, reexamine their assumptions, and reflect on what others have to say.

Resistance can be one of the most difficult aspects of educating about diversity and social justice. Often, we feel angry at resistant behavior and frustrated with the individuals. They can make us feel incompetent. It becomes hard to like or to connect with people who are being resistant. Most of us are painfully aware that we are least effective when we feel this way.

We can address those feelings and enhance our effectiveness by better understanding resistance. Rather than viewing resistant individuals as stubborn or obnoxious, we might see them as people who are afraid or in pain. This can increase our empathy and help us to develop strategies for intervention.

Socio-Political Factors

We cannot understand resistance without understanding the social context in which it occurs. If we consider the realities in which we live, it is hardly surprising that people become defensive when social justice becomes a topic of discussion. Our social, political, and economic systems create and reinforce worldviews and ways of acting that undermine an openness to true democracy and equity.

Most broadly, social relations in this country are structured based on a power-over (Kreisberg, 1992; Lappe, 2010) or dominator model (Eisler, 1987). This top-down model is characterized by inequality, ranking, domination, and intimidation. It fosters a dualistic, win-lose mentality, and the belief that people need to compete for scarce resources. Coming out "on top" or "ahead" is the primary measure of personal value. People assume that dominating others is natural, normal, inevitable, and desirable. Therefore, this view erodes investment in fundamental change or true social justice. (I discuss this further in Chapter 9.)

Although this type of social system perpetuates oppression, certain aspects of it are especially relevant to understanding resistance to social justice issues. The structures and values of hierarchy, competition, meritocracy, and individualism, along with the presumed normalcy and superiority of the dominant group and the material benefits to people from dominant groups are one aspect. The second aspect is the social climate and norms that dehumanize oppressed people and deny differences. I will discuss each of these more specifically.

Structures and Values

In general, the system is set up to the advantage of dominant groups. People from these groups gain *material benefits* from oppression. The very nature of being part of a privileged group means that one has greater access to resources, opportunities, and unearned advantages because they are denied to others. Social change threatens these privileges that have been taken for granted and alters the rules of the game. As Wellman (1977) noted, White Americans want to attend to Black's demands while avoiding the institutional reorganization that might cause them to lose ground (p. 216).

People have also been conditioned to believe in the *normalcy and superiority of people from privileged groups*. Through the messages from the dominant culture, individuals from privileged groups internalize (consciously or unconsciously) that they are somehow better and more "normal" than people from the oppressed group. It therefore can make little sense to make equal other people and cultures deemed inferior or to attempt to reduce the dominance of "superior" people.

Like oppression, which is grounded in dominant and subordinate relations, our social dynamics and institutional structures are based on *hierarchies*. Schools and workplaces are organized hierarchically; some people are considered better than and/or superior to others. Higher positions generally confer greater status and privilege. No matter where people are in the hierarchy, they usually strive to be "above" others and to stay "one up". The only alternative seems to be "one-down". Since people from disadvantaged groups are usually at the lower levels of the hierarchy, they serve to elevate people from dominant groups. Continuing to see people from subordinated groups as inferior justifies and maintains this stratification.

Competition is embedded in our hierarchical structures. In order to advance in the hierarchy, one needs to beat out others. This serves to create a zero-sum dynamic; one person's gain comes at another's expense. We often need to compete for status, power, and resources—be they material (e.g. jobs) or emotional (e.g. attention or respect). Since we are encouraged to see others as threats to our achievement or well-being, we have little incentive to enhance their situation.

A *belief in meritocracy* makes this competitive system seem fair. Increasingly, people from dominant groups assume that the playing field has been leveled and that people therefore get what they deserve. People from advantaged groups maintain that anyone can succeed if they have the ability and work hard. Lack of success is attributed to incompetence, laziness or cultural deficits. The existence or impact of inequalities and discrimination are minimized or discounted. "People who believe in a just world are most likely to see victims as meriting their misfortune and/or asking for it" (Rubin & Peplau, 1975, p. 71). A victim-blaming culture undermines concern for those in disadvantaged positions and reduces the perception that the current system needs to change.

Moreover, our culture promotes *individualism*. Unlike other cultures that emphasize group membership and a collective sense of self, the United States glorifies the autonomous individual (Bellah, Madsen, Sullivan, Swidler & Tipton, 1985; Sampson, 1988). "Look out for Number One" and "Pull yourself up by your own bootstraps" are common expectations and advice. This individualistic orientation fosters a preoccupation with self-sufficiency and advancing oneself, regardless of the impact on others. Individualism also impedes our ability to see ourselves as part of a privileged social group that unfairly benefits from inequality. Most people tend toward individualistic analyses of oppression. They attribute inequities to individual prejudices and discrimination. The focus, therefore, becomes trying to change bigoted individuals, rather than examining the cultural values and institutional structures that maintain oppression. There are those who claim that because they already are treating everyone nicely and fairly, they do not need education about diversity. Some people may resist exploring social issues for fear of feeling guilty or personally accountable for social inequities. There is an investment for people from privileged groups to retain this individualistic perspective. If people acknowledge a system that advantages their group, it may lead them to question their own accomplishments. This lack of larger social and historical perspective allows some people from immigrant white ethnic groups, whose families "made it" to assume that others today could do so as well if they just worked as hard.

Competition and individualism are mutually reinforcing. As people become focused on themselves, they increasing view others as rivals. The more people are defined as rivals, the harder it is to build an overall sense of community or to establish genuine connection. This leads to a greater focus on self and the erosion of social responsibility. Similarly, the more people are self-oriented, feel responsible for their own survival, and become obsessed with their success, the more they see others as competitors. Dominant groups may have the most intensified self-absorption since they have the most opportunity for mobility and aggrandizement (Derber, 1979).

Competitive individualism is fostered by the dominant culture, rooted in institutional structures and exacerbated by economic forces.

> People are cut adrift from any community providing economic security and thrown into a labor market that rewards individual performance, while making employment precarious and highly competitive; each individual must become self-oriented simply to subsist and succeed. (Derber, 1979, p. 91)

Theses values and ways our society is organized are joined with additional societal factors that influence one's perspective on the need and desire for social justice.

Social Climate and Norms

Public *scapegoating and the dehumanization of oppressed groups* further promotes resistance to social justice. Immigrants, people of color, gays and lesbians, and women (especially feminists) are frequently blamed for the ills and breakdown of society. There has been a rise in the backlash against immigrants, especially Latinos, and assumptions that most Muslims are linked to terrorism. Oppressed groups are often portrayed or discussed in less than fully human ways. For example, while debating a welfare bill, House Republicans compared welfare recipients to alligators and wolves (*New York Times*, July 19, 1996) and a lieutenant governor from South Carolina likened government assistance to the poor to feeding stray animals (Associated Press, Jan. 25, 2010). When Barack Obama was running for and elected president, there were many cartoons and jokes linking Michelle and him with apes.

Not only are people from oppressed groups scapegoated, they are also blamed for their own social situation. To account for social problems or inequality, this "blaming the victim" ideology (Ryan, 1970) locates problems in the individual rather than in the social structures. The marginalization of groups of people is attributed to their own failings; they are somehow deviant, lazy, unintelligent, or "culturally disadvantaged." Consistent with an individualistic orientation, the focus is on changing the individual, not society.

A *conservative political climate* contributes to this thinking. Since the 1980s, social programs have been dismantled and governmental efforts to address inequality have been eroded. Hate radio has boomed. Claims of "political correctness" have become popular and progressive social causes are no longer in vogue. The religious Right has gained enormous popularity and political power.

Despite this "public noise" about racism and other types of inequalities, there are *taboos against acknowledging differences and discussing oppression*. People are generally taught not to notice differences; to do so implies that one is prejudiced. The preferred stance is color blindness (or other types of denials of differences), what Ruth Frankenberg (1993) refers to as color- and power-evasion. In a country where most people consider themselves middle class, despite huge ranges in income and wealth, one is not supposed to acknowledge our class system. There is a publicly perpetuated norm to avoid honest, meaningful discussions about our social identities, social inequities, and our experiences because of them. People enter our classrooms and workshops with this internalized taboo, and a lack of skill or comfort in having these types of conversations.

These various interlocking factors provide little institutional or cultural support to engage in an exploration of social justice. We are discouraged from recognizing and discussing systemic inequality, and from developing a sense of community or social responsibility. Needless to say, this is not absolute; we receive contradictory messages as well—to help those less fortunate, to be kind to your neighbors, to treat others as you want to be treated. Nonetheless, the dominant values and social structures push us to act otherwise—to maintain the status quo and reserve our positions of power. Thus, this provides rich soil for the growth of resistance.

Psychological Factors

These social, cultural, political, and economic factors affect our psychology and worldview. There is an ongoing dialectic between the psychological and the societal, the personal and the political. As our consciousness is shaped by the dominant ideology and institutionalized practices, it influences how we act, how we view ourselves, and how we perceive others. We become conditioned to see the world in particular ways and to act accordingly.

Clearly, there is much in the dominant culture that lays a foundation for resistance to social justice. To some extent, we are products of our environment. However, these cultural values and institutional practices get internalized in personal and idiosyncratic ways. Based on our particular psyches, social identities, cultural backgrounds, and circumstances, we respond to these influences differently. Thus, while resistance has social roots, it is ultimately a psychological phenomenon. There are numerous psychological processes at work which help explain this need to resist new perspectives about social reality. While there may be intrapsychic dynamics involved, I will primarily focus on what I see as social-psychological issues.

Focus on One's Own Pain and Plight

In the previous section, I discussed how our economic and social systems, which reflect an "ethos of selfishness, materialism and cynicism", fuel fears, pain, and insecurities. Many people feel underappreciated and under-recognized. Accepting the notion of a meritocracy, they blame themselves for not being more successful. People often become resistant to social justice issues or the plight of others when they are focused on their own distress or anxiety. A generally narcissistic culture also contributes to people's absorption with their own lives and personal struggles. Preoccupation with self and self-concern can reduce one's attention to or caring about others (Staub, 1978).

I regularly hear people from privileged groups express concerns about their own well-being, some clearly tied to societal situations, others to more personal issues. Few people from dominant groups feel powerful or greatly advantaged. Even though they are the so-called benefactors of oppression, they may feel victimized as well. Many have personal stories about how they were discriminated against, excluded, or stereotyped. They often feel angry and hurt by those experiences. White people have recalled how they were snubbed by people of color and assumed to be racist. Others recount aspects of their socialization, which have had negative or painful consequences. People from wealthy families have discussed how they have felt isolated from other people, and received material goods instead of love and family connection. Men talk about how they were taught to hide and ignore their feelings and pretend to be someone they weren't.

People from privileged groups may also perceive that it is they who are really at a disadvantage in many cases. They complain that low-income people or people of color get various kinds of financial, employment, or academic support for which middle-class and White people are ineligible. Some White men feel that they are unfairly losing jobs to White women and people of color due to affirmative action and that they are cast as the scapegoats in society. Heterosexuals may believe that gays and lesbians are getting special rights. Regardless of the accuracy of their beliefs, their emotions and experiences are real. Even when not directly blaming others, they still have worries about paying for their education, getting affordable housing, obtaining quality childcare, or keeping their job in the midst of downsizing. This focus on their own concerns affects their openness and ability to participate in a self-reflective and critical educational process.

People from privileged groups who are strongly identified with one of their subordinated group identities may have little interest in exploring the areas of their lives where they are privileged or the oppression of other groups. They may be narrowly focused on the pain or difficulty they face as a person from a disadvantaged group. Since the experience of victimization or oppression is usually more salient, they may have difficulty acknowledging privilege. It is challenging to them to see how they are both privileged and oppressed and to consider how their privileged and oppressed identities intersect and interact. In Chapter 2, I discussed how people in privileged groups often try to minimize their dominant identity and emphasize their targeted identity. Being the "victim" is usually more attractive than being the "oppressor". This focus on their subordinated identity to the exclusion of other aspects of their identity may also be related to their process of social identity development, which I discuss later.

In some cases, it is unacknowledged pain that becomes the source for resistance. Swiss psychoanalyst, Alice Miller (1990) describes the "hidden cruelties of childhood" and "poisonous pedagogies"—the various ways children are abused, manipulated, objectified, and used to satisfy their parents' needs. She maintains that unless people have the opportunity to examine and work through these hurts, they are unable to acknowledge the suffering of others. They deny others' pain in order to resist facing their own pain. Unless people consciously deal with their mistreatment, they are more likely to lack empathy and to mistreat others.

Stage of Social Identity Development

In the previous chapter, I outlined some models of social (racial) identity development that can be useful in understanding people's self-concepts and worldviews (Hardiman and Jackson, 1992, 1997; Helms, 1992, 1995; Jones & Carter, 1996; Tatum, 1997). Resistance may be related to where people are in their development of social (racial) consciousness. Individuals are more likely to be resistant at certain stages, in particular, Reintegration (Helms model) and Acceptance (Hardiman and Jackson model). At these stages, individuals have internalized the dominant belief system about themselves and others. They may be invested in the status quo and most resistant to alternative ways of construing social relations.

During Reintegration (in the Helms model), as people deal with their awareness of racism, their feelings of guilt or denial may be transformed into fear or anger directed toward people of color. They revert to blaming the victim and to beliefs of superiority. There is the effort to restore their sense of privilege by idealizing Whites and White culture and denigrating people of color and their cultures.

In the Acceptance Stage, people also support the dominant ideology. In Passive Acceptance, people unconsciously collude with the unjust system. They participate in maintaining inequality, often without ill-intent, simply by going along with the status quo. While there may be some resistance from people at this stage as their assumptions are challenged, they are less vehemently entrenched in a worldview that maintains oppression. People in Active Acceptance, however, consciously subscribe to a worldview that supports domination and subordination. They intentionally perpetuate attitudes and actions that oppress other people. They are invested in a belief system that preserves their dominance. We can expect the most resistance from people with this perspective.

When people make the transition from Acceptance to Resistance (in this case, meaning the resistance to an oppressive ideology), they become more aware of systems of social injustice and more critical of them. In many cases, this state of disequilibrium creates an openness to new information. However, this period also can be marked by fear and uncertainty. People may worry about the implications of this questioning and self-examination. If the discomfort or fear is too great, they may feel overwhelmed and close down.

People in Active Resistance in a subordinated identity may also avoid dealing with their dominant identities or have minimal concern about people from other disadvantaged groups. At this point, many are steeped in their own feelings and process. They have little attention for things outside this scope. For example, a heterosexual Latino man in active resistance regarding racism may not be willing to recognize his heterosexual or male privilege or to connect to the experiences of heterosexism faced by gays, lesbians, or bisexuals.

Cognitive Dissonance

Another psychological factor that underlies resistance is cognitive dissonance. It is the discrepancy between what we currently believe to be true and other contradictory information. "One way to think about cognitive dissonance is as psychological discomfort" (Elliot & Devine, 1994, p. 67). We often resist things that challenge our views of self, other, and how the world operates. Thus, social justice education can be a very threatening process. If you've always believed that the United States was a just place or that certain groups were inferior, it is understandable to want to shut out contradictory information that forces you to question your whole view of the world and your place in it.

There are several ways people try to reduce cognitive dissonance (Simon, Greenberg, and Brehm, 1995). One way is to change the attitude, value, opinion, or behavior. Once individuals receive information that convinces them that their current view is inaccurate, they change their belief.

Another way individuals deal with dissonance is to seek out information to reduce the inconsistency. People may try to discount or explain away the discrepancy. Some will look for facts to support their opinion, and discredit the other view. Others find ways to blame the victim (they're less intelligent or lazy) as a way to justify the oppressive conditions.

The third way to reduce cognitive dissonance is to trivialize the issue in order to reduce the importance of that which is creating discomfort. For example, people may argue that the oppression experienced really is not that bad, that things have really changed, or that another group has it worse. Sometimes they complain that people from disadvantaged groups are being oversensitive, that they are making a big deal out of nothing.

Lastly, some people simply try to avoid or distance themselves from the issues. They may psychologically or physically withdraw. In educational settings, this may include cutting classes, not doing the assignments, or being inattentive or disruptive. All of the aforementioned strategies serve to reduce the dissonance and restore psychological comfort.

The emotional ramifications of cognitive dissonance also can lead to resistance. Cognitive dissonance can be particularly threatening when it involves questioning beliefs or values learned from one's parents or other respected individuals. This can disrupt one's trust in the people and precipitate a potential rupture in relationships. This concern may be especially salient for college students who are just beginning to forge their own identity, apart from their parents. It is also discomforting to acknowledge the limitations or prejudices of people who have been held in high esteem and with whom there is a desire to have a close relationship.

Avoidance of Painful Emotions

Students may realize that allowing oneself to fully acknowledge the injustice and suffering in the world may lead to disturbing emotions. Resistance can be a way to shield themselves from painful feelings of guilt, shame, sadness, anger, and power-lessness. Therefore, instead of being open to new information and exploration, they may choose, consciously or unconsciously, to shut down or push away.

Protection of Self-Integrity and Self-Worth

Like cognitive dissonance, in which people's beliefs and values are challenged, individuals may avoid situations they fear will challenge their self-concepts. Social justice issues are resisted to protect self-integrity. Most people believe that they are good and caring. They consciously hold an egalitarian, non-prejudiced self-image (Gaertner and Dovidio, 1986). Therefore, many people resist experiences or infor-mation that might induce guilt or awareness of negative aspects of themselves. They are often concerned that they will find out how prejudiced they are or feel badly when they realize their role in perpetuating the oppression of others. Moreover, many people, especially professionals, see themselves as competent, capable, and sophisticated. They are invested in maintaining this image to themselves and others. Therefore, in educational settings, they may be reluctant to appear ignorant, foolish, or naive. This prevents them from being open to new perspectives and activities that challenge their sense of competence and control.

Another reason to become defensive is to preserve one's self-worth. If one's identity is precarious and built on feeling superior to others, then questioning that system threatens one's sense of self. Even unconsciously, people may feel that their social group is more "normal" or "better" than others. Truly valuing and validating the traits and cultures of other groups diminishes this sense of superiority. More-over, in a competitive and presumably meritocratic system, we need to constantly prove ourselves and fend off feelings of worthlessness (Kohn, 1992). Putting down others is often a way to bolster self-esteem and a sense of self-worth.

Fears about Change

Most people fear change. The unknown is scary. Especially if one accepts the dominant worldview, there is greater reason to fear social justice. People from dominant groups frequently imagine that the sharing of power and greater equity will mean that they will become oppressed. The assumption is that the same social dynamics will be in place, but that they will be in the disadvantaged role. If the only alternative is a less desirable situation, it makes sense that they would resist the notion of social change. From this perspective, it also makes sense for people to want to ally with the oppressor rather than the oppressed.

Even if people do not fear a reversal of roles, they may still be concerned about what greater equity would mean for their lives. What would they have to give up? How might their lifestyle need to change? What privileges might they lose that they now take for granted? People's worries about how they could be negatively impacted by reducing inequality may keep them from exploring social justice issues.

Other Factors

Reactions to the Educator

Resistance can result from various types of reactions to the educator. Some people struggle with authority, regardless of the specific content or leader. They do not want to feel in a lesser position and thus seek to assert their power. Certainly, diversity issues are provocative and evoke resistance, yet the underlying dynamic is to challenge anyone who is in a role of authority and is seen as telling them what to do or think. This can occur with students in a classroom or participants in a workshop within an organization. Their reaction is likely to intensify the more they assume that this will be a lesson in "political correctness."

Others tend to blame the messenger for bringing them unsettling or painful information. The instructor becomes a target for their fear and anxiety. The leader is attacked for presenting issues that make them feel uncomfortable. They blame the educator who "made them" become aware of certain personal characteristics or social realities.

There are also dynamics that arise between students and teachers due to their social identities. Allsup (1995) suggests that there is a "bond of unstated but understood affirmation between white male students and a white male instructor" (p. 89). When a White male teacher reveals and challenges the system of White male privilege, White male students may feel betrayed. They may become angry when the educator acts in ways that violate the implicit norms that maintain oppression and the assumption that "he is one of us". Similar reactions can occur with other "isms" when the educator from the dominant group does not espouse the expected perspective and breaks the assumed sense of solidarity.

When teachers are members of the subordinated group, students from the dominant group are more likely to challenge their authority and credibility. A sense of superiority and entitlement (particularly from White males) allows them to feel freer to do so. White women and people of color, especially women of color, are often viewed as less competent and less qualified. Students may not take them as seriously and question their expertise. When educators address a form of oppression where they are in the disadvantaged group, they may be perceived as self-serving, complaining, oversensitive, bashing people from the privileged group, or imposing their opinion. In these various ways, people use the educator as an excuse or vehicle to avoid dealing with the material.

Religious and Cultural Beliefs

Many people use their spiritual/religious beliefs as a foundation from which to do work for social justice. (I discuss this further in Chapter 8). Individuals with strong religious or cultural convictions can be open to and respectful of other views, even if they ultimately do not accept them. Many people find ways to integrate new understandings and changing social dynamics into their religious or cultural belief systems. However, these beliefs can also promote intolerance and closemindedness which may manifest as resistance. Some people who hold strong religious or cultural beliefs use these as reasons not to consider other points of view. They rigidly maintain the correctness of their positions and dogmatically reject the validity of other perspectives or experiences.

White Men and Resistance

Given the various societal and psychological factors discussed earlier, it is not surprising that many educators often find White males to be most resistant to social justice. Male psychology, socialization, and social position encompass and often epitomize the previously described reasons for resistance. First, they tend to have an individualistic and separate sense of self. Landrine (1992) describes two ways of identifying with "self": the "referential self" which is egocentric and western in origin, and the "indexical self" which is sociocentric. The referential self focuses on the "rugged individualist", which is usually associated with White, male, middle-class Americans. Rarely do White men see themselves as part of a social group or understand how, as a group, they benefit from social inequality. Therefore, it is hard for them to understand oppression as a social system or their role in it by virtue to their social identity.

Second, they tend to imagine relationships as hierarchies with an emphasis on competition and maintaining or advancing oneself in this hierarchy (Gilligan, 1980/ 1993; Tannen, 1990). Their identity often has been based on a sense of superiority and on "making it" in society. Creating more equity changes roles and expectations, throwing into question their sense of identity.

In addition, most men have been socialized to suppress their feelings and fears. In an effort to deny and block feelings, they may resist emotion-generating experiences. It is threatening to acknowledge the pain of participating in an oppressive system and the ways they feel vulnerable or hurt others. They are generally less skilled in accessing their feelings and more constrained in expressing them. The denial of their own pain and emotions makes it more difficult to identify with the feelings of other people. This reduces their capacity for empathy, an important component of social justice work.

Several studies have reported that white men increasingly feel that they are unfairly blamed for social problems (Cose, 1995; Gallagher, 1997; Gates, 1993). White men often believe that other groups are getting advantages or special treatment that they are denied. I frequently hear White male students in my classes express anxiety about getting or keeping a good job. Narrowly focused on their own concerns about security, they have little interest in worrying about others.

Moreover, White men have received the greatest benefits from oppression and therefore have the most to lose. Since they have been "the norm" against which others have been measured, it can be frightening to become "decentered" and lose some of the privileges and superiority they have taken for granted. They often experience this shift toward equity as unfairness (since they're not getting as much as they used to). This generates a backlash against social justice efforts.

Conclusion

Clearly, the institutional structures and values of the dominant culture lay a strong foundation for resistance to social justice issues. Our society encourages people to be self-focused, to gain their sense of self-worth by feeling superior, to see others as threats, to protect their resources, and to blame people for their failures. These messages and worldview become internalized, to which people add their own personal issues. Psychologically, resistance is more likely when people are focused on their own struggles, are in particular stages of social identity development, try to avoid cognitive dissonance, and need to protect their sense of self. Despite this litany of reasons for resistance, all hope is not lost. By considering the range of societal and psychological reasons people may be resistant, I believe we can be more compassionate and more skillful in how we work with them. As we know, we *are* able to reach many (if not most individuals). We *can* help them become more open to a process of change. In the next chapter, I'll discuss how.

5

ADDRESSING RESISTANCE

The previous chapter discussed how many socio-political and psychological factors underlie the resistance we encounter when discussing social justice issues. Our dominant cultural values, structure, and social climate emphasize competitive individualism, hierarchy, a belief in meritocracy, blaming the victim, and the denial of differences. These increase people's drive for self-preservation and advancement at the expense of others. Psychologically, fears, pain, cognitive dissonance, and the protection of one's self-concept fuel defensiveness. In the long term, we need to work for systemic change in order to transform the societal beliefs and structures that maintain inequality and create the context for resistance to social justice. In the short term, we can look at how we can reduce the factors that promote defensiveness and resistance.

Resistance is an expression of fear, anxiety, and discomfort. It blocks people's openness to explore alternative viewpoints that question the status quo, analyze systems of oppression, and offer new possibilities of social relations. To address resistance, we need to create "psychological safety and readiness" (Friedman & Lipshitz, 1992). As discussed in Chapter 3, before people can deal with challenges to their current worldview or "contradiction", they need an affirming, supportive environment or "confirmation". As educators, we need to provide people with a balance of challenge and support.

> If someone needs challenge and they get too much support, they don't learn anything. If someone needs support and they get too much challenge, they will flee the learning situation. People in defense are heavy on challenge and need support. (Bennett & Bennett, 1992, p. 4)

Therefore, in this chapter I'll discuss how to provide support and "confirmation" in order to prevent, reduce, and address resistance. Some general approaches, as well as specific interpersonal and curricular strategies will be described.

Shifting our Perspective

As educators, the way we view resistance and people who act resistant affects how much resistance we encounter and how effectively we deal with it. Moreover, when a student is being resistant, we tend to locate "the problem" solely within the psyche of the student. This tends to lead to blame and judgment. We need, however, to look at ourselves as educators and the teacher–student relationship. It is helpful to consider what is happening between the instructor and the participant that is either facilitating or impeding the person's openness. I offer two metaphors from which to think about resistance and our relationship with students.

I have done an exercise with educators where I ask them to remember a time when they got defensive or acted resistant (if possible, about a social justice issue when they were in a privileged group). In reporting their feelings in that situation, they mention, among other things, feeling angry, frustrated, invalidated, and misunderstood. As a result, they withdrew, attacked back, defended themselves or shut down. They felt that the other person made assumptions, blamed them, and didn't listen. They wished the other person had really listened to them, checked out their assumptions, and treated them respectfully.

As their responses are listed, it becomes painfully clear that their feelings and responses are very similar to how resistant students act and feel. Imagine a resistant person as someone who has shut the door and won't come out. Our first impulse may be to try to convince him to come out. When that fails, we sometimes start talking louder. As we do, the student locks the door. As we start yelling and banging on the door, insisting that he open it and come out, he starts adding bolts. As the situation escalates, he begins pushing furniture in front of the door, barricading himself in. In our zealousness for students to "get it", we can end up "banging" so loudly that students feel they need to protect themselves. When they feel attacked and blamed, they are likely to try to defend their position rather than question it. Since most of us who teach about diversity issues are personally invested and passionate about these concerns, we can easily end up trying to convince students of the importance of these issues. A more useful image is gently talking with the student and developing enough trust, safety, and validation that he gradually opens the door, further and further, until he is ready to come out.

A second metaphor is that of a dance. The martial art, Aikido, teaches that instead of trying to directly confront or block the force of the opponent, to try to move with the energy. Aikido actually means "a way of blending energy." Thomas Crum (1987) has applied this concept to conflict resolution, and I think it apt in this context also. Often we experience resistance as an attack, and our impulse is to "fight back" (not physically, I assume, but verbally or psychologically). This is reflected in "banging on the door" in the aforementioned metaphor. Rather than opposing the energy, Aikido offers us three main principles. First, honor and acknowledge the energy given. Second, accept the energy. By aligning with the direction of the attack, it dissipates the power of the attack and allows the person to be led in another direction. Instead of trying to get rid of the energy, work with it. When we direct the flow instead of being pushed around by it, this creates a dance. Third, get out of the way and remove the object of attack. Expecting but not getting a rigid target, the attacker becomes off balance. When people express resistance, they are often testing the reaction of the educator and expect a strong response. When they don't get it, the intensity is usually diminished. If we push back, we set up a confrontation and usually block progress. If we acknowledge the feelings and work with them, we can create movement. Dance rather than struggle.

Both of these images, the door and the dance provide ways for us to conceptualize how to respond to resistance. Instead of setting up an adversarial relationship in which we become more forceful, we can think about how to engage and dance with the student. I know how difficult it can be to do this. There are several times, despite my best knowledge, that I have gotten emotionally hooked and found myself doing exactly what I knew I shouldn't be. In my conversations with educators about resistance, I have found a pattern among those for whom resistance was not particularly a problem. They conveyed the deepest sense of respect and empathy for the student and centeredness in their role of educator. I'll explore this further in Chapter 11 in Issues for Educators.

For now, let's consider how to apply the aforementioned metaphors and establish the kind of context that will most allow people to feel safe enough to take risks. I will first discuss ways to prevent and reduce resistance, then how to address it when it occurs. (Figure 5.1 provides a summary of these ideas.) I offer these as suggestions, not formulas or guaranteed solutions. Even though I've tried to describe them simply, the approaches are not meant to seem simplistic given the complexity of our situations, our students, and ourselves. The suggestions are geared for dealing with people from privileged groups, but most are relevant to all students. Similarly, many of the examples refer to classrooms, though the principles apply to other situations.

Preventing and Reducing Resistance

The key to preventing and reducing resistance is creating a space that allows people to let down their guard and feel comfortable enough to explore emotionally and intellectually challenging material. In Chapter 3, I briefly mentioned ways to create a confirming climate. I will now discuss in more detail some specific ways to do so. Particular strategies will be discussed under three main approaches: build relationships and trust; affirm, validate, and convey respect for participants; and heighten their investment.

Build Relationships and Trust

The longer I live, and the more I educate, I increasingly believe that everything is about relationships. In social justice education, one of the most important

---

Preventing and Reducing Resistance

Build Relationships and Trust:

- Talk with participants beforehand
- Get to know individuals—develop rapport
- Self-disclose appropriately
- Build a supportive educational environment
- Provide clear structure and expectations

Affirm, Validate, and Convey Respect for Individuals:

- Affirm people's self-esteem
- Avoid personal blame—emphasize cultural conditioning and the systemic nature of oppression
- Acknowledge feelings, experiences, and viewpoints
- Discuss common reactions and social identity development
- Validate and build on current knowledge
- Allow people to discover information themselves
- Provide opportunities for frequent feedback

Heighten Investment:

- Allow participants to have input into or help design the class/session
- Humanize the issue
- Frame diversity issue in terms of shared principles and goals
- Explore participants' self-interest in social justice and alternatives to systems of domination

Responding to Resistance:

- Avoid getting hooked
- Assess reasons for resistance
- Invite exploration of the issue raised
- Contain the behavior (e.g. set a time limit, summarize and move on)
- If the group is resistant, go with the flow
- Provide a time-out (e.g. journaling, free writing, reactions in pairs, a break, etc.)
- Arrange a private meeting

FIGURE 5.1 Addressing Resistance to Social Justice Issues from People from Privileged Groups

determinants of whether there will be resistance is the stance of the teacher and the relationship between teacher and student. The more we are able to "join" with the students or participants, the less resistance we will encounter and the more able we will be to constructively offer challenges.

Talk with Participants Beforehand

When I anticipate that I will encounter a lot of resistance, I try to meet with people before the actual sessions. If I will be training in an organization where I know there is hostility around the issue, I try to do some needs assessments or data gathering that provide me with an opportunity to talk with people who will be involved in the training. This usually helps to diffuse some of the resistance since those individuals get to be heard. It also allows them to get to know me, to see that I'm a reasonable person, and to understand what I intend to do. It also alerts me to what some of the particular issues might be. Knowing the root of the resistance provides opportunities to develop ways to address it. This approach can also be used before other types of meetings, classes, or workshops. Whenever possible, before the session talk to people on the committee or in the group who are likely to block what you want to accomplish. Beyond just meeting with the participants beforehand, actually involve them in designing, or facilitating planning the sessions.

Get to Know Individuals—Develop Rapport

During a class or training, we can make an intentional effort to connect with individuals who are being resistant. Chat during breaks, before or after class, and encourage visits during office hours. Developing some rapport reduces the resistance. Even if students don't agree with some of the material, they feel less need to be defensive or disruptive if they can trust or like the educator. I have also found that the greater the rapport with students, the easier it is for me to effectively deal with them. When I am in touch with my caring for the students, and I know that they believe that I care and have their interests at heart, it provides a greater range of educational options. I feel freer to use (appropriate) humor and physical contact, and to be more direct. I can more easily trust my responses and know that the students will take my actions as intended and in turn, will be more responsive.

Self-disclose Appropriately

Self-disclosure on the part of the teacher can enhance teacher–student rapport and help increase safety. Appropriately sharing personal experiences with discrimination, our process of coming to understand oppression, our mistakes made in dealing with diversity, and our struggles to overcome prejudices can make the teacher more human, less "perfect", and easier to identify with. It can also make students feel more comfortable to disclose or acknowledge their concerns, feelings, and vulnerabilities. Some educators will be very intentional about when and how they self-disclose. They will choose some things to share at the beginning of the class, and others to reveal as the course progresses. Particular stories will be saved until predetermined points in the class to correspond with the issues that are being addressed. Teacher self-disclosure is a way to promote and sustain openness and trust. However, educators should always be thoughtful about what they share, ensuring that it is for the benefit of the students, not simply self-serving.

Build a Supportive Educational Environment

Class/workshop ground rules are a central part of developing a confirming climate. While these guidelines can be suggested by the educator, I prefer to let the group develop them. Given the content and structure of the class, I ask students to identify the things that would make this a sufficiently safe and productive educational environment for them. Invariably, students include items such as respect, confidentiality, no put-downs, really listening, and being non-judgmental. Often I will ask people to clarify what they mean by certain general terms, such as respect or being non-judgmental. I will also make suggestions to the list, as necessary and agreed to by the students, often including the importance of speaking from one's own experience. Trust is built in the process of constructing the list, since they get to discuss some of their needs and concerns and come to agreements. Furthermore, students subsequently feel greater ownership and investment in the rules they have created. Throughout the course, the students and I will refer back to the list, especially if we are embarking on a difficult discussion or if some guidelines have been violated.

It is also helpful to acknowledge the feelings people have as they begin the class or training. Frequently people are concerned about saying the wrong thing, what others will think of them, finding out how prejudiced they are, of conflicts in the group, or of being forced to accept information they don't believe. Surfacing these concerns lets people know they're not alone and that it's all right to have some reservations. One activity I do that addresses this is called "hopes and fears". Give each person an index card and ask them to anonymously write on one side a hope they have for the class/session, on the other side a fear or concern they have. Then collect and redistribute the cards, asking each person to read the card they have received. People just listen to what people have written. We can then discuss how to address the hopes and concerns people have (often the guidelines are a good way to do this). In groups with higher trust, I'll ask people to share this information in pairs, and then have them report out.

Other types of ice-breaker activities also allow people to get to know each other and become more comfortable. There are many activities, usually fun and engaging, that loosen people up and begin to get them involved with the class/training. Exercises that give people the opportunity to work in pairs or small groups, to share (low risk) things about themselves, and to begin to think about the content of the class are usually effective. A particularly adaptable format is "rotating pairs". People are asked a series of short questions, each time pairing up with a new person and answering the question. (They can also do this as concentric circles, with the inner circle facing a partner on the outer circle. After each question, the outer circle moves to the right, so they get a new partner.) The questions can range from asking about a favorite activity, where they would rather be than here, one thing they like about their cultural background, a challenging situation in dealing with diversity, a time they experienced discrimination or stereotyping, or when they first became aware of racism. The questions can be geared toward both getting acquainted and generating content for the class.

Provide Clear Structure and Expectations

Some people enter learning situations with a host of concerns about what will happen and what will be expected of them. They may assume that they will have to espouse what is considered "politically correct", unwillingly reveal personal things about themselves, participate in embarrassing activities, or face arbitrary grading/evaluation based on whether or not they agree with the instructor. In any educational situation, it is helpful for people to know upfront generally what will occur and what is expected. It allays people's anxiety and their related resistance to hear what the agenda is. It reassures them to know that no one will be forced to do anything they do not want to do (they have the option to "pass" in an activity), and that the point is to learn and consider new information not to blame people or convert them. If the instructor conveys this with genuineness and respect, most people feel somewhat relieved and are more able to be open to the experience.

In classroom situations, where grading is an issue, we need to be especially clear about how students will be evaluated. They need to be assured that they will not be pressured to adopt particular beliefs or graded on how prejudiced they are. Instead, grading can be based on their ability to understand, articulate, and apply the material; to engage in critical analysis; to write effectively; etc. It is important to have a syllabus that clearly describes assignments, grading procedures, and class expectations.

Affirm, Validate, and Convey Respect for Participants

Many people from privileged groups enter classes or workshops on diversity issues concerned that they will be made to feel badly about themselves, and therefore immediately become self-protective. If students believe that they will be attacked or vilified for who they are or what they believe, they are likely to shut down or fight back. We are more likely to face resistance if participants feel they are being condescended to, underestimated or forced to accept particular views. Therefore, it is essential to create a space where people feel seen, heard, and valued.

Affirm People's Self-esteem

If individuals have positive self-concepts, they can more easily sustain threats to their worldview without becoming defensive (Steele, Spencer, & Lynch, 1993). If people's self-esteem is sufficiently intact, they can more easily engage in the sometimes difficult self-reflection required in social justice education. We can create ways to support a positive self-concept as people examine dynamics of oppression. People can explore their own ethnic or cultural background, becoming more aware of the specific traits and strengths of their culture, and ways their social group has overcome obstacles. They can discuss ways they have effectively dealt with diversity, supported equity, or acted against injustice. They can read about or research people from their dominant social group who have worked for social justice. These various activities reinforce that just because they're White or men (or part of a privileged group), this does not make them bad people. Throughout the course, they can have opportunities to participate in socially responsible activities such as letter-writing, boycotts, petitions, fund-raising, volunteering, mentoring, or other kinds of activism. These kinds of activities not only build self-esteem, they also counter powerlessness.

Avoid Personal Blame—Emphasize Cultural Conditioning and the Systemic Nature of Oppression

When students from privileged groups understand that it is not their fault that they hold biased views or unintentionally act in oppressive ways, they are less likely to become defensive. They did not ask to develop these attitudes and behaviors. Individuals are conditioned to develop distorted views and have been socialized into narrow roles. To illustrate how pervasive and insidious this conditioning is, students can do exercises in which they recount stereotypes they have heard about different groups. Their lists are usually remarkably alike. Similarly, they can be asked to discuss the messages they got about how to act as a male or female growing up. Again, within the male groups and the female groups, the socialization tends to be very similar, despite differences in age or culture. It is useful for students to understand this conditioning, so they can be more authentic and challenge it.

Nor are they personally responsible for oppression. While individuals play a role, systems of inequality are rooted in history and social structures. People from privileged groups certainly have a responsibility to address inequality, yet they alone are not the cause. When the maintenance of structural inequality is reduced to the actions of individuals, it moves the focus away from the need to challenge the dominant ideology, institutionalized policies, and unjust systems. It is more constructive to have participants think about their role in challenging injustice than feeling blamed for it.

Acknowledge Feelings, Experiences, and Viewpoints

The opportunity for people to voice their feelings, experiences, and viewpoints and to have them acknowledged is central to the process of confirmation. It validates their concerns and communicates that divergent perspectives are welcome in the class. Not only does this help people feel heard and respected, it also provides educators with information about the needs and concerns of students. This can inform the class content and process. In addition, it allows students to hear themselves. This can help them to sort out and work through some of their experiences and reactions, and provide a point from which to compare their views later in the course. (See Tatum, 1992 for a good illustration of using student self-interviews at the beginning and end of the course.)

There is another reason students need the opportunity to voice their feelings and concerns in a confirming environment: when people are focused on their own pain and needs, they are frequently unable to attend to or care about the misfortune of others. As noted in the previous chapter, people also may need to become more conscious of their past mistreatment and how this has impacted their current attitudes and behavior. Therefore, we need to provide the opportunity for individuals to explore some of their feelings about their own experiences before moving on to consider other people's treatment. Alice Miller (1990) suggests,

> It's not possible for someone really to clarify his situation and dissolve his fears until he can feel them rather than discuss them. Only then is the veil lifted and he realizes his true need: not a tutor, not an interpreter, not a confessor; he needs space for his own growth and the company of an enlightened witness on the long journey on which he has set out. (1990, p. 184)

The importance of bearing witness is illustrated in the popular film, *The Color of Fear*. Though this film can be read and interpreted in many ways and on multiple levels, it struck me as a powerful example of how people need to acknowledge their pain in order to reduce their resistance. The video documents a gathering of men from different racial backgrounds who come together for a weekend to discuss racism. Several of the men of color try to get one White man, David, to acknowledge the existence of racism. They repeatedly provide information, tell their stories, and share their experiences with various types of racial discrimination. They speak calmly, angrily, rationally, and passionately; they do everything short of standing on their heads. David remains steadfastly unmoved. He continues to minimize and invalidate their experiences. He maintains that they are being over-sensitive, assuming racism where there is none, and not making the effort to "fit in" or take advantage of opportunities that do exist. He continually blames the victim. Near the end of the weekend, there is some movement. David reveals that he was abused as a child by his authoritarian father. He emotionally recounts how he heard racist comments and jokes, learned to obey in order to survive, and protected himself from emotions. He realizes that as an adult, he has tried to avoid dealing with the pain and strife of the real world; thus, he has minimized the feelings of the men in the group so that he would have to deal with them. He admits how unaware he is of the dynamics of racism. It was not until David acknowledged his own mistreatment that he could begin to recognize the pain systematically inflicted on people of color.

Of course, people have various kinds of pain, degrees of mistreatment, and different levels of need to address it. For some people, dealing with their experience of discrimination and prejudice may be a pre-requisite for engaging in the exploration of the mistreatment and oppression of other people. People from a privileged group who also have a salient subordinated identity often need to express their experience with that oppression and have it validated before they can allow other oppressed groups to be the focus of discussion. If not, they may feel that the others' oppression is seen as more important than their oppression. For example, White Jews can be reluctant to fully engage in a discussion of racism if they feel their experiences with anti-Semitism have not been recognized as another legitimate form of oppression.

Similarly, men of color may resist discussing sexism and owning their own involvement in it until they feel racism has been adequately acknowledged. Moreover, we need to acknowledge the multiple and intersectional nature of one's identity and how that affects one's lives. People do experience privilege (and subordination) differently depending on their other identities.

In telling their stories, people from privileged groups may need others to recognize how their lives have not been full of benefits and the ways that they have been hurt by social inequity. Few people from dominant groups feel powerful or greatly advantaged. Even though they are the so-called benefactors of oppression, they often feel victimized as well. As noted in the previous chapter, they usually have personal accounts about how they were mistreated and how they feel they are now the ones being discriminated against.

The issue is not whether we agree with their interpretation of events or how we feel about their situations. The point is to help them deal with their feelings so they can become engaged with exploring social justice issues. We are trying to create an openness and ability to participate in a self-reflective, critical educational process. Although it is important to acknowledge different experiences and perspectives, this of course does not mean that they need to be accepted as the only reality. Regardless of the accuracy of their beliefs, their emotions and experiences are real. Students as well as teachers need to develop the skills to actively listen and to be empathic, without having to accept all views as equally valid. Listening empathically and understanding does not necessarily mean agreement. We can assist students in gaining more information and in linking the personal with the political to consider how their individual experiences are related to social conditions.

As teachers, we need to make careful choices about the best way to allow students from dominant groups to voice their feelings of pain and mistreatment, without alienating other students, invalidating people from subordinated groups, or derailing the class. We should not be therapists or attempt to make the class into a therapy session (though referrals for some people may be appropriate). There have been a variety of ways I have tried to allow students to express their experiences and perspectives. These choices depend on the dynamics and make-up of the class, time available, personalities of the students, and my state of being, among other factors. Students should be reminded of the class ground rules as necessary.

Time can be created in the class for people to share their feelings and experiences as part of the regular whole class discussion. Another option is to have paired or small group discussions. Students initially could talk with others who share their background. Or, students could participate in self-selected heterogeneous groups of people with whom they have a personal relationship. In these contexts, students could have greater time and freedom to discuss their experiences with people who are likely to be supportive. Subsequently, there could be a more limited sharing with the whole class.

Students can also do free-writing during class in response to the readings, discussion topics, or focus question, which could then selectively be shared with the whole class. Journal-writing is another effective way for students to express and reflect on their own experiences without the concern for other students' reactions and judgments. Responding to (not evaluating) their journal entries, enables us to recognize the student's feelings and can allow a dialogue between student and teacher. We can invite students who require more attention than is available or warranted in the whole class or in these assignments to speak with us after class or during office hours.

It can be one of the more challenging tasks to listen to people from privileged groups talk about their concerns and mistreatment, especially when it may seem relatively insignificant or distorted. Nevertheless, I have seen important growth and openness occur as a result—for the students themselves, for their classmates, and for myself. Even students from marginalized groups have reported that hearing experiences and feelings have helped them to humanize and better understand people from privileged groups. We can also help all students make links between their own feelings and experiences and those of other people, promoting empathy, and a broader understanding of the dynamics of oppression.

Discuss Common Reactions and Social Identity Development

It can also be helpful to discuss with students at the beginning of the class some common feelings and reactions people have as they learn about multicultural issues. We can go beyond just acknowledging their feelings at the moment, to helping them to anticipate what they might experience as the class progresses. Describe the tendency to want to avoid threatening material, the anger, guilt, or sadness that may arise, or the desire to discount information that challenges currently-held views. Have them think about how they might deal with their feelings should they occur in the course of the class.

Sharing the stages of social identity development can help students make sense of their experiences as they explore social issues. (See Chapters 3 and 11 for a review of social identity development models.) They can better understand their own attitudes and responses as well as those of their classmates. Like educators, when students have a way to understand their own and others' perspectives and experiences, it can make them less threatening; they are part of a normal process. This can pre-empt some of the resistance, normalize students' feelings, and provide language to discuss resistance as it occurs in class.

Validate and Build on Current Knowledge

One way to both convey respect and minimize resistance is to acknowledge and build on what people already know. This avoids coming in as the expert who is going to tell them the right way to think. It reduces people's issues with authority and concerns about political correctness. Adults especially respond well to having their experiences and expertise validated. Case studies are particularly useful in letting them share what they already know about an issue, about what is effective or ineffective, and about solving problems. As they struggle with and debrief the case, it also allows them to notice where they need more information or ideas.

Often people make generalizations based on their own experiences (e.g. my immigrant family succeeded in school without bilingual education, therefore other immigrants don't need it). Thus, their view may be limited and incomplete. We can acknowledge their piece of the truth and expand on it, offering a broader and more complex picture. Other times, people may share information that is only partially correct. Again, we can affirm the correct aspect and provide a more accurate perspective.

Allow People to Discover Information Themselves

In general, and especially when there is resistance, people learn the most when they discover the knowledge for themselves. When information is presented that people disagree with, it can feel to them like it is being imposed. Instead, let *them* acquire the information. They can gather statistics (e.g. the racial and gender breakdown of employment in various levels and positions in an organization, or the ratio of students of color in tracked classes or special education classes); review the representation of people in the media (e.g. the number and types of roles of gay and lesbian characters); find out how much welfare recipients actually receive and the constraints on their lives; interview people from a particular group about their experiences (e.g. what it's like to be a person with a disability on campus), conduct research on a topic, using various sources; do a survey (e.g. of people's experience with sexual harassment) or observe in an organization (watch for gender or racial bias in classrooms).

In one class, after watching the film, *Still Killing Us Softly* about the images of women in advertising, a number of male students discounted the validity of the video. They claimed that the ads portrayed were exaggerated and biased, that they didn't fairly represent current advertising. I asked the class to do their own research and bring in ads from the magazines they read to compare them with what they saw in the video. They were amazed at how sexist the ads were; the males acknowledged it was worse than they thought.

People's learning can also grow out of their own experiences, whether real-life situations or simulations. Telling people information is never as convincing as actually experiencing it. The effects of inequality and the inaccuracy of blaming the victim are more powerfully conveyed by spending time in a homeless shelter, a battered women's shelter, or a poor inner-city school—and then discussing those experiences. Attempting to explain the effects of exclusion has less impact than having people go through an exercise in which they are excluded or asking them to draw on their own experiences of exclusion. There are a variety of simulations which help people understand these issues in powerful ways. Providing learning experiences where people can come to their own insights and conclusions reduces resistance and creates more meaningful learning.

Provide Opportunities for Frequent Feedback

Resistance often occurs when people feel they do not have a voice. In addition to sharing ideas and experiences in class, it helps to provide opportunities for frequent feedback about the class process and content. We can do this through short anonymous written evaluations at the end of each class (or every few classes) or longer ones periodically, through journals or through verbal check-ins at the beginning or end of classes. This provides several advantages: less will be stifled which may erupt inappropriately in the classroom, it allows for a connection with quieter students, we can engage with students in a less public way (possibly, providing more safety for them to express their views), and it reaffirms that we value students' feelings and opinions. It is then essential that their feedback is acknowledged in some way and that the educator is seen as responsive to their views. This can be done by summarizing the feedback, by making changes in the class, by allowing for some flexibility, by responding in writing in the journals, or by inviting students to talk with you further about their concerns.

Heighten Investment

We are more effective if we consider why participants would care about the diversity and social justice issues we are discussing. The content and structure needs to draw in and feel relevant to our students. As educators, we need to think about how to present the material in ways that enable them to connect, reflect their language, address their concerns, speak to their frames of reference, and allow them make a connections to their own lives.

Allow Participants to Have Input into or Help Design the Class/Training

When people have a say or role in designing the class, they feel more invested in it. It will more likely reflect their interests, reduce their sense that this is being forced on them, and increase their feelings that they are being respected. There are varying degrees to the role individuals can play. Students can be asked at the beginning of the class what questions or topics they would like to see addressed and the syllabus can be constructed to include these. They can be given choices in assignments and classroom activities, which they could have a role in leading. Students or participants can work together with us to decide the content and as well structure of the class/training. If resistance is expected, try to include some key individuals who can influence how the training will be received. If they have a role in designing it, they will be more likely to set a positive tone and encourage people to be appropriately engaged. We are also more likely to address issues that people will find relevant and useful.

This strategy was particularly effective when I was doing some training with a police department. Many of the police officers felt that more training, especially by someone who was not a police officer, was forced upon them. I worked with a couple of officers from the department who were well-respected and in positions to potentially sabotage the whole thing. Not only did they have input into the entire design, but I specifically asked them to create a few case studies that they felt would be most meaningful. The training was now seen as something done in collaboration with their department, not simply as something that was imposed from the outside.

Humanize the Issue

It is easier for people to argue facts and dismiss a topic when it is in the abstract. People can more easily turn-off information when it's impersonal or theoretical. If they are exposed to social inequities on a human level, they may get more drawn in. Consider putting a human face on the issue. Participants may be more open to exploring a topic if they see how if affects actual individuals or can relate to the situation from their own experience. Seeing and hearing about real people who deal with specific consequences of oppression—whether it be classmates, other students or colleagues or community members, can soften resistance and increase interest. As I will discuss in depth in Chapters 8 and 9, empathy is a powerful force in developing care about others. It can be used to reduce resistance as well as to motivate action.

Frame Diversity Issue in Terms of Shared Principles and Goals

Resistance is likely if people see the class or training as interfering with, irrelevant to, or contrary to their goals and values. If we can frame the issue in a way that is consistent with their principles or mission, people usually are more receptive. There will be greater buy-in if they see it as useful and aligned with their philosophy.

In organizational contexts, I will try to relate the training to their mission statement, goals or long-range planning. (The more relevance the mission statement has, the more effective this is. Unfortunately, there are often great things written on paper that have little connection to actual practice.) Agencies or businesses are usually concerned with productivity, effective teamwork, and good customer/client service (not to mention avoiding lawsuits and bad public relations)—all which impact the bottom line. Sensitivity to diversity and equity therefore helps people to work more productively in teams, to attract and retain diverse clients and customers (and talented employees), and to foster a positive public image. Schools tend to highlight meeting the needs of diverse students, creating a safe and respectful school community and fostering high achievement. In this context, attention to diversity and equity enhances their ability to teach diverse students (improving their test scores and their attentiveness in class), decreases intergroup tensions, reduces fights, and creates a more inclusive environment. I find there is always a way to connect social justice issues to a wide range of goals. In Chapter 8, under appealing to self-interest, I discuss ways to address particular needs and concerns of individuals and organizations.

More broadly, educators can appeal to people's commitment to democracy, fairness, and equality. Most people believe in these core national principles. The class can be framed as examining what these words mean and how well our country lives up to these goals (see, for example, Andrzejewski, 1995). There is ample evidence that convincingly demonstrates that we have not yet reached these ideals despite the many justifications for various inequities. Allow people to do their own assessment of how well reality matches these stated values. In general, instead of being seen as anti-American or against national or organizational principles, discuss social justice issues in the context of already established goals and commitments.

Explore their Self-interest in Social Justice and Alternatives to Systems of Domination

By helping participants reconceptualize social change, we can reduce the defensiveness that often occurs when we propose challenges to the status quo. Students are likely to resist perspectives or strategies that they deem detrimental to their current or future well-being. While people from marginalized groups tend to be more able to see how changing the status quo can be positive for them, often people from dominant groups see efforts at progressive social change as a win-lose situation (in which they will lose). Given this vantage point, it is not surprising that we encounter defensiveness.

One approach is to help reframe the discussion from a win-lose model to a view that everyone could benefit from the elimination of oppression. As students from privileged groups see how they have been limited by oppression and why it is in their self-interest to foster social change, it can help reduce resistance and increase their investment in social justice. In classes and workshops, people have shared a range of stories that reflect their understanding of some of the costs of oppression. White students have spoken about being ostracized from their families for dating a person of a different race and their fear of engaging with people of different races or cultures. Heterosexuals have acknowledged how their homophobia has led to the loss of friendships and family relationships with gays and lesbians. Men have expressed feeling pressure to assume certain "masculine" roles and behaviors that limit who they can be. People from wealthy families have talked about the guilt they experience about their privilege and the inability to relate to those from other class backgrounds. Many people can see that violence and social decay is directly related to unfair social and economic systems. This is not to pretend that there are not real advantages to their privileged status. Nonetheless, we can help individuals from dominant groups understand what they have to gain, not just what they have to lose, by creating greater equity. We can also help them see that there are alternatives to systems of inequality that can be better for all people. (In the following chapters, I describe at length the costs of oppression to people from privileged groups, some of the benefits of social justice, how to appeal to people's self-interest, and alternatives to systems of domination.)

Responding to Resistance

Even with our best efforts to prevent and reduce resistance, we still may be faced with it throughout the course or sessions. This a good time to remember the images of the door and the dance. The more we can maintain our perspective and composure, the more effective we will be, and the more we will enjoy our work.

Avoid Getting Hooked

Because resistant behavior is likely to trigger our own feelings, we need to be particularly careful not to fall into certain traps. For each of us, there are probably particular types of resistant individuals and resistant behaviors that are more likely to hook us. While we may try to avoid or ignore these individuals, we often end up focusing our attention on them at the expense of attending to the rest of the group. One trap is arguing with them and trying to convince them of our position or prove them wrong. Another trap is trying to engage people who do not appear interested or attentive. We zealously may try to capture their attention and generate some responsiveness. Usually we are reacting to our own issues and needs, and not considering what is best for the whole group.

Assess Reason for Resistance

As previously noted, there are many reasons why people become defensive. They may be feeling blamed, overwhelmed, forced to accept things they're not ready or willing to accept, or trying to protect their self-concept. Their reactions may be related to their stage of intellectual or social identity development. The more we understand what is going on, the better able we are to decide how to respond. It can be helpful to revisit the ideas suggested in the section on preventing and reducing resistance. Often, we need to reestablish safety and connection, acknowledge people's feelings, affirm their sense of self, and slow the pace.

Invite Exploration of the Issue Raised

If individuals make a statement that you perceive as resistant, you can ask them to further elaborate on why they think or feel this way. Many times, if people aren't immediately shut down and do have a chance to be heard, they can then listen to others. So, when a student says angrily, "The problem isn't with discrimination. Someone just has to be willing to work hard," instead of quickly trying to prove them wrong, we could say calmly, with genuine interest, "It sounds like you have strong views about this. What has led you to feel this way?"

In the course of their explanation, we can acknowledge their feelings and perspective, and look for ways to lead the conversation into a broader exploration of what might account for differences in achievement or success. It is extremely important to invite other perspectives, especially if one individual is tending to dominate the group. We can ask, "What do other people think?" "Are there any other opinions?" If people are reluctant to speak, we can offer some other alternatives, such as

> Some people think that people have internalized a sense of inferiority and therefore feel hopeless, lack self-confidence and don't bother trying; others believe that people face systemic discrimination in hiring and promotion, especially when they don't fit the cultural norms or expectations. They need to be twice as good to be seen as competent. What do you think of these possibilities?

I handled it another way when Brian, a White male undergraduate student in my class on diversity once became agitated that there was so much sympathy for people on welfare. He said that if he could make it, other people could too. When asked why he had such a strong feelings, he briefly recounted his own life history: growing up in a single parent dysfunctional family, running away from home, becoming involved with drugs, and finally getting himself straight and struggling to work and pay for school. Both his other classmates and I validated his experience and the strength it took for him to be at this place in his life. After that process, I asked the class to brainstorm reasons why other people might not be able to do what Brian was able to do. In the course of ten minutes, the board was full of ideas including discrimination based on race, gender, disability, or sexual orientation; having children; internalized oppression; limited English skills; poor communication or writing skills; addictions; lack of connections; mental illness; and homelessness. (There were many obstacles on this list that Brian did not confront.) We did not discount Brian's experience or try to convince anyone of anything. But brainstorming other reasons allowed people to think about this issue more broadly and from other perspectives.

If you perceive that something is said to intentionally be adversarial, as a bait and a challenge, there is little likelihood that they really want to engage in an open, productive discussion about it. Instead of debating individuals' personal views, raise it to a larger issue and explore it as a commonly held viewpoint. Don't bite the bait. Instead, use it constructively. Rather than responding to their particular comment, such as "Women can avoid being sexually harassed if they wanted to and they really just like it," use this remark to explore aspects of sexual harassment. We could say, "That's an interesting point. Some people feel women are responsible for the sexual attention they receive and should just say no if they don't like it. Let's look at the dynamics involved in sexual harassment." Then discuss responsibility in sexual harassment, power relationships, blaming the victim, laws and policies, etc. Don't engage with whether they are personally right or wrong, but use their comment to look at the issue and the views that many people hold. Use the comment as a point of departure, shifting the discussion from the personal to the general.

As an issue is being explored, and even as we acknowledge different opinions, we need to provide accurate information and have people adequately support their views. We cannot simply allow an opinion to be accepted as fact. Invite the expression of views and feelings, acknowledge them, *and then* help people to do more critical thinking. As mentioned before, people can be given information or be asked to do research themselves.

Contain the Behavior

When one or two individuals are disruptive and continue to assert their views or raise inappropriate questions, their behavior needs to be curtailed. Often, the squeaky wheel gets the most grease. It is easy to get pulled into allowing one or two individuals to derail the class and to become the focus of attention. After they have had ample opportunity to express their views (see previous suggestions), acknowledge and summarize their perspective and indicate the need to move on. "I understand that you feel that affirmative action is reverse discrimination, and you don't believe anyone deserves preferences. Clearly, people hold different opinions about this issue. Let's leave this topic now, and move onto talking about other laws intended to prevent discrimination." They can also be given a time limit to address the issue before moving onto other topics. "Take a couple of minutes to finish what you'd like to say about this, and then we need to discuss other issues." We can also invite them to discuss the issue further at another time (outside the session). In a group situation, other people and other issues need attention. People in the group will appreciate your efforts not to allow one person to control the class.

If Group is Resistant, Go with the Flow

I have found that when the whole group or a large part of it is being resistant, there is little I can do in the moment to stop it. I have realized that you can't fight the tide. When this occurs, the Aikido principles become particularly helpful. Be flexible and work with the energy. Allow the group to discuss their issue and see how you can connect it to the class topic. One time, when I was trying to do training on diversity with teachers in a school system, I encountered a lot of resistance. Every time I would try to engage people in exercises or discussion, they would complain about how they were forced to be there and how the administration was really the problem. After unsuccessfully trying to push them to be involved, I stepped back and allowed them to vent their feelings and concerns. This led to some strategizing, some connections between their feelings and those of the students, and how this was related to diversity issues.

As most trainers can attest, there is a favorite game of some groups informally called "kill the trainer". Whatever anger, resentment, fear or powerlessness the group is feeling toward management or their institution gets projected onto the trainer. The trainer becomes a convenient target upon which to vent their emotions. The trainer will surely lose if s/he attempts to confront this head on and get into a struggle with the group. Again, it will likely be more productive to try to dance with the energy, not being a rigid target, to try to join with the group and move with them to address relevant issues. In training situations, I have learned to try to do as much assessment as possible before I go in to determine if this is an appropriate time and manner to do training, so I can void being "set-up". With adequate pre-assessment, some of this can be avoided.

Provide a Time Out

If resistance becomes intense, and either the group or we need some time to think about how to handle it, we can call a "time out". This can take the form of a break where people get a few minutes to cool off, talk informally, and just break the flow of energy. We can create a more structured process by having people react for a couple of minutes in pairs, free write about what they're thinking and feeling right now, write their opinion of the issue with supporting evidence, or come up with how they would like to proceed with this issue (continue in a particular way or revisit it at another time). We can also lead a few minutes of breathing and silence. Time outs allow both the educator as well as the participants to collect themselves, refocus, and decide how to move forward.

Arrange a Private Meeting

If there is strong or ongoing resistance, meeting with the individual(s) might be warranted. It is important to do this in an inviting, not a punitive manner. If people feel they are going to be scolded or attacked, they will become more defensive. Expressing interest and concern sets a different tone. Saying something like, "I notice you're having a hard time with the class/training. I'd like to talk with you more about it and hear some of your concerns. Could we find a time to talk?" During the meeting, try to express genuine interest and respect, and listen empathically. We can affirm their views while also helping them understand your perspective and the impact they are having on the rest of the group. Try to problem-solve about how to address the situation.

Conclusion

While there may be no magic answers, clearly there are a range of options to prevent, reduce, and address resistance. Most people, if given the right opportunity, would rather be engaged than anxious and defensive. Those who are unable to participate appropriately and enjoy a disruptive role can be dealt with in ways that do not prevent others' learning. While we cannot make people grow in the ways we might like, in my experience, there are few cases where someone has begun and ended in the same resistant manner. When sufficient trust and rapport has been built, and interesting material and activities presented, people often become productively involved, sometimes despite themselves. Making and sustaining these connections can sometimes take a tremendous amount of energy and patience. Yet, unless we can approach people with respect and compassion, we will likely face more difficulties. It is to our students' and our advantage to create a space in which people are engaged.

6

THE COSTS OF OPPRESSION TO PEOPLE FROM PRIVILEGED GROUPS

In the previous chapter, I discussed how resistance could be reduced if people from dominant groups reconceptualize how they think about social justice. Although change for most people tends to be difficult, it is even more so for those who feel they are on the losing end. People from privileged groups often see social change as a win–lose situation in which they lose. Even though greater equality would undoubtedly involve giving up and sharing power and resources, social justice could also enrich their lives.

Living in a society where there are systematic, institutionalized inequities affects everyone, whether in advantaged or disadvantaged roles. It has profound ramifications which influence and limit how we think about ourselves and others, how and with whom we interact, and the opportunities and choices we have about how to lead our lives. While in some instances there are positive effects, there are costs and harmful consequences for all of us, though in different ways.

Most efforts to understand the social and psychological effects of oppression have focused on the experiences of those in disadvantaged groups. Yet, systems of oppression also affect people in advantaged groups. When the experiences of people in privileged positions are considered, they tend to be compared to those who are oppressed. The focus is usually on how people from dominant groups oppress others or benefit from the inequalities. Of course, this is critical. Most theorists have paid less attention to how oppression has negative consequences for people in the advantaged group. However, our understanding cannot be complete unless this is fully explored as well. As members of an interdependent society, what affects some people inevitably affects us all. Martin Luther King reminds us, "All men [sic] are caught in an inescapable network of mutuality, tied in a single garment of destiny. Whatever affects one directly, affects all indirectly" (1991, p. 7).

One way to address resistance and to foster meaningful, long-term involvement in social change is to help people in privileged groups understand how they are harmed by structural inequality. In this chapter, I will first present specific ways people from dominant groups are adversely affected by oppression and how they can benefit by its elimination. Then, I will consider how systems of oppression more generally undermines their sense of humanity and human potential. As I have said before, most people are part of both advantaged and disadvantaged groups. The focus here is on their experience as someone from a privileged group, even though their other social identities always affect this experience.

Specific Costs of Oppression to People from Privileged Groups

We need to name the damaging effects of social injustice on people from advantaged groups without ignoring the larger dynamics of social power in which they occur. Recognizing the ways in which dominant groups may be negatively affected by oppression in no way equates that reality with the experiences of people in oppressed groups. Whatever the costs are to those in dominant groups, it is not the same as the loss of power, dignity, opportunities, and resources faced by people in disadvantaged groups. In this sense, I am not suggesting that people who are in privileged groups also are "oppressed"; they still have disproportionate social power. While keeping this in mind, I still believe it is useful to discuss the price paid for privilege and dominance in order to more fully understand the dynamics of oppression, and to develop strategies and visions for change.

There has been little in-depth exploration of the costs of systemic inequality to dominant groups. The pro-feminist men's movement has probably most clearly articulated the harmful consequences of sexism for men (Kaufman, 1993; Kimmel & Mesner, 1989; Kivel, 1992) and offered new models of masculinity. Others have described some of the negative ramifications for privileged people in relation to classism (Bingham, 1986; Mogul & Slepian, 1993; Wachtel, 1989), racism (Bowser & Hunt, 1981/96; Feagin & Vera, 1995; Kivel, 2002), and heterosexism (Blumenfeld, 1992; Thompson, 1992). Even though each form of oppression has its own particular effects on those in the advantaged group, there are numerous similarities that illustrate some common dynamics of systems of domination.

Drawing on the aforementioned works and my own teaching experiences, I will discuss the psychological, social, moral/spiritual, intellectual, and material costs of oppression to people from dominant groups. Although these different consequences will be discussed separately, their overlap with and impact on each other is extensive. In addition, even though people may experience these costs on an individual basis, they are the result of larger social patterns, structures, and ideology. They grow out of our particular systems of domination and inequality. Other oppressive societies with different forms of social organization may have both similar and different negative effects on those from privileged groups.

The themes cited highlight consequences or issues that pertain to dominant groups across different forms of oppression. The quotes are taken from participants in classes and workshops I have conducted in the past several years. Some of the effects are very personal and center around the individual and her/his interpersonal relationships. Others involve societal ramifications that impact the individual as a member of society.

Psychological Costs: Loss of Mental Health and Authentic Sense of Self

Systems of oppression constrain the ability of people from dominant groups to develop their full humanity. Pressures to fit prescribed roles and to limit one's emotional capacity hinder one's self-development. Diminished self-knowledge and fears further thwart healthy psychological growth. I will describe several aspects of how overall mental health is compromised.

Socialization into Roles and Patterns of Behavior

People in dominant groups are socialized to conform to certain rigid standards of behavior. This impedes the exploration of aspects of themselves that do not fit with these expectations. For example, heterosexuals may constrain their feelings and relationships with people of the same sex, while men may block their emotional expressiveness or pursuit of interests considered "feminine". People from upper-class families are prevented or discouraged from considering non-professional occupations or career interests outside the family's established sphere. Individuals' efforts to conform to expected roles can undermine their ability to know who they are, what they can do, and what they really need.

Denial of Emotions and Empathy

Personal growth is further limited when people attempt to deal with the contradiction between what they are often taught (equality, love, and kindness) and what they are expected to do (treat people inequitably). This may occur when they divert their eyes from a homeless person or treat a person in a service role as a lesser human being. As a result, people may disregard or not perceive the feelings of other people. While clearly damaging to people in disadvantaged groups, it also requires people in advantaged groups to deny their own emotional capabilities, sensitivity, and mutuality. This stifles emotional honesty and hinders the development and use of empathy.

Limited Self-knowledge and Distorted View of Self

People from dominant groups are routinely denied information and opportunities to understand their role in an unjust social system, as well as honest feedback from people in oppressed groups. As a result, they are denied self-knowledge. This skewed self-awareness has numerous ramifications.

People from privileged groups often obtain a positive sense of self (consciously or unconsciously) based on the diminishment of others. They feel good about themselves because they can point to someone else who they believe is inferior. However, this positive self-esteem is shallow, artificial, and false. After marrying a Latino from Central America, one White woman reports that "because of my own 'privileged' background, I felt somehow better than him and his people. When I began to accept responsibility for myself, I had to 'eat' my own response to this racism. It wasn't easy, but it was necessary."

People from advantaged groups often develop a sense of superiority or a distorted sense of self to rationalize the inequality. Promotions, opportunities, and access to resources are inequitably distributed in an unjust, hierarchical system. Often these are not truly gained by merit, but by connections or by belonging to a certain race, sex, or class. To justify these greater advantages, people from dominant groups often convince themselves that they are better than other people and therefore more deserving, even if they are somehow aware this is not so. In order to reconcile themselves to this situation, they may maintain the belief in their own superiority. They can easily draw on the dominant culture to create and reinforce this view.

Despite these efforts, they may find it hard to trust their gains and to believe in their abilities. They may wonder whether their achievement was based on privilege or merit. McIntosh (1985) labels this "feeling like a fraud". While these feelings can arise for a variety of reasons, success in a rigged system can rob people of faith in their capabilities and diminish their sense of accomplishment.

Discrepancy between External Perceptions and Internal Realities

There is often the discrepancy between external appearances and internal realities. People do not feel like the "powerful" "privileged" people they are assumed to be. On the surface, it may appear that privileged people "have it all", especially those with wealth. Yet internally, people often feel isolated, lonely, cut off from one's self, others, and "the real world". Even though there may be material success, there can be emotional and spiritual emptiness.

Fears and Pain

There are numerous fears, many of which have social ramifications (and are addressed in the following section). Even when people recognize the irrationality or unfoundedness of some of their fears (of certain types of people, of new or different situations), they still find that these fears inhibit their lives and cause psychological distress. Some people are afraid of losing entitlement and privileges. They worry that people in oppressed groups may retaliate and mistreat them as they have been mistreated. If marginalized groups are given greater social power, they fear this will be used against them (i.e., women will deny men employment opportunities, people of color will subjugate Whites to second-class treatment).

For those with close relationships with people from dominated groups, there can be fear for the other's well-being. People from dominant groups find it painful to witness and share in their suffering and mistreatment. Whether this involves common encounters with discrimination or a more dramatic occurrence, it can be distressing to see and feel the effects on one's friend or relative. This is particularly evident when a daughter or wife gets raped; a friend of color is harassed by police; a low-income friend is unable to find work or housing; a gay friend gets beaten; or a Jewish friend's synagogue is defaced. Parents from dominant groups who have children from disadvantaged groups (of color, gay or lesbian, or with a disability) are often concerned about their treatment and safety.

People from dominant groups who support justice often describe the pain they feel when they hear offensive remarks made about disadvantaged groups. Others from their social group often assume that they will share the prejudiced view. It is both psychologically and emotionally upsetting to listen to such disparagement about other people. When there are other more serious acts of hatred, it is even more painful to realize that fellow human beings are capable of such cruelty.

Diminished Mental Health

Thomas Pettigrew (1981) identified six criteria for positive mental health. Among them, he cites self-awareness and self-acceptance, degree of actualization of one's potential, relative independence from social pressures, adequate perception of reality, and the integration of psychic functions. As reflected in the aforementioned costs, being socialized into an unjust system negatively impacts our ability to obtain these components of psychological health. In particular, people from dominant groups tend to develop unhealthy psychological mechanisms (such as denial, false justification, projection, disassociation, and transference of blame) to deal with their fears of minorities or people from oppressed groups (Fernandez, 1996). One woman describes this process. "As a White woman I cannot easily own the negative parts of myself. I disavow them and project them onto others (people of color). As a result, I am cut off from important parts of myself." Middle-aged people, in an effort to deny their own mortality, may marginalize and discard elderly people; or heterosexuals, who cannot accept their feelings for members of their own sex, may act out in homophobic ways.

Social Costs: Loss and Diminishment of Relationships

The lack of trust between groups, a social climate which rarely supports relationships across differences (except for men and women of the same backgrounds), and our socialization, which has fed us misinformation about ourselves and others undermines relationships. Internalized oppression and social taboos often interfere with positive interpersonal relations among diverse people. Fears, avoidance of different people, and limited experiences and knowledge of others result in less human connection and more isolation. The social costs are immense.

Isolation from People Who Are Different

The separation people experience from those who are different may be due to an individual's psychological or emotional issues and to the social structures and norms in society. In the former case, fear and discomfort prevent people from reducing the distance. "I often felt so isolated from most people and yearned to be able to connect but my fear of the 'unknown' was so prevalent. It overpowered me. How very sad and how I regret this!" Opportunities for deep, important, gratifying relationships with diverse people are lost. An able-bodied man recounts,

> I literally often avoid contact with the disabled because I'm unsure how to act—to walk the line between acknowledging a difference in ability and being rude; between helpfulness and patronization. My social distance grows as I don't make efforts to interact fully with the disabled.

In the latter case, various forms of oppression restrict where we work and play, and the ease with which we can have meaningful relationships across differences. Often we have no contact with certain groups of people, or only in limited ways.

> As an able-bodied person I did not come into contact with handicapped people until I was old enough to participate in volunteer work in junior high. Though I have done extensive work with them, I still don't feel natural being around them. They are not part of my life. I feel like I am missing out on the opportunity to be friends with a certain number of the population.

Barriers to Deeper, More Authentic Relationships

Even when there is contact, it is difficult to have meaningful relationships. It is often hard to develop deep, genuine relationships with people from diverse backgrounds. Numerous barriers interfere with this process.

First, people from dominant groups often carry a host of fears because of their social position and socialization in an unequal society. A very common fear is of people who are different and of participating in other cultural experiences. Because they have had limited contact with and received negative messages about people who are different, people are fearful of going to places or having relationships across social group boundaries. When and if they do deal with people from dominated groups, people from privileged groups worry about saying or doing the wrong thing and being offensive.

> I hear negative messages about racial groups that my grandparents used to say and I fear that someday I will use them out of my subconscious. On a conscious level, I do not want to believe or use the terms they used, but I fear some aspects of racism were ingrained at an early age.

Often, people talk of "walking on egg shells". With the constantly shifting social norms, even many well-intentioned people are confused or frightened about what is acceptable and what is not. At times, it can seem easier to do nothing at all than to risk pain or embarrassment.

Second, stereotypes or pre-judgments may prevent contact in the first place or impede real relationships once there is contact. People from dominant groups recognize that their stereotypes of others (especially, in a context that encourages segregation) inhibit their ability to get to know people from oppressed groups or to develop those relationships. One White woman spoke of her loss of a potentially important relationship due to her own racism and the segregated social environment.

> I had a male friend in college who was African American and my friends told me he really liked me. I never made any advances (and neither did he) because the idea of going out with a Black man made me nervous. I think I missed out on an opportunity to become involved with a sensitive and caring man because of how separated/segregated my experience was when I was growing up. If I was confronted with why I didn't go out with him, I would have denied racism vehemently. But in hindsight, I know that this is the truth.

Third, people from privileged groups recognize a lack of trust. On the one hand, they realize it will be harder and slower for people from oppressed groups to be open and honest with them. In relation to heterosexism, one person writes, "I lost out in the ability for people to share their [gay men and lesbians] lives fully."

In addition, the lack of trust makes it less likely that they will broach difficult subjects or try to work out troublesome interpersonal dynamics. A White woman spoke of how racism affects her ability to have real and honest interpersonal relationships with people of color.

I am hurt or limited by the fact that I cannot honestly state some of my feelings and concerns about the subject for fear it may be considered racist. I feel that if there is not honest dialogue about people's true concerns, we will never be able to reach real solutions. We will just walk politely around the issues and put band-aids on problems as they jump up and hit us in the face. This is no different than communication between a couple or close friends. If you're not really honest about how you see things, you will either just learn to live with things as they are or pull away even farther from the situation. You will not really make a positive long-term change.

People from the dominant group also complain that they are stereotyped by people from the subordinated group and not seen for who they are. They may be judged and avoided based on their social group identity, which may feel frustrating and unfair.

Quite at odds with their own experience and self-image, a man may be seen as a potential rapist and not trusted by women, a wealthy person viewed as an elitist snob, or a White person as an unconcerned racist. Two White women describe this experience:

When attempting to assist with problems of others that are not White, it is looked upon as charity or I'm told that I don't care because I'm White, or that this trouble doesn't concern me. This was said without regard to my feelings about the situation or my beliefs as an individual. There was a simple presumption that I would only offer to help because I believed I was superior to them, solely based on the color of my skin.

This was echoed by another person:

> ... not being taken for who I am but assuming I am part of the stereotypical dominant race who are stereotyped as uncaring, rich, selfish, biased, unaccepting of other cultures, rude, snobby, better than others, etc., by the minority race who holds negative opinions of the White race.

As a result of feeling like they will be judged, people from privileged groups choose to hide aspects of themselves. Hiding aspects of who one is undermines an open and honest relationship. People most often discuss this in terms of class.

> As a product of a middle/upper class environment I often feel that I am pre-judged. People think I'm spoiled or have been given everything on a silver platter. They think I'm pretentious or a snob or that Daddy is going to do everything for me. Consequently, it is an aspect of my life that I don't usually reveal.

Disconnection, Distance, and Ostracism within Own Group

As people from dominant groups speak about barriers to relationships, they often refer to the distance that is created in their own communities and families. As before, this distance may be due to their own or others' attitudes. One type of disconnection is due to differences in other social identities.

Among people with a shared subordinated identity, some individuals may also have a dominant identity that creates a rift within the social group. Middle- and upper-class people of color frequently mention feeling disconnected from poor and working-class people from their own racial/ethnic group. Sometimes, it is they who feel excluded. "As a Black woman it is a constant issue that I am upper-middle class. I am often made to feel that I must hide this fact because of the attitudes and judgments from Blacks." Other times, people feel they have little in common with people from lower socio-economic classes. The distance is due to their own discomfort, estrangement, and/or privilege. "As an upper class Black person in a wealthy White community, I often ended up oppressing people who looked just like me but didn't have money".

These dynamics, which lead to disconnection, also occur within families. A women recounts how this occurred in her family due to class differences.

> As a result of classism, I don't know my father's side of the family. My mother's family is middle class and educated. Dad's are farmers and fishermen. They are seen by Mom's side as 'not worth knowing', so I don't even know cousins I have.

In addition, because of heterosexism, heterosexual siblings or parents may reject a gay child, forfeiting that primary relationship.

Other times, people are ostracized for the choices they make that violate the accepted norms of behavior within their own group. This strains or breaks bonds with family members, friends, peers, and co-workers. Men can be teased and become a social outcast for not being "one of the guys".

> In my peer groups at work, I often get 'knocked' because of my feelings and values, and my openness and willingness to express them. I definitely feel my male peers expect certain 'male ' behavior and attitudes from me.

If individuals date or marry outside their racial or class group, they can be disowned by or estranged from their family. One White woman from the U.S. tells how after she married a Guatemalan man, she "experienced the pain of rejection, abandonment, discrediting, and almost complete discounting" from her family. Another woman relates the "numerous issues with my father due to his belief that I should not date out of my race. His anger at my dating of a Black man has also led to physical violence toward me by him."

Moral and Spiritual Costs: Loss of Integrity and Spiritual Center

Most people like to see themselves as decent, caring individuals and having principles of fairness. However, they live in a society where there are pervasive inequities, reflected in homelessness, poverty, violence, and job discrimination, to name a few. Many people grapple with the discrepancy between the reality in which they live and their moral/spiritual beliefs.

Guilt and Shame

Some people feel uncomfortable with the fact that some people have so much, while others have so little. They may feel embarrassed or guilty for having more than others. People frequently feel guilt when they know that others do not share their privileges or standard of living. In response to these increasingly apparent inequities, people often "blame the victim". Yet, for many people, the guilt and shame still haunt them. Do I deserve to have so much when some people have so little? What is my responsibility to "them", to myself and family? How can I see myself as a good caring person, yet do nothing to really change the system or their conditions?

As people become more aware of injustices, these feelings and questions become harder to ignore and these moral naggings intensify. People from advantaged groups may feel bad or defensive about who they are ("I may be White but some of my best friends are Black"). It is shameful to think about how one benefits from the pain or exploitation of others. Often people feel guilty for not doing more to change inhumane or unjust conditions, for not responding to offensive comments and jokes, or for not taking a stand against an injustice.

Moral Ambivalence

Often people feel torn between acting in accordance with their personal integrity and risking family or societal disapproval, such as giving up significant money to social change efforts or marrying "one of them". They may be faced with decisions of doing the "right" thing or going along with social pressure—selling their home to gays, Jews or people of color in an otherwise (apparently) homogeneous neighborhood, or hiring a person with a disability knowing that clients or staff would be uncomfortable and resistant to accommodations. They may also question their negative feelings about a person from an oppressed group, wondering whether their personal dislike or perception of incompetence was due to prejudice or to a fair and reasonable judgment.

Spiritual Emptiness or Pain

Many people's religious or spiritual beliefs maintain that we are all "Children of God", part of the same Oneness, or interconnected and interdependent beings. Perpetuating oppression violates this sense of connection. It also belies the notion of God or Spirit in each person, and undermines the inherent integrity of each individual. As one person stated, "I believe when one group suffers, we all suffer for it is an indication of our own lack of 'soul'."

Intellectual Costs: Loss of Developing Full Range of Knowledge

Neither their formal education nor their own experiences tend to provide people from dominant groups with sufficient and truthful information about their own or other social groups. The lack of relationships and the lack of (accurate) knowledge about people from dominated groups furthers ignorance. People's ability to expand their minds is thwarted.

Distorted and Limited View of Other People's Culture and History

People from privileged groups are uninformed or misinformed about much of the human race and the contributions of many other kinds of people. These include aspects of culture such as music, food, arts, values, philosophies, and social systems. When people in privileged groups are only exposed to the ways and accomplishments of people like themselves, they develop a distorted worldview. When history is recounted from the perspective of the dominant group, they receive only a partial picture of our past. This ignorance leads to limited and skewed views of different lifestyles, viewpoints, perspectives, and people. They become out of touch with reality and lose the ability to consider other more productive and effective ways to live their lives and to understand the lives of others.

A White woman recounts her experience in an African-American community:

> I was so enriched when I worked with African-American families and came to see a different worldview of collectivism—families taking care of family members, communities, themselves. What a loss had I not experienced this other possible worldview. It has changed my life and my priorities.

However, more often, ignorance allows people to retain the misinformation and stereotypes about other social groups. This, coupled with fears, fosters the avoidance of people and experiences that might challenge their view of the world. This distorted perspective also has social consequences.

> As a member of the upper middle class, classism and 'blaming the victim' prevented me from knowing and reaching out to those who are less privileged than I am. I was prevented from seeing others as 'human' until I learned more about my own privilege.

Ignorance of Own Culture and History

People from privileged groups not only lose a clear understanding of others, but of themselves. History books, in addition to omitting and distorting the experiences of people from oppressed groups, misconstrue the experiences of people from dominant groups. In the section on psychological costs, I discussed the loss of individual self-knowledge. However, people also miss a more accurate understanding of their own cultural group. For example, racism has caused many Whites to let go off their particular ethnic backgrounds in order to assimilate into mainstream White society, with its resulting privileges. In addition, when we ignore the wisdom and stories of our elders, we lose important perspectives and information, particularly about one's own history. "Ageism has cost me a rich resource of knowledge from the past. From the mouths of elders in my own family, I have lost their life experiences which I cannot pass on to my own children."

Material and Physical Costs: Loss of Safety, Resources, and Quality of Life

Oppression creates social conditions that not only affect people from privileged groups very personally and directly, but indirectly as well. Due to social injustice, we lose and waste both material and human resources. Many factors related to one's safety and quality of life are negatively affected.

Social Violence and Unrest

Oppression and inequality tend to breed social unrest. As people feel increasingly mistreated, hopeless, and disconnected from the larger society and its benefits, violence and anti-social behavior increases. Although people from dominant groups often have more opportunities to try to hide from this reality, its effects are inescapable. They may try to avoid people and experiences that make them uncomfortable, creating a smaller and smaller world in which to live. People may put up walls and live in gated communities, becoming prisoners in their own homes. Their access to places is restricted as they increasingly feel it's just not safe to go there. People become more fearful to move about in the world and spend more time, money, and energy trying to protect themselves and their belongings.

Negative Health Implications

People in privileged groups experience high degrees of stress and stress-related illnesses as they feel increasingly fearful and disconnected from other human beings. Pressures to achieve and maintain status in a hierarchical, competitive social and economic system further undermines health. Studies find there are higher morality rates for both wealthy and poor people in geographic areas with high-income inequality (Lynch, et al., 1998; Wilkinson & Pickett, 2009).

Higher Costs

As it becomes more difficult to find homes and schools that are safe and of good quality, the ones that do exist become more expensive. It becomes more challenging to maintain a good standard of living. Basic economics teaches that when there is high demand and short supply, prices go up. This also occurs in the labor market. When groups of people are systematically excluded from the labor pool (because of stereotypes, discrimination, lack of preparation, etc.), there are fewer people to chose from, which creates higher wage costs. Employers therefore need to spend more to attract qualified people.

Waste of Resources

Keeping an unjust system in place is also extremely expensive. A significant amount of our taxes and economic resources go to supporting law enforcement, the judicial and penal systems, and providing social support services, etc. Economic and human resources are directed at addressing the effects of social inequalities as opposed to ensuring opportunities for all. For example, one study (LaVeist, Gaskin, & Richard,

2009) finds that 30% of direct medical expenditures for African Americans, Asian Americans and Hispanics were excess costs linked to health inequalities. Eliminating those inequalities would have saved the US economy 1.24 trillion dollars.

Loss of Valuable Employees, Clients, and Customers

When groups of people are impeded from having decent jobs and earning living wages, they are less able to purchase goods and services. This is turn, negatively impacts the economy. When restaurants, universities, businesses, and other organizations are seen as inaccessible, discriminatory, or unfriendly to different oppressed groups, they lose clients, customers, and students. This tends to translate into financial loss for the owners and less job security for employees. Similarly, it is more difficult to attract and retain talented employees from marginalized groups who would enhance organizational success. When they are hired, if they are unable to bring their whole selves to work (including aspects of their identity or culture) or have to constantly deal with prejudices, they are less creative and productive.

Loss of Knowledge to Foster Societal Growth and Well-Being

When groups of people are disenfranchised, given limited opportunities, or have their cultures ignored or obliterated, the society as a whole loses their contributions. We know that different cultures and life experiences can bring fresh perspectives to current problems and issues. When these are discounted, or individuals not given the chance to develop their abilities, we have lost the potential for new ways to think about old and new concerns. We also miss the contributions to the arts and sciences that enrich and advance our country and the world. As one person noted, "I believe that we simply 'miss out'. As a culture we lose some of the inventive, creative contributions that could be made by many people who are denied a chance to flourish."

Diminished Collective Action for Common Concerns

When attention and energy is directed at addressing the effects of oppression and on individual (or group) survival, it is diverted from other issues that would enhance societal well-being. This keeps us separated and impedes our ability to work together to address larger common concerns (the environment, education, health). Even collective action in a narrower sense, such as in unions, is hindered by the intentional or unintentional exclusion or marginalization of oppressed groups.

Interconnections and Variations

Though described separately, in fact, many of these costs are overlapping and mutually reinforcing. They build and feed on each other, often creating a vicious cycle. When people do not have contact with others who are different and do not

---

Psychological Costs: Loss of Mental Health and Authentic Sense of Self

- Socialized into limited roles and patterns of behavior
- Denial of emotions and empathy
- Limited self-knowledge and distorted view of self
- Discrepancy between external perceptions and internal reality
- Pain and fears (of doing and saying wrong thing, of retaliation from oppressed groups, of revealing self for fear of judgment, of different people and experiences)
- Diminished mental health (distorted view of self and reality, denial, projection)

Social Costs: Loss and Diminishment of Relationships

- Isolation from people who are different
- Barriers to deeper, more authentic relationships
- Disconnection, distance, and ostracism within own group if one acts differently

Intellectual Costs: Loss of Developing Full Range of Knowledge

- Distorted and limited view of other people's culture and history
- Ignorance of own culture and history

Moral and Spiritual Costs: Loss of Moral and Spiritual Integrity

- Guilt and Shame
- Moral Ambivalence (doing right thing vs. social pressures and realities)
- Spiritual Emptiness or Pain (disconnection from other human beings, violation of one's spirtual values.)

Material and Physical Costs: Loss of Safety, Resources, and Quality of Life

- Violence and unrest (restricted ability to move about freely; increased fear for self and others; limited desirable places to live, work, go to school, recreate)
- Negative health implications (e.g. stress and stress-related illnesses)
- Loss of valuable employees, clients, and customers
- Loss of knowledge to foster societal growth and well-being
- Waste of resources (to deal with effects of inequality)
- Diminished collective action for common concerns

FIGURE 6.1 Costs of Oppression to People from Privileged Groups

have accurate information about themselves or others, they develop fears and stereotypes which make it harder to establish contact. This leads to more discomfort, avoidance, ignorance, and fear. They, therefore, are more likely to support social policies that are oppressive or ineffective at addressing the issues, which, in turn, helps to perpetuate the inequality.

Even the same general cost may affect various areas of one's life. The disconnection from others may have psychological, social, moral/spiritual, intellectual, and material costs. For example, one is likely to develop fears or be limited in one's self-knowledge, to lose out on meaningful interpersonal relationships, to feel cut off from other human beings who are subject to injustice, to not know about others' lives and perspectives, and to miss out on valuable talent or knowledge. As one woman aptly summed up, "This separation causes a kind of blindness to others' suffering and experiences, and a narrowness of viewpoint which can affect one's political, social, intellectual, and spiritual development."

In their work analyzing the effects of economic inequality on health and social problems in various countries and within the United Sates, Wilkinson and Pickett (2009) found that physical health, mental health, drug abuse, education, imprisonment, obesity, social mobility, trust and community life, violence, teenage births, and child well-being are substantially worse in more unequal societies. These problems are often many times worse than in more equal societies. It is the degree of inequality, the gap between people, that is divisive and socially corrosive. This inequality increases fear, erodes trust, impedes human relationships, and diminishes involvement in community. People at all levels, including those near the top, experience negative material and psychological effects from inequality, including mental illness, violence, drug abuse, and teen pregnancy. In particular, they are subject to stress and anxiety due to status competition—how they will be judged by others. Overall, societies are less healthy which negatively affects all its members.

How people from dominant groups perceive and experience the costs of oppression to themselves varies among individuals. Sometimes people may not even recognize something as a cost until it is named by someone else (e.g. the expense involved in maintaining oppression). They may take for granted certain ways of being or social arrangements, assuming these are normal (e.g. sex roles or conflicts among different groups). One's other social identities clearly play a role in what is seen or felt to be a cost. I wonder about gender differences. In general, males may be less likely to identify costs since they are more advantaged by our current social system. Yet, since males, overall, are socialized into roles of dominance and are more constrained by rigid sex roles, those who are socially conscious may be more sensitive to the pressures to act in ways that deny their own and others' humanity. Women, who are allowed (and encouraged) to be more emotionally expressive, and often experience more flexibility in their ways of behaving (and thus experience less of a cost), may be more attuned to the loss of connection with others (due to being White, heterosexual, middle/upper class, etc.). We cannot expect all individuals to experience the costs in the same way. It is useful, however, to be able to illustrate the various effects and to help people to identify the relevant ways they as individuals and as members of society are negatively affected by oppression.

General Costs to People from Privileged Groups

When we collectively consider the range of costs of oppression to people from privileged groups, it becomes clear that they cannot escape the consequences of the systems of injustice. In order to maintain inequality, people from advantaged groups must be psychologically conditioned to assume their roles in the social order. The current ideology and social structures reinforce the kind of thinking and behavior that perpetuates injustice which ultimately diminishes all human beings. As we participate in the dehumanization of others, which we inevitably do by participating in institutions, practices, and social relations that support societal inequality, our own freedom, authenticity, and humanity is diminished. Several prominent social activists have acknowledged the intertwined fate of the oppressor and the oppressed.

According to Paulo Freire (1970), "humanization is man's [sic] vocation." "As oppressors dehumanize and violate their [the oppressed's] rights, they themselves also become dehumanized" (p. 42). "Dehumanization, which marks not only those whose humanity has been stolen, but also (though in a different way), those who have stolen it, is a distortion of becoming more fully human" (p. 28).

Nelson Mandela, in his book, *Long Walk to Freedom* adds,

> I knew as well as I knew anything that the oppressor must be liberated just as surely as the oppressed. A man who takes away another man's freedom is a prisoner of hatred, locked behind the bars of prejudice and narrow-mindedness. I am not truly free if I am taking away someone else's freedom, just as surely as I am not free when my freedom is taken from me. The oppressed and the oppressor alike are robbed of their humanity. (1994, p. 544)

Martin Luther King, Jr. (1991) also noted this connection.

> I can never be what I ought to be until you are what you ought be, and you can never be what you might be until I am what I ought to be. (p. 7)

In his writing about racism, Robert Terry (1981) addresses the loss of authenticity. He maintains that authenticity "describes the press in all of our lives to make sense out of our world and act purposefully in it" (p. 121). This involves being true to ourselves and true to our world. Like other forms of oppression, racism distorts authenticity since it distorts our relationships to ourselves, to others, and to our society.

One of the fundamental human desires is to know and be known. We seek relationships with others that allow us to fully "see" them and to have others fully "see" us. People want to be recognized for who they truly are. Oppression prevents this process of mutual recognition. It thwarts our ability to become our authentic selves and to fully know ourselves. It also impedes others from knowing who we are. It is often with much pain that people from dominant groups recount stories of how they feel mis-seen and misjudged, especially by people from oppressed groups. The full complexity of their history, backgrounds, and experiences are not acknowledged. Instead, they are perceived more one-dimensionally. Certainly, we know this occurs to people from subordinated groups. Even though they are not experienced in the same way by people who are in advantaged and disadvantaged positions, dehumanization, inauthenticity, and misrecognition are inherent aspects of all forms of oppression.

Benefits of Social Justice

As people from privileged groups gain an awareness of these costs, it can lead to an understanding of how systems of oppression are not necessarily or fully in their best interest. From there, they can more readily think about the advantages of living in a more just society. In fact, Wilkinson and Pickett (2009) illustrate the actual benefits of greater equality to all people based on data from current societies. Their research showed that people at any level of income, education, or occupational level are better off in a more equal state. They are more resilient and live longer and happier lives. Specifically, they have less mental illness, communities that are more cohesive with more trust, more social mobility, and better health, are less likely to have drug addictions, experience less violence, and the children do better in school. Based on their data, they suggest that if the United States were to reduce its income inequality to something like the average of the four most equal of the rich countries (Japan, Norway, Sweden, and Finland), the proportion of the population feeling that they could trust others might rise by 75%—presumably with matching improvements in the quality of community life; rates of mental illness and obesity might similarly each be cut by almost two-thirds, teenage birth rates could be more than halved, prison populations might be reduced by 75%, and people could live longer while working the equivalent of two months less per year (p. 261).

At times when I ask people from privileged groups to describe the negative effects of oppression, I also ask them to identify how they might benefit from greater social justice. Since we have yet to live in a truly just society, the benefits they identify are based on what people imagine life would be like as well as their experiences when they do have moments of freedom, authenticity, and equity (in relationships, personal pursuits, workplaces, social/religious organizations, etc.). As the costs imply, with greater social justice people could have a fuller, more authentic sense of self; more authentic relationships and human connection; greater moral consistency and integrity; access to cultural knowledge and wisdom; and improved work and living conditions. There would also be the potential for real democracy in our government and institutions.

In one session, after discussing the benefits of social justice for dominant group members, the participants reminded me that it wasn't simply that there would be less fear, better relationships, or improved quality of life. There also would be more joy and fun. This is a wonderful example of how health is not simply the absence of illness, that wellness transcends the mere removal of the sickness. They spoke about how people could more fully experience life and truly enjoy themselves and others. There is a freedom and exuberance that is captured by the word "joy" that more fully reflects the liberation that a just and caring world could offer us. (This was before I considered exploring the "Joy of Unlearning Privilege/Oppression", the next chapter.)

Whether experienced personally, theorized or grounded in research, there is ample reason to believe that people from privileged groups have something to gain from greater equity. Yet, simply helping people from privileged groups to understand the personal and societal limitations of oppression does not mean that they will readily work to change the current system. There are many incentives to maintain the status quo. However, it does create an opportunity for critical thinking and for challenging the win-lose paradigm. In the next chapter, I'll present specific ways individuals from privileged groups have benefited from unlearning privilege/oppression which further illustrates how challenging systems of oppression can have positive results for all of us.

7

THE JOY OF UNLEARNING PRIVILEGE/ OPPRESSION

Unlearning racism and other "isms" has been one of the best things I've done in my life. I've spent many years working on these issues. I've attended countless workshops, classes, and groups. Sometimes it's been really hard and uncomfortable. I've had my share of tears, guilt, and anger but it's been worth it. It's been such a liberating experience.

At this point, people in my diversity classes or workshops are usually looking at me with a mixture of mild disbelief and curiosity, but almost all with rapt attention. Mine is a perspective they rarely hear. Typically, when a White person thinks about unlearning racism or a man has the opportunity to examine sexism, their first response is usually negative: "It will make me feel bad", "I'll just feel guilty", "I'll just be bashed and blamed for all the problems in the world." These common reactions led me to believe that something was missing. People from privileged groups needed to understand the benefits of engaging in meaningful, ongoing unlearning privilege/oppression work. They needed a vision of what they had to gain, if they overcame their preconceptions and opened their hearts and minds.

I knew my view of unlearning privilege/oppression as valuable and transformative was not unique. As I discussed this with others, people quickly offered their own metaphors and adjectives for how this work has been deeply gratifying. Most often people spoke of it as *healing, freeing,* and *liberating.* Quite the contrary to the negative associations, people who have actually participated in a process to unlearn privilege and oppression have found it to be an overwhelmingly positive and profound experience. I could see there was a bigger story to tell.

I struggled with finding words to capture what I meant by *unlearning privilege/ oppression.* I wanted to convey that it is a *multifaceted and comprehensive process which includes both self-reflection and social analysis.* Unlearning privilege/oppression includes examining one's biases, socialization, attitudes, behaviors, and worldview. It also entails understanding 1) the historical and contemporary manifestations of the oppression, 2) how inequality is systemic and institutionalized, and 3) the privilege and oppression experienced by the dominant and subordinated groups. It means learning how to be an ally and challenge injustice. In addition, I wanted a term that was inclusive of different forms of social inequality. I decided to expand on the more commonly-used term *unlearning racism* and use *unlearning privilege/oppression*. I wanted to use both the terms *privilege* and *oppression* since for people from dominant groups, it was particularly important to be looking at privilege in addition to the oppression more generally. At the moment, this is the best word or phrase I could find to capture this complex process.

I also grappled with using the word *joy*. I chose the title *The Joy of Unlearning Privilege/Oppression* as a play on *The Joy of Sex* or *The Joy of Cooking*. I wanted to capture the irony of connecting unlearning privilege/oppression with something joyful. While not everyone got the joke, the term *joy* actually did speak to many people's experiences. I do not intend for this language to be flip or trivializing of the hard work involved in unlearning privilege/oppression or of the oppression suffered by people from marginalized groups. I do hope it captures people's attention and helps them think about what this work can mean in their lives.

Theories of racial/social identity development, discussed earlier in Chapter 3, describe changes in how people perceive themselves, others, and social issues. They capture both a sense of process and a state of more complex awareness. These frameworks describe movement through different levels of consciousness or schemas related to one's racial or social identity, implying an unlearning process. For example, Helms (2007) refers to the evolution from a racist to a non-racist White identity. While none of these theories suggests that one reaches a final, discrete "stage", they do describe perspectives that indicate greater consciousness and complexity. Yet, they say little about how people feel about themselves and their lives once they achieve this level of consciousness. My research on the joy of unlearning privilege/oppression described in this chapter can be seen as building and elaborating on these theories by offering illustrations of how people experience the capacity to live with this greater awareness.

I solicited people's experiences of unlearning privilege/oppression when they are in the privileged group through workshops, conferences, and list-serves, collecting dozens of verbal and written responses. In addition, I conducted in-depth interviews with people from various privileged groups. Responses were primarily in relation to sexism, racism, and/or heterosexism though other "isms" were referenced as well. Most people focused on one form of oppression as their basis for discussion and then added thoughts about unlearning others. In many cases, people had a deeper passion about one "ism" even though they clearly recognized and cared about other forms of inequality, and injustice in general. The quotations in this chapter are the words of the respondents.

As I analyzed people's responses, I noticed an interesting relationship between the main benefits of unlearning privilege/oppression and the results of my study on the costs of oppression to people from privileged groups described in the earlier chapter. Even though I conducted the research for these two studies years apart, with completely different people, the themes strongly correlate. The main costs of oppression identified are: the loss of mental health and authentic sense of self, the loss and diminishment of relationships, the loss of developing a full range of knowledge, the loss of moral and spiritual integrity, and the loss of safety and quality of life. These very same qualities are what people felt they had gained or reclaimed as a result of their unlearning process. The joys of unlearning privilege/oppression seem to mitigate the costs of oppression, at least on a personal level; they were able to remediate many of the negative affects on themselves and their relationships. The costs of oppression provide a useful context and backdrop when reading about the joys of unlearning privilege/oppression.

In this chapter, I will first discuss the benefits of unlearning privilege/oppression identified by people from privileged groups, which are grouped into five main themes: knowledge and clarity; an enriched life; greater authenticity and humanity; empowerment, confidence, and competence; and liberation and healing. There is overlap among the themes since the benefits gained are clearly interrelated and mutually reinforcing. As people discuss their present experiences, their comparisons are to their lives before they seriously undertook unlearning privilege/oppression. Later in the chapter, I describe what the respondents identify as the key factors that have helped them unlearn oppression and that help them stay on this journey.

Knowledge and Clarity

Unlearning privilege/oppression provides information and perspectives that give people new lenses for viewing themselves and the world. This enables individuals from privileged groups to be more conscious, informed, and insightful. As a result, they develop not only intellectual knowledge about how society operates but personal knowledge as well. People expand their ability to analyze and understand the dynamics of oppression as they manifest in society and in their own psyche. One person considers unlearning privilege/oppression a "sociological and personal study."

By its very nature, systems of oppression misrepresent and ignore wide realms of knowledge about people, cultures, history, and social realities. Gaining information and frameworks for analysis is a compelling part of the unlearning process. "Nothing is more interesting, thought-provoking or rewarding." Respondents refer to unlearning privilege/oppression as "a mystery to unpack" and "deeply fascinating." "I think more complexly and ask what am I missing or not seeing?" a person explains.

Very often, systems of oppression feel confusing and irrational. People know something is wrong but cannot necessarily name it or articulate it. A greater understanding of oppression helps people figure out the world in which they live and their role in it. It "creates meaning in a system that doesn't make sense" and "intellectually connects the dots." As one woman expresses, "I feel more humane and sane in a culture that often does not feel sane to me."

One aspect of intellectual growth involves rethinking what one has accepted as true and considering perspectives one has never considered before. As people from privileged groups unlearn oppression, they recognize how much they have missed and how limited their world and thinking has been. As one person puts it, "I busted out of my own head." Unlearning privilege/oppression also encourages people from dominant groups to reexamine their notions of who and what is to be valued.

> Whole groups of people were unknown to me. I was taught not to see them as offering valuable perspectives. I had a narrow, hierarchical view—a sense of superiority. But now those people, that information and those perspectives are available to me.

Understanding different forms of oppression and how they manifest allows me to feel less "stupid". I can follow and respond appropriately to conversations about personal experiences or current events. I can appreciate political analyses and offer my perspective. I much prefer feeling like I "get it" to feeling "clueless." I'm sure this is preferable to the people I'm talking with as well.

Intellectual understanding is only one facet of deepening one's knowledge and clarity. Unlearning privilege/oppression also enhances self-understanding. It offers opportunities and tools for self-examination. As people unlearn oppression, they investigate and uncover aspects of themselves previously hidden, distorted, or ignored. One respondent explains that it "gave me a way to examine my experiences with more consciousness and capacity to understand things." Another adds, "I'm a more whole person psychologically. I better understand my personal experiences and history." Individuals can explore their personal traits, socialization, and life path in the context of the larger dynamics of privilege and oppression.

A critical component of examining one's identity is looking at how one has internalized the messages of the dominant culture. Unlearning privilege/oppression is becoming aware of one's biases, attitudes, beliefs, and behaviors that reflect and perpetuate systems of oppression. Respondents realize that denying that they have prejudices or that they are unscathed by living under systems of inequality precludes the possibility of working toward greater personal consciousness and liberation for all. As the respondents make clear, acknowledging their biases is not simply accepting and justifying them, but bringing them to light so they can be worked through. This allows them to dispel their stereotypes and correct their erroneous thinking.

Increased self-knowledge and clarity also helps people realize that despite their biases and internalized superiority, they are not bad people. They, therefore, feel less mired in guilt or shame. People from privileged groups can be deeply and genuinely committed to social justice but still embody oppressive conditioning, regardless of whether it is conscious or intentional. One woman describes being able to "accept myself as being both a racist and anti-racist. That those two aspects co-exist together in me." People who are unlearning privilege/oppression acknowledge that they will never be completely enlightened and thus, must live with themselves in their imperfect state while they strive to become their best selves and create greater justice.

These insights into themselves are not only personally helpful, they also allow people to be clearer when dealing with others. The better they can separate their issues or biases from those of others, the better they can take responsibility for their thoughts and feelings. "I don't project my own stuff and judge others, especially others from dominant groups." Individuals can more quickly recognize their "baggage" and how it affects their reactions and interactions. "I know there are unconscious ways I get triggered, but I can stop them and not act them out as much." They are more conscious of how their attitudes or assumptions may impact their behavior. People become increasingly adept at recognizing ways they enact and reinforce dynamics of superiority/inferiority. "The more open one is to one's racism, the less it gets acted out."

Some respondents particularly note that they can take things less personally. They can better discern when reactions or situations are about them in particular or more generally about people from their social group. This is heard most frequently from White people in relation to people of color or about White people's role in racism. For example, a White woman can hear the anger from a woman of color and not assume it's directed at her personally. Another White woman tries to explain how she feels a collective responsibility for historical racism and the benefits she derives from it, but recognizes that she is not responsible for every act committed by every White person. "I can listen to stories from people of color or Whites and not feel personally responsible for past history as much as I don't feel responsible for the invention of the telephone."

Awareness of different social realities also helps people from privileged groups develop perspective on their own lives. They take less for granted and have greater appreciation for what they have. Several mention that they realize that "other people's plights can be worse than yours. It helps you to step back and gain perspective." Despite the focus on their own development as they unlearn oppression, understanding others' subjugation helps them become less self-absorbed.

An Enriched Life

People who have been unlearning privilege/oppression feel their lives are richer and more fulfilling in numerous ways. One is living with greater meaning and purpose. They have found issues they feel passionately about and engage in efforts that feel significant. Work for social justice gives their life depth and direction.

Their process of unlearning privilege/oppression has also introduced them to new relationships and new worlds. Several people highlight this point:

> If you have true, genuine interest in others and value them, it opens you to enriching experiences and relationships with a broader range of people.
>
> It [unlearning privilege/oppression] exposed me to other ways of being, an awareness of other oppressions and the different ways people are in the world. I'm more open to everyone and everything.

Respondents have been able to make connections with a greater array of people, particularly with whom they previously had limited relationships. Their expanding relationships are usually due to being in a wider range of places and engaging in more varied activities that bring them into meaningful contact with others. As a result, they have a more diverse community of friends and acquaintances. "Because of this work, people have come into my life and my children's lives." In addition, as people become more aware and comfortable, they find they can more easily engage in situations they may have avoided before. A man explains, "Unlearning privilege/oppression expands the relationships and people I can be comfortable with. I can be in spaces where I'm the 'only one' and be comfortable." In return, respondents find other people are more interested in them as well. "I have an 'enriched community'. I'm more open to others, others are more open to having me as a friend."

Openness to new experiences and relationships gives people from privileged groups exposure to the cultures and wisdom of marginalized peoples. They increasingly explore and learn from others' worldviews, literature, history, art, philosophy, music, theater, and spirituality. For example, men discuss being enriched by learning about women's spirituality and more collaborative ways of engaging; White people find value in more collectivist worldviews and the histories of people of color. While there can be concerns about appropriation and exploitation, there are also appropriate ways to embrace other cultural contributions and perspectives.

Relationships with people from their dominant group often improve as well. On the one hand, people who have developed greater awareness sometimes have less interest or patience with people from their privileged group, if those others are also not raising their consciousness about social justice. On the other hand, many find that their unlearning process allows them to develop more compassion and connection with others from their dominant group. One White person explains, "I feel less judgmental. I don't judge other Whites, I don't project my own stuff." Another adds, "I used to have a White identity in opposition to other Whites. Divide and conquer, racist or not. I came to a place of deep love for White people and see myself as part of White people."

Moreover, when people engage with others from their privileged group in unlearning privilege/oppression, it can deepen their relationships. Men are often part of a men's group while White people often meet with other Whites to work on their racism. These shared experiences require openness, trust, and support, moving people beyond a superficial level of interaction. Several people mention that when they and their partner are both involved in unlearning the same oppression, it brings them closer together.

These more diverse networks of connections and deeper relationships can reduce feelings of isolation. In the process of unlearning privilege/oppression, people often need to reevaluate their current friendships and sometimes let go of relationships as their attitudes, behaviors, and priorities change. They may feel alone or worry about losing their social network. This may remain true for some, however most of these respondents ultimately feel more connected, not less. One man explains it this way:

> People often fear the loss of family and connection. Rather than feel more isolated, I feel less isolated. I have an extended sense of family and community, like we're all in this together. Often we feel like we're on the fringe when we're part of the social justice community, but I'm part of a community.

Since my life, like many others, is often segregated along racial and class lines, it is often through social justice work that I can develop relationships with a broader diversity of people. It is a context where we can come together with some shared interests and values and work together toward common goals. When I don't have these relationships, my life feels sterile. Being with people who share my dominant group identities can have its comforts, but this homogeneity lacks the vibrancy that makes me feel more stimulated and engaged. For many respondents, a wider range of relationships and greater sense of community is something that most enriches their lives. They cherish having connections with more diverse people and feeling part of a larger human community as well as part of a group of people committed to social justice.

Authenticity and Greater Humanity

Respondents repeatedly discuss a deep desire to feel more authentic within themselves, in their relationships, and in their lives. Being authentic refers to feeling more genuine and true to oneself. They want to know who they are without the limitations of their conditioning and to have meaningful connections with others. Individuals describe "gaining a sense of wholeness and feeling more complete" and "connecting at a deeper level and living closer to my core values."

Unlearning privilege/oppression clearly enables greater authenticity. Because of his work unlearning privilege/oppression, one man reports, "I am authentic now in ALL relationships. I am who I am wherever I am and now stand up for my beliefs." Another person explains,

> I wished to live "authentically" within my own shell. Upon deeper examination, at age 45, much of what I was, had accumulated and been provided felt inauthentic. Admitting that inauthentic feeling was a *huge* but crucial step. Pursuing my own unlearning process these past 12 years has allowed me to

see privilege when it's presented, and to question myself in ways that I have never needed to question before. The result is an inner calmness with my self-perception, but it is coupled with a persistent desire to educate and keep the process of awareness-raising alive in myself and for others.

Some respondents find they can be more truly themselves, regardless of how their identity is usually socially constructed. People are more able to reevaluate societal expectations, refuse to fit into the prescribed boxes, and make choices about how they want to be. One woman describes her experience:

As a heterosexual woman athlete, I was not the stereotypical female. I had to deal with my own fear that if I act outside the traditional gender norms, people would think I was a lesbian. I developed the confidence to be myself: confident, loud, strong physically. I could live with myself easier, feel better in my own skin.

A heterosexual male explains how he came to terms with his male identity and embraced different aspects of himself. "I now see that everything is a spectrum. I don't have to put myself in a category; I don't have to pigeonhole myself."

The authenticity of people from privileged groups is hindered by internalizing beliefs about their group's superiority and the other group's inferiority. This is the foundation upon which oppression is built. A significant piece of unlearning privilege/oppression work for people from dominant groups is understanding and rejecting this ideology. As people are able to do this, they no longer need to elevate themselves and their social group while diminishing the oppressed group. They can experience a truer sense of their own humanity, as well as that of others. "Learning to let go of the clearly erroneous but often covert sense of one's own superiority helped me feel more fully human."

Becoming more authentic and more human also entails reclaiming one's full emotional capacities. Living in unfair and unequal societies encourages people to suppress and deny their feelings in order to dull the effects of oppression. "Privilege requires us to shut down emotionally, to shut down from other people. I can now be in touch with feelings." Unlearning privilege/oppression helps people regain their ability to feel and be empathic.

Feelings for and about other people grow as one's knowledge of systemic inequality increases. "The deeper my understanding of oppression, the wider my capacity for compassion, care, presence and generosity." People can better appreciate how everyone is trapped in dysfunctional and harmful social systems. Having a systemic, rather than just an individual focus, helps people feel more empathy. It shifts away from blaming the victim or blaming individuals from privileged groups for their oppressive behavior by considering the larger social context and conditioning. One woman found, "I am more able to forgive others from dominant groups when I'm in the oppressed group."

In addition, several people note that they have become more focused on being true to themselves and their ideals, and less concerned with being liked or appreciated by people from the oppressed group. "I've shifted from wanting to be thought well of by people of the subordinate group to being accountable to them. I'm striving for internal consistency. I want to be authentic and consistent—to see myself and have others see me that way." While relationships and accountability are important, seeking "approval" from others is not the driving force.

Overwhelmingly, respondents focus on how much they long for and value authentic relationships across differences. As individuals feel more authentic themselves, they can be more authentic with others. Not only do people have a broader range of relationships, those relationships are also more genuine and fulfilling. People maintain that these more meaningful relationships are a direct result of their unlearning privilege/oppression. One man more pointedly says, "A fulfilling relationship with my partner is only possible because of the work I did on sexism." People from the privileged group are able to engage in more honest, conscious, and caring ways, and feel more trusted by people from the oppressed group. This creates a stronger relational foundation that allows both parties to be more vulnerable. Some respondents tell how humbling and moving it is when people from the oppressed group openly share their experiences and struggles with oppression. In discussing her relationships with friends of color, a White woman notices, "I can be authentic—warts and all—and I will still be liked." She did not have to worry about being perfect or fear that making mistakes would undermine the friendships.

Unlearning privilege/oppression allows individuals to experience their own humanity and see the full humanity of other people. Often, when White people say, "I don't see color, I just see people" or "I've transcended race", they are expressing a discomfort with acknowledging race or an ignorance of the significance of racial differences. (This can also occur in relation to other social identities.) One of the benefits of the unlearning process is being able to relate to others as "just people", while simultaneously recognizing the importance of social identities and the complexities of who people are. One of the greatest joys I experience is when I can be with someone from a subordinated group and connect unself-consciously as two human beings, while still being mindful of our various social identities and their relevance. There is neither the anxious focus on a particular identity nor the erasure of it.

In general, people from privileged groups describe feeling less guarded and more spontaneous in their relationships with people from the subordinated group. They do not have to constantly self-monitor. For myself, humor (and gentle sarcasm) is part of my cultural style. If I don't feel comfortable enough to joke around, I cannot be fully myself and I feel stilted. I love being able to use my humor freely feeling comfortable enough to trust what will come out of my mouth and that it will be received as intended.

As a result of unlearning privilege/oppression, many people feel they can live more authentic lives and feel more inner peace. There is greater congruence with who they want to be, what they do, and how they live. Respondents repeatedly express sentiments such as, "I know I'm doing the right thing. I'm closer to who I want to become." Many specifically talk about how this moral/spiritual alignment allows them a sense of spiritual integrity. "I can sleep well at night, knowing I did the best I could to challenge injustice and raise awareness in others." "I could meet my maker and hold my head up—that's priceless." People feel more serenity within themselves and with the way they can be in the world. "As a result of this work, I no longer feel inauthentic and have a genuine peacefulness with who I am, what I stand for and where I am making a difference." Another echoes, "I have an inner peace knowing I'm not acting in ways that harm others and I'm less likely to perpetuate racism." This inner calm has wider implications. As one person recognizes, "The more internal peace I have with who I am, the more peace I can extend to others."

Often respondents report experiencing spiritual growth and strength as well. "My spirit is more whole, more nourished." For some people, their moral/spiritual values are a driving force from the beginning. Others suggest that these became more central as they became increasingly involved with social justice issues. In either case, the desire to live in a way consistent with their vision of themselves and the world they want to see is a strong component of many people's unlearning work.

Empowerment, Confidence, and Competence

A deeper understanding of oppression, a clearer sense of themselves, and more diverse relationships builds empowerment, confidence, and competence to address social justice issues. One person labels unlearning privilege/oppression as "agency enhancing." Another person notes, "Doing this work has provided me with a fearlessness and a feeling of strength in what I do." Rather than feeling overwhelmed and hopeless about creating change, many people report quite the opposite.

> "Understanding privilege is a powerful antidote to the immobilization of guilt because it enhances your ability to take concrete action."

> "I feel more powerful, not powerless—to do what I can do."

> "It frees up a lot of energy to take action. I'm not in constant conflict internally."

Respondents' increased confidence and trust in themselves makes them more willing to acknowledge their limitations and mistakes. They are not as fearful of being imperfect. It is easier to admit their errors, learn from them, and keep going. As one man explains,

> I am no longer afraid of making mistakes. Trust me, I make plenty of them, but I know more about how to own them and I'm willing to look at their origins, which helps me to avoid them the next time around.

Most respondents highlight that they have become less defensive. As one person puts it, "I have enough confidence in myself and my commitment to take in feedback and move on." They can listen to critical feedback from others and not just shut down or push back. "I am willing to take risks, learn from mistakes, hear criticisms as constructive feedback and not be devastated." This is a key quality since I do not know anyone involved with social justice work who has not struggled at times with feeling defensive when they said or did something offensive or ignorant.

As a teacher and trainer, I have many opportunities to make mistakes and be challenged by participants from the subordinated group regarding oppression issues. As I continue to unlearn oppression and feel more confidence in my knowledge and skills, I find it easier to stay present and try to understand what those individuals are saying rather than immediately to defend myself or feel overwhelmed. When I do get defensive or mess up and feel demoralized, it is easier to recover. I can remind myself of all the times I have been effective and use my support network to help me learn from mistakes and keep them in perspective.

Whether formally or informally, most respondents are educating others about social justice issues. Their own unlearning privilege/oppression is inextricably tied to their competence and effectiveness in doing so. As one person puts it "steps for self, become steps for the work." The more knowledge and experience one has in dealing with oppression issues, the more one has to draw from when engaging others. "I've been in circles I wouldn't have otherwise been in which gives me access to information, perspectives, and experiences that I can then share with others." As people are clearer about how systematic inequality operates, they can be more articulate when teaching others. The more grounded they feel in the content, the better they can explain it and respond to questions and challenges. Increased knowledge not only leads to greater clarity but also lets people feel more self-assured and comfortable. "A deeper grasp of the material gives me more confidence in dealing with it and helping others see it."

Many people describe feeling better able to work with and serve people from marginalized groups. Several different facets of this are mentioned. One aspect is being able to connect more effectively with them. "When you're able to truly see people from subordinated groups as equal, you can better build relationships and be flexible." Moreover, people can be more conscious of how they unintentionally may be enacting oppressive dynamics and how someone from the marginalized group might view them. They can better understand the initial distrust or anger directed at them because of their dominant identity and professional role.

Another facet is appreciating and adapting to other ways of being and doing. People are not as limited in their thinking or behavior. "As I was able to overcome some of my male conditioning, able to be less adversarial, more collaborative, I could build relationships and problem solve with women I worked with." Consciousness and flexibility enhance any kind of working relationship with people from other social groups.

The third way is recognizing how the problems of clients/students/employees are related to the oppression they experience. It allows practitioners to appreciate that individual issues are often reflections of larger social/political dynamics and structures. This helps alleviate the tendency to "blame the victim" or focus solely at an individual level, without also addressing the greater context.

As people do their own consciousness-raising work as a member of a privileged group, they are usually better at working with others from dominant groups, whether the same or different from their own. They can connect with more patience and empathy. Some of this compassion comes from realizing that, like themselves, other people from privileged groups are shaped by the conditioning of the larger society. This perspective can also help them understand and address the resistance they encounter. They can see themselves in others.

Many people find that they can now be a positive example for individuals from privileged groups. "It feels good to be able to be a role model, to do anti-heterosexism work and be a resource for other heterosexuals." When people from a privileged groups work with people from the oppressed group as co-trainers, they can model equitable, respectful relationships which value each other's styles and perspectives. They can also illustrate that all of us have internalized biases and make mistakes but can learn from them and grow. "The more I can laugh at myself (about my own mistakes), the more disarming and more able I am to help others take risks." By sharing their process of unlearning, they can make it feel safer for others to do their own self-exploration.

Another important component is being able to show others from privileged groups how to be an ally. They can talk about how they have worked against oppression and some of their experiences doing so. "I try to share both my successes and mistakes in trying to be an ally. I want people to realize that there are ways they can be helpful but also realize some of the pitfalls." As people unlearn oppression and increase their effectiveness being an ally, they can pass this wisdom onto others and support their involvement with social change.

Liberation and Healing

In the broadest sense, unlearning privilege/oppression is liberating and healing for people from privileged groups. It is a transformative process that infuses their whole being and permeates their entire life. "Generally, I'm a better person—happier, with a more interesting life, better mental health, and smarter."

It is liberating to let go of beliefs, feelings, and patterns of behavior that have been limiting or destructive. It's like a burden has been lifted or a constriction has been loosened. "I feel so much lighter" one woman reports. Another states, "It's a way to freedom." Overcoming fears is central to this experience of liberation. They no longer feel preoccupied with worries about what they'll find out about themselves, engaging with those who are different, doing or saying the wrong thing, offending others, or how their life would change for the worse.

This sense of freedom is in contrast to the negative effects of living under systems of oppression. As one respondent puts it, "White supremacy depends on so many things that are bad for us—numbing, violence, silence." Another similarly expresses,

"Privilege looks like it makes life easier but really it increases fear, stress, and soul death."

Individuals who are unlearning privilege/oppression strive to break free from this deadening, unaware state:

> I think White privilege and White supremacy for so long have placed us all in a trance, and doing this work, studying our history and better understanding the nature of this work and the need for it helps me get out of the trance. I continue to read and study history and it feels like layers are peeling away, like I'm waking up. Slowly.

Many respondents discuss how unlearning privilege/oppression is a means to heal from the myriad ways people from privileged groups are damaged psychologically, emotionally, intellectually, socially, and spiritually. Healing occurs when they let go of guilt and fears, when they gain a clearer understanding of the world, when they become more authentic in themselves and with others, when they live their lives in morally consistent ways, when they have meaningful relationships across differences, and when they can take action to foster social justice.

For myself and the other respondents, the benefits of unlearning privilege/oppression undoubtedly outweigh the risks or costs. The joy of reclaiming one's humanity, living an enriched life, and creating a better world is a satisfying and motivating force. In the following sections, I explore what assists people on their journey of unlearning privilege/oppression.

Key Unlearning Experiences

When I asked people what was most helpful or significant in their process of unlearning privilege/oppression, a range of influences were cited. These include experiences with different people, opportunities for self-reflection, information and frameworks for analysis, and mentors. The most influential factors may change throughout their lives. What may have stimulated them early in their journey is different from what may have most impact later on.

Not surprisingly, access to theories and information prove particularly valuable. All respondents have done readings or attended classes or workshops on issues of oppression. Sometimes, personal experiences occurred first and the theory came later. "Trainings offered frameworks and analysis for what I was already seeing and experiencing." Other times, learning about privilege and oppression motivated further exploration. A class or workshop prompts the interest in these issues and the desire to seek out more knowledge and contacts. Regardless of which occurs first, respondents recognize the value of both first-hand experiences and relationships, and theory, analysis, and information.

Overwhelmingly, people talk about relationships with people from oppressed groups as critical in their unlearning process. Most salient is the opportunity to have meaningful conversations over time, which include talking about privilege and oppression. These conversations may occur in the context of a professional relationship, a friendship, or a family relationship. They all allow for a deepening connection, a growing trust, and the sharing of feelings, experiences, and perspectives in an increasingly open way. They permit people from the privileged group to gain an intimate understanding of the experiences of the marginalized group.

Another aspect is being able to be in the places and spaces of people from the oppressed group. So often, people from privileged groups meet people from marginalized groups in places that are defined by the dominant culture. It can be very different to be with people from subordinated groups in the spaces in which they are most comfortable or in which they are the majority. It is not that people from privileged groups just insert themselves into places where they are not welcome or in voyeuristic ways. They are invited into spaces because of a relationship or because of a mutually beneficial collaboration.

These contacts and relationships lead to growth in several ways. It forces people to acknowledge their biases, either due to their own awareness or by being confronted by the person from the oppressed group. It allows people to see the struggles first hand, to appreciate what living with that oppression is like. It also lets someone be known enough to see them first as their friend, as a whole human being, not first as a person from a subordinated group. In addition, people can make connections with their own oppressions. They can draw similarities between the oppression they face in another aspect of their identity and what this group experiences. As one person realized, "I wanted to be recognized as a Black woman. I realized gays wanted to be recognized too."

In addition, experience with one oppressed group helps in understanding other "isms". While there are great differences in how people experience subordination, there are also many commonalities. As people intellectually understand one form of oppression and develop caring relationships with people from that oppressed group, they can transfer some of that knowledge and concern to other forms of inequality. Furthermore, the openness required to unlearn oppression can carry over into other situations. As one person says, "Unlearning heterosexism made me generally more tolerant of other things and people."

Several people describe being called on their oppressive attitudes and behaviors as significant moments in their unlearning process. Even when they are deeply humiliated or angered when they are confronted, it spurs growth. Generally, when the challenge comes from people they value, it is easier to take it in. "Some of my key learning experiences were from people who were willing to confront me, who cared about me, and loved me enough to do so."

In some instances, respondents are confronted by people from their own privileged group. In referring to his experience in a men's group, " I wasn't attacked, but my defenses crumbled. It was harder to discount what they were saying." Other times, it is from individuals from the oppressed group. As one White woman recalls, "I was confronted by the people of color I was training with. I was playing out my internalized dominance in my attitudes and behavior. I had to own my past and current behaviors." In the moment, people have different feelings about being challenged, but ultimately they recognize it as a valuable experience.

None of these experiences or information would have been as significant to the respondents' unlearning process, if there were not the willingness to engage in deep self-exploration. Individuals recognize that the way out is through; we need to acknowledge and accept all parts of ourselves in order to be and act differently. If we try to disown or disengage from these "negative" aspects, they never get addressed or keep us locked in destructive feelings. "Coming to terms with my own history allowed me to move out of shame and guilt." Another person elaborates on this point.

> I found that acknowledging racist or sexist thoughts loosened the shame. It allowed the letting go of shame—of thinking, "I'm bad for having objectifying or bigoted thoughts." I realized it's part of cultural conditioning— "normal". It was better not keeping it hidden—that's unhealthy, it gives it power, it keeps it alive, digging inside.

Several people stress the importance of self-compassion as they do this personal work. "It's like meditation. It got easier when I let go of self-judgment which just compounds fears and bad feelings." This is echoed by another:

> I see this path as a Buddhist path. We need to mindfully look at and contemplate who we are. With loving compassion, we need to come to acceptance of who we are with all our faults. ... The more open one is to one's own racism, the less it gets acted out. In trying not to be that, we are more that.

The value of looking honestly at oneself is especially important to recognize. Many people resist self-examination as part of unlearning privilege/oppression since they fear what it will reveal. They may fear getting stuck in the pain, guilt, or negative feelings about themselves. Yet, delving into these feelings is what allows people not to get trapped in them.

Staying on the Journey—Then and Now

People from privileged groups can more easily make the choice not to think about or unlearn oppression. So, why and how have people stayed on this journey—in the past and in the present? Respondents are quick to note that there is always more that they could do and more they need to know. They are aware of contradictions in their lives. Yet, they have stayed committed to continuing this process and to living in greater congruence with social justice.

One response to why they have stayed on the journey stood out. It is that it feels good. Again, this is in stark contrast with people's assumptions that there will only be pain. There are a wide variety of experiences that give people positive feelings. A sampling of responses are listed below:

> "The times I 'get' it."
> "My relationships and friends."
> "Meeting my own expectations for how I want to be. I set the bar and the closer I get to it is rewarding."
> "When I feel more clarity and integrity."
> "I continue to be enriched."
> "I get a high when I see people shift."
> "I am re-energized when I effectively confront and negotiate my biases."
> "The passionate feeling I have is hard to stay away from."

As seen in the other sections, when people feel more powerful, more aligned with their values, smarter, more passionate, more effective, and more authentically connected to themselves and others, they naturally want to continue on this path.

For many people, unlearning privilege/oppression addresses their personal needs. Overwhelmingly they crave authentic relationships with all people, but especially with those from the oppressed group. Many describe an intrinsic "zest for growth" and need for continual personal and spiritual development. Some are motivated by a desire to deal with their own pain and discomfort or to make amends for past mistakes. "I felt bad much of the time when I wasn't dealing with it (racism). I had much more fear. Denial and fear of judgment just led to wasted energy and pain."

There are also more concrete needs as well. Several mention the need to keep their job (usually as a trainer or educator). Others talk about their desire to keep their friends and to continue to expand their social connections. A number of people recognize that their privilege allows them the time or money to pursue opportunities to unlearn their oppression. They could more easily follow their desire for growth or connection. "'I didn't have to worry about my survival—other privileges make it easier to focus on doing this work."

Support from others is critical for staying on this journey. It comes from a number of sources in a variety of ways. It is not always warm and fuzzy, but ultimately people feel cared for and encouraged. Being connected to others who share their commitment to social justice is mentioned often. Respondents are sustained by "other allies and by being part of caring communities." One person explains, "I stay engaged by actively seeking and maintaining communities of support and accountability with people who share my identities and people who have different identities." A number of people have families or partners with whom they can share the journey or mutually encourage each other's growth. Some find support from being part of groups or organizations that address social justice issues. At times, people actively need to seek out like-minded others so they do not feel alienated or alone.

Relationships with both people from the subordinated group and people from their privileged group are needed. Having other allies to talk with and process with is salient for many respondents. This gives them a space to figure things out or deal with their feelings, apart from people from the oppressed group. They can share common experiences and struggles. Many also refer to the support from individuals from the subordinated group who are willing to challenge and hang in there with them. The trust bestowed on them from people from the marginalized group enhances their confidence and desire to continue their learning.

In addition, role models from the past and present are frequently helpful. It allows people to feel connected to a larger movement and history, to learn from the risks others took, to find examples of how to be an ally, and to have a vision of how they want to be. Role models offer inspiration and build courage.

Respondents clearly feel a commitment and responsibility to continue their unlearning process and to create social justice. This may be derived from their religious or spiritual teachings, political principles, personal beliefs, and/or inner calling. Several people indicate that their relationships with individuals from the oppressed group are central. They feel an increased responsibility to continually earn their trust, not to be hurtful, and to work to alleviate the suffering and inequality people face. "I can't forget the people I love and they won't let me forget." Another person adds, "I feel a responsibility to show up and be more useful."

A number of people who are also members of oppressed groups make the connection between their own oppression and that faced by other people. They know what it's like to be oppressed and they do not want to inflict that on others. "I have an acute understanding of being oppressed. I *do not* want to participate in another's oppression." Another adds, "I connect to my own struggle as a Black woman and being marginalized."

Those who are parents or have close relationships with children express the desire to leave them a better world. They also feel the responsibility to educate their children to be less biased and to understand injustice. People want to be able to effectively talk with their children about oppression, so they can notice, analyze, and intervene when there is inequity.

Moreover, it's important to be able to support children to be who they are, particularly if they are part of an oppressed group, so they can feel empowered and self-accepting.

> You don't know who your kids will be. I want to be there for my kids or the kids of friends and neighbors. If you don't do the work, you'll just be part of a system that makes them feel bad or creates obstacles, and contributes to them being someone who they're not.

Being able to be on and stay on the journey of unlearning privilege/oppression seems to require that people can value discomfort and trust that it will bring them to a better place. They see discomfort not as an enemy to be destroyed, but a teacher to be embraced. Being uncomfortable means that there is growth. They accept that they will be uneasy, but "discomfort is not such a bad thing. Change requires discomfort." Others state, "Comfort can mean complacency, not being alive." "Discomfort keeps me motivated. Racism isn't comfortable and shouldn't be. If there is no discomfort, it's a red flag I'm getting complacent."

Not only is discomfort unavoidable and welcomed, it is tolerable and worth it. This is clearly counter to those who try to avoid feeling uncomfortable and fear that it will be unbearable and destructive. "Yes, it can be painful and incriminating at first … but the results of getting 'unstuck' are well worth the messiness." Another explains,

> There is a profound freedom in getting honest and talking about these things (talking about racism and her family's involvement with it). Despite the fact that it makes my ancestors and people of my race look and feel awful. So what. It's all about healing. And healing hurts sometimes. So I guess you could call all anti-racism work and White privilege/White supremacy awareness work "joyful pain."

In addition to accepting discomfort, a number of people speak about needing to trust the process, to believe that this will be worth it. You need to be "willing to surrender, to let go, to trust that you're going to get to another place." When discussing how to engage others, one woman says, you need to "help them see the promise of going to an uncomfortable place". Unlearning privilege/oppression can be uncomfortable, but people survive and thrive as a result.

None of the respondents feels like there is an option of turning back, of undoing or stopping this journey. It is part of who they are and how they live their lives. People describe it as: "I'm beyond the point of no return—I can't close that 'third eye'". "Not being part of social justice is just not an option".

Respondents recognize that they are continually a work in progress. People are quick to add that they still have much to learn, that they make mistakes and that they see this as ongoing. "This isn't an end product; it's a process. The highs and lows of the work are constant. I continually disappoint myself and others." No one wants to give the impression, that despite all they have learned, that they are "done".

> I recognize that being an ally is an everyday endeavor, and each day I need to turn in and subsequently re-earn my ally identity. Being an ally is like being funny. You should not need to tell people that you are it, it should be apparent.

Others express, "There is no final place of Nirvana." "I'm keenly aware that it takes constant vigilance, self-reflection, and analysis." I can concur. No matter how long I do this work, I'm always finding new issues to learn about, ways to understand myself, and avenues to challenge inequality.

Conclusion

What is striking from all these stories is the overwhelming sense of how valuable and significant this work has been—how liberating it is, how much better people feel about themselves, how their lives have been enhanced, how good it feels. While I initiallychose the word "joy" as ironic, it fits much better than I expected. These feelings challenge two main reasons people resist engaging in unlearning privilege/oppression: 1) that I'm fine, and there's no purpose in subjecting myself to this and 2) that it is just going to hurt and not be worth it. As one woman explains, "It's hard to know what's missing or how life could be different until one experiences it."

In some ways, this process is like psychotherapy or counseling. (I am not saying as educators we should be doing therapy with our students or that our classes/work-shops are counseling sessions!) There are some issues or some dis-ease impeding our life that draws us into therapy. Therapy can be painful and uncomfortable at times; it can reveal things that are hard to acknowledge about ourselves, the people we're close to, and the situations we're in. But its goal is not destructive, it's restorative. It is not meant to harm but to heal. It's about becoming healthier and more whole. Ultimately, we come out the other side with a clearer view of ourselves and others and an enhanced capacity to deal with life. It is not that we are now the model of mental health and that we live our lives with perfect clarity and balance. But we have changed in significant ways. Like unlearning privilege/oppression, hard work and discomfort are part of a healing process that brings us to a better place from which we keep evolving. We are more equipped to continue to learn from mistakes and new situations. We are better able to take more risks, to become the person we want to be, and to help create the world we want to live in.

There seems to be a point in the unlearning privilege/oppression process where people get "over the hump"—where the scale tips toward feelings of growth and healing and less toward discomfort and guilt. Sometimes, people are overwhelmed with reevaluating previous beliefs and integrating new perspectives. Someone described it as feeling like standing in quicksand or in shifting sand. Eventually, people find more of a foundation from which to progress. It may also be harder in earlier phases to appreciate how this effort will be beneficial. The costs and struggles are most salient. Consistent with social/racial identity development theories, there may be times in the beginning and middle of the process where one is more likely to feel guilt, shame, anger, or pain rather than joy or liberation. I was doing a workshop on the "Joy of Unlearning Privilege/Oppression" where I asked people to identify how they had benefited from unlearning privilege/oppression and one woman responded, "I'm not feeling much joy!" One interviewee shared that feeling but now feels differently, "I felt a lot of guilt before it felt liberating. The liberating part comes from the work we do for justice, that I'm doing the right thing." It can be helpful for people to see that staying with the process will be worth it.

Unlearning privilege/oppression reminds me of a mountain-climbing adventure. A mountain guide is telling you how great it is, but like most of the people you know, you enjoy the comfort and security of your couch. You don't know where this journey is leading. You worry there is too much risk, that it's going to be too taxing and not much fun. Yet, on some level you realize that you may be missing an opportunity, that there is something exciting out there and that sitting on the couch may not be the best way to live your life. It helps that the guide is skilled and supportive. It's hard to resist her enthusiasm and reassurance. You trust her enough to take the first steps.

You find you're not alone on this journey, that there are other travelers on this path with your guide. Some start out slowly like you. Others are eager to bound ahead, feeling more sure-footed. As you start out, you're tentative and out of shape; it's hard. There aren't any views. People suffer to varying degrees from blisters and sore muscles. You think about turning back. But there is something about the mountain air and the nature around you that feels stimulating and healing. With the guide's support, you keep putting one foot in front of the other. You have the camaraderie of the other hikers who trudge along with different amounts of enthusiasm but you help keep each other going. You observe other hikers far ahead of you who seem to be enjoying the outing.

Gradually you notice the beauty around you. You get glimpses of views. Eventually, it gets easier as you get in better shape and feel more comfortable on the terrain. You hike higher and higher, seeing beautiful vistas and wildlife. You feel healthier than before and begin to appreciate why the effort was worth it. You reach a top of a mountain and get a rush of the wonder of nature. But the hike still continues over the endless range of mountains. People continue on different paths over the ridges. You find other hikers to join on this ongoing adventure. While there are always new vistas and beauty to experience, there are also the ups and downs of the trail, descents into valleys, stumbles, blisters, and bug bites. You realize that those too are part of the journey that continues to lead you to new levels of fitness, greater competencies, and breathtaking panoramas. There is no turning back.

As educators, people need to trust us as their guides. We can offer them challenge and support in their unlearning process. They need to hear that there is something meaningful to be gained that is worth the effort. As one respondent says, "I was closed off, but didn't know it because I didn't know differently." Through these stories about the joy of unlearning privilege/oppression, we can help people know differently. We can hold out the vision of greater humanity and liberation.

8

WHY PEOPLE FROM PRIVILEGED GROUPS SUPPORT SOCIAL JUSTICE

> Our obedience to the demands of justice can bring us the possibility of a far deeper happiness, security and sense of integrity than can any commitment to individual wealth or personal comfort.
>
> (David Hilfiker, 1994)

I am often asked why people would want to change a system from which they benefit or why I, as a White person, am committed to eliminating racism. There are obvious reasons why people from dominant groups resist challenges to the status quo. There are also plenty of reasons why they remain apathetic and uninvolved. Yet we know from history and our current experiences that people from privileged groups also assist, and often take leadership in struggles for social justice. Instead of just focusing on why people from privileged groups *don't* support equity, I have been exploring what motivates people to do so. Supporting social justice can occur on different levels—from supporting a particular project, to being committed to dismantling a specific form of oppression, to working to change the structures and values which underlie all systems of domination and subordination. As I'll discuss, some people just may be willing to act in limited ways under narrow circumstances, while others may be deeply committed and devote large amounts of time and energy. I will consider both the similarities and differences in motivation for these types of support.

Why do some men support feminist initiatives, some heterosexuals work for gay and lesbian rights, or some Whites challenge racist practices? Why have you tried to address inequities experienced by people from a subordinated group as a member of the privileged group? I have been asking people in classes and workshops that question.

People's responses tend to fall into three distinct, though interrelated, categories.[1] In the first category, people speak about a personal relationship they have with an individual from an oppressed group, of how they can relate from their own experiences to the experiences of others, or how they feel a sense of connection or "we-ness". I call this type of response *empathy*.

Others speak of their need to act morally and their discomfort with the discrepancy between what they believe and what they observe around them. Some talk of unfairness, of how certain groups don't deserve their disadvantaged status, and of their desire to fulfill the American ideal of equality. A spiritual belief in the inherent worth and dignity of all people motivates others. I call this type of response *moral principles and spiritual values*.

In the third category, people recognize how oppression affects them as members of the dominant group and the potential benefits of greater equity. They speak of wanting to live in a society with more harmonious intergroup relations, of wanting a world safe for their children, and of seeing the survival of the planet predicated on creating greater justice. Others personally desire more diverse friendships, broadened knowledge, and more varied cultural experiences. Some acknowledge the benefits to their organization through increased enrollments, retention, or profits. This group of responses I name *self-interest*.

I will first describe and discuss each of these sources individually. I will then explore the interconnections among them. In the following chapter, I discuss how to actually foster and appeal to empathy, moral or spiritual principles, and self-interest in order to gain support for social justice concerns. I am not suggesting that these are the only qualities that inspire people to work for equity, but that these are key motivators that encourage people to do so.[2]

Empathy

Empathy involves being able to identify with the situation and feelings of another person. It incorporates affective and cognitive components, requiring both the capacity to share in the emotional life of another, as well as the ability to imagine the way the world looks from another's vantage point. Chinua Achebe refers to this as "imaginative identification" (1989, p. 153, as cited in Lazarre, 1993, p. 4). It is "our capacity to understand and feel the suffering of others even though we have never experienced that particular suffering ourselves" (Lazarre, 1993, p. 4). Being empathic, or taking the perspective of another person and imagining how that person is affected by his or her situation, can be useful for promoting more positive attitudes and inspiring action. Research suggests that empathy and the desire to help is a natural human inclination (Kohn, 1990).

Empathy is not the same as pity. With pity, we hold ourselves apart from other people and their suffering, thinking of their condition as something that makes them fundamentally inferior or different from ourselves. Pity is seeing a homeless person on the street and while feeling sorry for that person, thinking "that never could be me". Empathy, however, is more like compassion. It recognizes our shared vulnerability while also acknowledging the differences between ourselves and others. Compassion is seeing the homeless person and thinking "that could be me". We acknowledge our susceptibility to situations of misfortune or subjugation as fellow human beings.

Empathy and Social Justice

Many theorists have discussed the significance of empathy in social relations (See Kohn, 1990 for a review of the literature). The presence of empathy can foster positive social action whereas its absence can perpetuate injustice. Suppressing empathy for people in oppressed groups is a powerful tool in maintaining oppression. When we fail to see our common humanity with people we perceive as different from ourselves, we can more easily ignore their plight. It also allows us to dehumanize others, seeing them as less than human or unworthy of care and respect. This sets the stage for the acceptance or perpetuation of violence (a common strategy during wars) (Grossman, 1995). The more one dehumanizes people, the more likely one will commit violence. This, in turn, increases the need to dehumanize them. "By making the objects of our violence less than human, we do not experience the guilt associated with killing or harming fellow human beings" (Sampson, 1991, p. 322).

There are many ways people from oppressed groups are depersonalized and dehumanized in our society. Depersonalization and dehumanization occurs through stereotypes (defining gay men as child molesters), images (depicting African Americans as animals), and language (using derogatory names—Gook, bitch, wet back). In sum, perpetuating the sense that the "Other" is sufficiently different and less human than ourselves erodes the capacity for empathy, and thus, the propensity for care and action.

On the other hand, empathy can be a powerful tool in promoting social responsibility. Empathy helps us connect with and subsequently care about others who seem different. "Coming to see others as more simply human than one of Them, represents so drastic a conceptual shift, so affecting an emotional conversion, that there may be no greater threat to those with an interest in preserving intergroup hostility" (Kohn, 1990, p. 145). Empathy makes it more difficult to use derogation as a means of maintaining a belief in a just world—vilifying or blaming victims for their circumstances, in order to continue to believe that society is fair. Instead, empathy tends to encourage prosocial action to remove the injustice (Batson, et al., 1997). It also helps to counter the egoistic desire to avoid personal costs and maintain relative advantage.

There is an important difference between using empathy to motivate altruistic or helping behavior and using empathy to encourage social activism and support for social justice. Most research on empathy and altruistic or prosocial behavior is confined to studies of people responding to someone's immediate distress (often in laboratory conditions). A single act will often suffice to alleviate that distress. It is usually focused on helping an individual in a particular situation, regardless of their social group membership or connection to social oppression. Prosocial activism, on the other hand, is "sustained action in the service of improving another person's or groups' life condition by working with them or by trying to change society on their behalf" (Hoffman, 1989, p. 65). People are more likely to engage in prosocial activism if they respond empathically to a victim's or group's long-term plight rather than just an immediate situation. This involves understanding that the other person(s) is part of a social group and recognizing the chronic nature of the victim's distress.

Although I will draw upon the research on empathy and prosocial behavior to discuss why people act in caring and socially responsible ways, the research on prosocial activism is most relevant to social justice efforts. As I will discuss, it is important that we encourage people to see beyond just aiding an individual in a particular situation. We need to foster their support for societal changes that will improve the lives of those who suffer systemic victimization.

Types of Empathic Responses

An empathic connection with someone who is suffering tends to elicit two kinds of affective responses (Hoffman, 1989). One is *personal or empathic distress*. This is when the empathy generates uncomfortable feelings for the people who are empathizing. This "negative arousal" may make people feel anxious, upset, disturbed, guilty, or shameful. With empathic distress, individuals have a personal reaction of distress to the situation of another. For example, when I see the unsafe, overcrowded, and inadequate conditions of the schools for children in the inner city near where live, I often feel guilty and upset.

The second kind of affective response is *sympathetic distress*. This is what we tend to think of when we think of empathy or compassion. It involves caring about and feeling for the person in distress. In response to the aforementioned school conditions, I may also feel sorry for the children and families who must live with these circumstances (sympathetic distress). Hoffman (1989) has suggested that sympathetic distress also may elicit other related feelings. These can include feelings of empathic anger—anger on behalf of the victim toward the party responsible for the suffering, and empathic injustice—feeling that the victim's treatment is unfair and undeserved. For example, I may also be angry at the politicians who don't attempt to remedy this school situation (empathic anger). Or, I may feel outrage since these children don't deserve to be forced into these oppressive conditions (empathic injustice).

Motivations to Care and Act

Once people have empathized and feel some kind of empathetic or sympathetic distress, they have to decide what to do about it. Different types of empathic responses tend to produce different motivations to respond to the person (group) in need. While these motivations are independent and distinct internal responses, they are not mutually exclusive and often occur in conjunction with each other.

Two main motives for acting on empathy are egoistic motivations since they are primarily concerned with addressing one's own needs (Batson, 1989). The first motivation is based on acting in *compliance with internalized standards*. Through socialization, people internalize standards or expectations for appropriate actions or behaviors. These may be based on social expectations (societal or group norms) or self-expectations (personal norms). The motivation to act is driven by their desire to live up to these standards. By complying with these expectations, they can antici-pate receiving rewards or avoiding punishment. These rewards or punishments may be explicit and obvious, such as obtaining an award, peer approval, monetary remuneration, gratitude from those helped, or public censure. Often they are more subtle, and in compliance with internalized needs such as avoiding guilt, seeing oneself as a good person, receiving esteem in exchange for helping, or gaining a sense of adventure. Continuing with the aforementioned example, I may decide to participate in a campaign for school finance reform because I think of myself as a caring person, my friends are involved in social justice causes, and I want to live up to the expectations of myself and my peers.

The second type of motivation is *aversive arousal reduction*. The motive is to reduce one's own distress that was generated by empathizing. There is the desire to do something to reduce feelings of guilt, anger, or discomfort. From this perspective, I may work for school finance reform because I want to relieve my guilt that my children attend a high-quality school while other children do not, to dissipate my anger at their unjust treatment or to relieve my discomfort at having to walk by there everyday.

The third motivation is *altruism*, which is focused on addressing others' needs. The motivation to act is not focused on addressing their own distress, arousal, or needs, but on responding to the needs of the other person (group). The concern is simply to improve the welfare of the other, regardless of whether they, themselves will benefit. They may still experience some kind of positive effect, but that is not a motivating factor. My social action might be based on my concern about the chil-dren and my desire that these children get the kind of education that all children deserve.

People's motivation to act on empathic responses can be based on any one or all of these motives, and often the line is blurry. Though isolating the specific reason is not crucial, it can be helpful for educators to understand people's motivation in order to better foster and channel their emotional energy.

Moral Principles and Spiritual Values

Morality deals with questions of right and wrong. Research suggests that people are intrinsically motivated to behave fairly and to seem moral and good (Kelman &

Hamilton, 1989; Tyler, Boeckmann, Smith, & Huo, 1997). Value systems affect people's judgment of a situation and their determination of whether it violates their moral or spiritual code. When someone considers something morally or spiritually wrong, it provides an impetus to act to remedy that situation. Even though people from privileged groups may be inclined to justify their advantage as fair, studies demonstrate that concerns about justice affect both the feelings and actual behaviors of the people in privileged positions (Tyler, et al., 1997). Despite the assumption that self-interest most influences people's decisions in the political arena, research suggests otherwise (Orren, 1988; Sears & Funk, 1990).

What is far more likely to predict someone's position on an issue of public policy is a deeply held principle. Attitudes about issues ranging from desegregation to unemployment tend to reflect value commitments more than they do one's personal stake in a given policy (Orren, 1988, p. 24). In fact, many actions toward social justice are done to uphold ethical or spiritual values (Colby & Damon, 1992; Daloz, et al, 1996; Hoehn, 1983; Oliner & Oliner, 1988).

Types of Moral Reasoning

There are two commonly recognized modes of moral judgment. One is a person-oriented, ethic of care; the other is a principle-oriented, ethic of justice (Gilligan, 1980/1993; Lyons, 1988; Reimer, Paolitto, & Hersh, 1983). The dominant ideology in the United States that espouses values of fairness, equality, and equal opportunity reflects a justice orientation. Each of these moral orientations and their developmental sequences has implications for motivating support for social justice.

A morality of justice, long believed to be the only system of moral reasoning, is focused on rights and fairness. This form of morality is concerned with upholding principles or standards. It is rooted in a formal sense of equality and reciprocity (treating others as you would want to be treated). When using this type of moral reasoning, people make moral decisions by applying logical, abstract, and impartial rules or principles. People contend that something is unjust when it violates these accepted standards which often involve equal rights, equal opportunity, or role-related obligations.

A morality of care is focused on relationships and responsiveness. This form of morality is concerned with promoting the welfare of others, preventing harm, and relieving physical or psychological suffering. Using this type of reasoning, people arrive at moral decisions inductively, motivated by the desire to maintain connection, and avoid hurt. From this perspective, individuals contend that something violates their moral code when people are being harmed or not cared for.

People may therefore agree that something is morally wrong but arrive at that determination in different ways. Take, for example, a situation of housing discrimination based on race. A justice perspective might focus on its unfairness, since it violates laws that assert equal opportunity. A care perspective might focus on the harm to the family looking for a home and the suffering it causes them.

Most people tend toward one type of moral orientation, though they often use both. Since a morality of justice is the norm, even people who prefer an ethic of care are fluent in and can use an ethic of justice perspective. Studies have suggested that women tend to use an ethic of care more frequently than men (Gilligan, 1980/ 1993; Lyons, 1988).

Developmental Sequences

Even within the same moral orientation, there is a developmental sequence of moral reasoning that reflects distinctions in how people make moral judgments within that framework. Again, although people may engage in similar *actions*, their *reasons* for doing so may be different. I'll use an example of a college administrator charged with recruiting and hiring more faculty and students of color to illustrate the different perspectives.

Within an ethic of justice there are three levels, each with two stages, that reflect the development of moral reasoning. *Level One—Preconventional* is concerned with the concrete interests of the individuals involved, not with what society defines as the right way to behave in a given situation. People consider what the specific consequences would be for acting in a particular way. The administrator reasoning from this self-oriented level might not even feel there is a moral problem (racial discrimination or exclusion) to be addressed. However, he may comply because he fears losing his job if he doesn't or because he thinks that he will be more marketable if he does increase diversity. He might also believe that this will give him more leverage with the student organizations or faculty groups that support diversity when he has to deal with other issues, such as an alcohol policy.

Moving away from a self-centered focus, *Level Two—Conventional* involves an identification with the expectations of others and the rules and norms of society. This level is most common among adults. The administrator might pursue this effort because it is what his peers are doing at other colleges, people he respects expect him to do so, and it is commonly recognized in academic circles that there needs to be more inclusion of underrepresented groups at colleges. He also might be concerned with conforming to affirmative action laws, campus policies, or other statutes that mandate equal opportunity and outreach.

In *Level Three—Postconventional or Principled* the focus shifts to abstract ideals of justice. These may include abiding by the social contract (laws, rules, and values) which consider the welfare of all and protect all people's rights. Individuals may also be guided by "universal ethical principles" which involve the equality of human rights and the respect for the dignity of human beings as individuals. People will abide by laws and social agreements to the extent that they correspond with their universal principles. The administrator might support efforts to create a more diverse and inclusive college to benefit all—providing a better educated workforce that can value diversity and utilize the talents of more of its citizens. He may believe that all people should have the freedom to pursue knowledge and be able to fulfill their potential.

The ethic of care also has a developmental sequence of moral reasoning. This three-position sequence begins with *Survival* where the concern is for caring for oneself in order to ensure survival. The second perspective is *Goodness* which involves caring for others and being "good" according to conventional definitions. The last perspective is *Truth* which considers care for oneself as well as others, recognizing the interconnection between self and others. Care becomes a self-chosen moral principle with the injunction to prevent or condemn harm and violence.

Similarly, different considerations might motivate the administrator using a care perspective. From the view of *Survival*, he may comply with this strategy in order to keep his job so he can pay his bills and support his family. From the view of *Goodness*, he may feel that being a "good" administrator means caring about all potential students and faculty, and being liked and respected by his colleagues and the campus community. From the third perspective of *Truth*, he may realize that exclusion hurts people of color by denying them opportunities and harms Whites by denying them a fuller educational experience. He may feel that ultimately the collective well-being is better served by a more diverse campus.

Spiritual Values

Spiritual beliefs may fall within these moral frameworks or have their own ethical codes. Spirituality or religion always has an ethical orientation since it seeks to respond to the moral question of how we ought to live our lives (Daloz, et al., 1996). Some talk of upholding the Golden Rule, of treating everyone as a child of God, of the importance of relieving suffering, or of recognizing that "there is that of God in every person." In their study of people committed to working for the common good, Daloz et al. found that for many individuals, religion and spirituality played an explicit or implicit role in their development of commitment and in their larger meaning-making system. They frequently alluded to a principle of inter-dependence. This sense of the interdependent nature of life informed their public commitment. These individuals also found a way to continually reframe and expand their religious understanding and practice to include and respect others and the complex diversity of the world. Some spoke of a sense of spiritual imperative, feeling called, and compelled to respond to the needs of the world. Despite their many differences, most religious or spiritual belief systems share a common mandate to care for those less fortunate and to treat people humanely.

We can be more effective at appealing to moral and spiritual values, if we understand how people determine what is ethical or just. As these frameworks and sequences suggest, different moral orientations and reasoning can motivate people to support social justice. The early stages in both moral frameworks are self-oriented, more focused on one's own needs than those of others. However, as we'll see in the next section, self-interest is not necessarily selfish concern. Self-interest can also be a healthy aspect of working for social change.

Self-Interest

I previously discussed some of the many costs of oppression to people from dominant groups. These various psychological, moral/spiritual, intellectual, social, and material/physical costs provide a basis for why people from privileged groups might support greater equity. They may seek greater authenticity and integrity, better interpersonal relationships, safer communities, or more effective organizations. I also described some of the benefits or "joys" people from dominant groups gained in their process of unlearning privilege/oppression and being allies for social justice. These responses as well point to how justice can be in the self-interest of individuals from privileged groups.

However, the term self-interest tends to have a negative connotation. In fact, the primary dictionary definitions refer to it as selfish concern and personal advantage. These common definitions of self-interest imply that one gains at the expense or exclusion of others; that it is a zero-sum game. This is consistent with economic exchange theory and the dominant worldview that envisions people as separate individuals competing for positions of advantage or superiority. While this may reflect one aspect of self-interest, it ignores the possibility that what may be in my interest might also benefit others.

People also tend to assume that there is something inherently wrong or less "pure" in considering one's own interests or needs, especially in doing work for social justice. As Carol Gilligan (1980/1993) has suggested, in interdependent relationships, we need to put ourselves in the "web of care" and consider our own needs as well as the needs of others. A healthy self-concern is not the same as selfishness. We do not need to ignore or act against our own needs in the process of working for justice. But to do so, we need a broader understanding of self-interest (cf. Lappe & DuBois, 1991 and Kohn, 1990 for a discussion of alternative conceptions of self-interest). The term "enlightened self-interest" has been used in a general way to describe the understanding that the interests of the individual and the common good can converge. I will propose a more complex conception of self-interest and suggest that it is a useful, if not necessary, component of motivating people from privileged groups to support greater equity.

Continuum of Self-Interest

Instead of defining self-interest simply as selfish concern, we can define it more broadly to include benefits to oneself that do not necessarily exclude benefits to others as well. Self-interest can incorporate the interests of others as well as one's own. It can range from a very narrow, selfish perspective to a more inclusive,

Individualistic	Mutual	Interdependent
"Me"	"You and Me"	"Us"

FIGURE 8.1 Continuum of Self-Interest

interdependent perspective. There are two key factors that distinguish different types of self-interest: one's conception of self (separate/autonomous or connected/relational), and a short- or long-term perspective (whether one focuses on immediate or long-run interests). Moreover, as evidenced in the costs of oppression and joys of unlearning privilege/oppression described earlier, the benefits for people from privileged groups may take various forms, from the psychological to the material. I will describe a continuum of self-interest (see Figure 8.1) and provide some illustrations of the various perspectives.

On one end of the continuum is *individualistic* or "me-oriented" self-interest. This coincides with the common equation of self-interest with selfish concern. People operating from this type of self-interest may support social justice efforts solely for their own perceived personal gain. The concern is for the self; the fact that it benefits someone else is incidental or secondary. The prime motivation to support social justice is seen in terms of what it will do for me. Appealing to this type of self-interest may be getting someone to do the "right thing" for what may seem to be the wrong reason. It is a short-sighted and short-term perspective, concerned with immediate, and usually material, benefits.

For example, a politician may support rights for people with disabilities because it will provide votes among a needed constituency. Similarly, an individual or organization may give money to a shelter for battered women or anti-poverty program because it will be good public relations and help their reputation. A male student may help organize campus events about violence against women as a vehicle to meet women or fulfill an extra-credit assignment.

Further along the continuum, self-interest involves a consideration of what benefits others as well as oneself. A *mutual* perspective sees benefits for both—"you *and* me". Moving away from a narrow, self-oriented perspective, this reflects a more *relational* view of self-interest. The action is based on real concern for others. The personal benefits may be of many types. Someone may volunteer in a food kitchen because it makes them feel good about themselves and allows them to feel they are doing something helpful (psychological) or to learn more about homelessness (intellectual). At the same time, they may also genuinely want to do something to address the disadvantaged situation of others. People may join the Peace Corps or other service organizations both for the sense of adventure and to meet new people (social), as well as to aid in the development of poor communities. Individuals might work on campaigns for welfare reform and living wages to relieve their guilt about their privileged economic background (moral) in addition to assisting people in need. A heterosexual father of a gay son may be involved in passing gay non-discrimination laws. It reduces his own anxiety over his son's experience of homophobia and benefits his son and other gays and lesbians. There may be material benefit when the decision to sponsor a "diversity week" is based on both the desire to respond to the concerns of marginalized groups, while also seeing it as a strategy to quell greater demands and accusations that the organization doesn't care about diversity.

My assumption is that for the majority of people who support social justice efforts there is some sense of mutual benefit. Even though they might like to believe or have others believe that it is solely on behalf of the oppressed group (in which case it would be pure altruism with no self-interest), I suspect that most of us get some other personal satisfaction from engaging in such actions. This in turn motivates further involvement.

The *interdependent* perspective has a greater relational view that blurs the boundaries between you and me and sees "us". As Sampson (1988) explains, "When the self is defined in relation, inclusive of others in its very definition, there is no fully separate self whose interests do not of necessity include others" (p. 20). Various feminist theorists have been developing relational theories of self (cf. Robb, 2007). Work on behalf of others is simultaneously work on behalf of ourselves. From this interdependent perspective, since our lives and fates are intertwined, social justice efforts are being done for our collective benefit. A heterosexual person who fights against homophobia might feel that all of us need to be free from rigid sex-roles, limits on sexual expression, and lifestyle constraints. Likewise, a person without a disability might advocate the humane treatment of people with disabilities believing it reflects on how society views and values all human beings.

Interdependent self-interest may require that people work against what appears to be their immediate self-interest. However, a relational sense of self and a more long-term perspective allows them to see the benefit to themselves and others in the long run. Wealthy people may support higher tax rates or caps on executives' salaries (which impact their earnings) in order to create a more equitable distribution of wealth. They may believe that since a more peaceful society depends on people having quality educational and work opportunities, and decent living conditions, there needs to be a fairer allocation of resources. White men (or women) may support affirmative action, even though in the short run it reduces the likelihood that they would be hired. They support a practice that they feel will lead to the kind of world they want to live in—one with great equity and the inclusion of important voices that have been silenced. People who have an interdependent sense of self-interest are likely to recognize their privilege, to seek ways to give it up, to not take advantage of it, or to use it to promote social justice.

The Connections among Empathy, Morality, and Self-Interest

By themselves, empathy, moral and spiritual values, and self-interest can provide an impetus to support social justice efforts. However, they often operate in conjunction and can be addressed in combination to strengthen the appeal to action. I will provide some examples of how they can be used to bolster each other.

Empathy Joined with Moral Principles and Self-Interest

The use of moral values along with empathy can help transform feelings into action. Instead of just feeling badly, moral or spiritual principles can create a sense of responsibility to act to alleviate the suffering or injustice. The experience of empathy may lead to the invocation of moral principles. In addition, since empathy generally requires that people see the situation or suffering as unjust, moral principles can allow people to come to that understanding or interpretation.

Self-interest is implicit in much empathically-motivated behavior. People often act in socially responsible ways to address their empathic distress. They are motivated by a desire to reduce their negative arousal or to be consistent with their internalized standards. After an empathy-generating experience, self-interest can be useful in helping them deal with their reactions. It can motivate and sustain action once their empathy has been aroused.

Moral Principles Joined with Empathy and Self-Interest

Empathy can help move one's moral concern out of the abstract and impersonal. Some people are rule, not person or other oriented. Kohn (1990) suggests that if people are overly concerned with rules, ideology, or abstract principles, this actually may interfere with their sensitivity to the suffering of real people. In these cases, empathy can help put a human face and a personal connection to the moral injustice and thus, enhance their commitment to address the situation. Feeling a human connection can also help expand one's sense of who is included in one's moral community. The more others are seen as similar or sharing a close relationship, the less able one is to maintain the cognitive distortion to justify the status quo. Also, empathy may be evoked once some human contact has been made after the initial action was taken out of moral principle.

Moral values promote action in part to maintain self-integrity. It is in people's self-interest to protect their self-esteem and self-image. Self-interest can also be tied to the level of moral reasoning and the motivation to act morally. For some, as earlier examples illustrated, self-interest is central in their process of making moral judgments. For those with more principled reasoning, a more mutual and collective sense of self-interest strengthens their ability to follow through on their moral convictions. Since people generally weigh the personal costs before acting on their moral values, increasing the sense of personal benefit helps shift the balance toward acting.

Self-Interest Joined with Empathy and Moral Principles

Empathy can shift people out of narrow individualistic self-interest by fostering a concern for others. It can strengthen their feelings of connection and promote interdependence. This can help move them toward a more mutual and collective sense of self-interest.

Moral principles can encourage people to act not just out of selfish motives or short-term advantages but also out of ethical considerations. It provides people with other guidelines to make decisions about their behavior. Since we want people to be engaged in social justice work with commitment and integrity, enhancing their emotional and intellectual investment leads in this direction.

Research on activists (though not necessarily working on issues in which they are part of the dominant group) suggests that they are highly developed in their sense of empathy, morality, and collective self-interest (Berman, 1997). Indeed, these factors are intertwined. Activists have a sense of self defined by moral values and a sense of connectedness with others, especially with those suffering injustice and with the world as a whole. This relational sense of self fosters a sensitivity to the feeling of others, an understanding of the connection between others' well-being and one's own, and leads to a commitment to relieve suffering and oppression. This connected sense of self underlies and promotes empathy, a morality of care, and an interdependent sense of self-interest.

For most activists, seeing themselves as a moral being was also a central part of their sense of self. This unity of self and morality fostered activism and erased feelings of self-sacrifice. "No one saw their moral choices as an exercise in self-sacrifice. To the contrary, they see their moral goals as a means of attaining their personal ones and vice versa (Colby & Damon, 1992, pp. 300–301). Commitment to honesty and openness to new information and change were also cited as common characteristics of activists.

In addition, studies suggest that

> roots of activism also lie in the desire for a sense of meaning that takes one beyond oneself. To be bigger than oneself, to feel one is contributing to the welfare of others and society, not only motivates action, but sustains it over the long term. (Berman, 1997, p. 68)

Similarly, as we saw in the previous chapter, people from privileged groups who were allies for social justice found that regaining a sense of authenticity, humanity, liberation, and meaning was a motivation and result of their work.

Conclusion

As reflected in this chapter, the reasons people from privileged groups may support social justice are varied and multi-layered. No one source of motivation—empathy, moral and spiritual values or self-interest will inspire all people, nor will the same approach appeal to every person in the same way. My impression is that educators often emphasize one of these aspects—usually empathy or morality—to the exclusion of others. Some people address these sources of motivation generally, without considering some of the complexities within each. Becoming more conscious about which we use, how we use them, and in what combinations, enhances our effectiveness with the various individuals and issues that we deal with. It provides some direction for our educational and social change efforts. When we build on empathy, moral and spiritual values, and self-interest in conjunction with each other, and along with the desire for meaning, purpose, and connection, we also promote more long-term activism. In the following chapter, I will discuss how to develop these qualities in our students and how to encourage social action.

9

DEVELOPING AND ENLISTING SUPPORT FOR SOCIAL JUSTICE

In the previous chapter, I discussed how empathy, moral and spiritual values, and self-interest can motivate people from privileged groups to support social justice efforts. This chapter will focus on how these sources of motivation can be developed in our educational and social change work. In the first part of the chapter, I describe how to foster and appeal to empathy, moral and spiritual values, and self-interest in order to engage people in actions that advance equity and social justice. At the end of the chapter, I discuss the importance of providing positive alternatives to our current system.

Empathy

Fostering Empathy

To increase people's empathy, both their intellect and emotions need to be engaged. In general, to foster empathy, individuals need to maximize their personal knowledge of and heighten their emotional attunement to others. By imagining someone else's point of view and feelings, they can better understand another's situation. In order to minimize emotional and physical distance and the anonymity of others, which impede empathy, it is helpful if people actually get to know real individuals and experience their life circumstances. There are many strategies we can use to increase the empathy of people from privileged groups toward people from oppressed groups. Some of these are discussed next.

Develop Perspective-Taking

Since perspective-taking fosters empathy, provide frequent opportunities for people to develop their ability to take the perspective of others and consider other points of view. This can be done through stories or historical accounts that reflect different perspectives, simulations, role plays, and case studies. Have students articulate how others might be feeling and thinking or have them represent a particular viewpoint that may be different from their own. It is especially important to have students consider or adopt the points of view of people from marginalized groups.

Expose People to Other Life Experiences

While there are a variety of ways we can expose people to others' realities, such as through books, movies, panels, and personal testimony, hearing the information in person tends to be the most powerful (though this has a higher risk since there is less control over what people say and do). Educators can invite an individual or a panel of speakers to discuss their lives. One of the more effective programs in my work with faculty on addressing issues of diversity and equity in the classroom has been to have students from marginalized groups (students of color, gay and lesbian students, poor students, etc.) talk about their experiences in classes. After hearing the panel, faculty are usually more receptive to discussing how to be more inclusive and sensitive in their teaching.

It is important to include a variety of experiences from within a particular social group to show the diversity (as well as commonalties) of experiences. If there is only one individual, it needs to be clear that this person does not speak for all people with this identity, though discussion can include how aspects of her/his experience may be shared by many others. Educators need to be careful that an individual is not seen as an exception to or atypical for their social group, especially if they do not fit the stereotype.

Have People Share their Own Experiences

We can ask people to reflect on and share their own experiences with discrimination and oppression. Nearly all people are members of at least one oppressed group. And, everyone has some experience of being stereotyped and treated unfairly. People can better understand the feelings of others by considering how they felt in similar circumstances. Individuals who have experienced the effects of oppression in one aspect of their identity can often use this to relate to the experiences of someone from a different marginalized group. In one class, a heterosexual African American woman acknowledged that she was homophobic and expressed some discomfort at listening to a panel of gay, lesbian, and bisexual people share their stories. After the session, she remarked, "They deal with a lot of the same stuff I do!" She could relate to their feelings of internalized oppression, marginalization, and fear of violence. By using her experience as a person of color as a reference point, as a heterosexual, she now had new insight into (and tolerance for) gays.

This can be a helpful starting point to make some connections and develop compassion, but further discussion is needed so that this identification goes beyond emotional catharsis. We do not want people to overlook differences or equate iso-lated incidents with systematic, socially sanctioned mistreatment. Just because the aforementioned woman could use her experiences as an African American to con-nect with the experiences of gays and lesbians, this does not mean that she knows what it's like to be gay (or vice versa). Moreover, a man's exclusion from a women's only support group is not the same as women's exclusion from men's organizations or positions that serve as vehicles for the sharing of social power and promotion.

Furthermore, if we want people to be engaged in social action, they need to understand that a person's experiences of subordination are not just an individual issue. Someone's lack of opportunities or disadvantage are due to larger societal conditions which require addressing social inequalities. People need to understand that the situation of this individual is symptomatic of some form of oppression that also affects many others like them.

Give people the opportunity to have first-hand experiences. We can provide people with the chance to get to know actual people and experience others' situa-tions directly. In a diverse class, cooperative learning and group projects can help achieve this end. Internships, extended visits to different neighborhoods, work in community organizations, volunteer activities, and service learning can reduce both emotional and physical distance. Even helping that is initially done non-empathically can lead to empathy (Kohn, 1990). People who help tend to develop a more positive view of those they have assisted, become more concerned with their well-being, and feel a greater responsibility to continue to help them (Staub, 1989). In conjunction with these activities, it is important that students are engaged in a process of self-reflection and discussions of privilege and social inequality, so that they can make sense of their experiences and avoid paternalistic attitudes. Even though service learning can be beneficial for both students and communities, there is also the potential for it to undermine the goals it seeks, such as by reinforcing stereotypic beliefs, a colonialist mentality or sense of superiority, and exploiting the community for the benefit of the student (cf. Reardon, 1994; Cruz, 1990; Kendall, 1990).

Hoffman (1989) found that activists' direct and repeated contact with dis-advantaged groups intensified their initial empathic and sympathetic distress. It also diminished their intellectual remoteness and challenged their stereotypes. Their empathic and sympathetic distress was transformed, in part, into empathic feelings of injustice, empathic anger at society, and guilt over their own relatively privileged position. This led them to question their own ideology that assumed that society was basically caring and just.

The power of empathy is seen in this community effort in Tennessee. After failed efforts to get Whites to support additional funds for poor Black schools, a group of African Americans invited a group of Whites (through an interfaith organization) to visit their schools. After this first-hand experience, Whites were willing to support the additional funds and also joined forces in fighting for school-based management.

The politicians were unable to split the Black and White communities on these issues (Bate, 1997).

Potential Pitfalls of Empathy

Although empathy is a powerful force in acting for justice, we need to be careful in our efforts to help people from dominant groups empathize with the experiences of people from marginalized groups. Elizabeth Spelman (1995) spells out some of the paradoxes of these efforts and dangers to watch out for.

In Spelman's *paradox of appropriation*, there is the tendency, in the process of seeing oneself in the experiences of another, to erase the specifics of the other's situation, and to equate the two experiences. While we want people to connect to the experiences of another and to a sense of shared humanity, we do not want them to expropriate that experience. It is the danger of falling into the trap of thinking, "I know just how you feel!"

In the *paradox of identification*, the danger is overemphasizing the similarity of experiences by ignoring the differences and the larger social and historical context in which these experiences take place. This overlooks the implications of differential social positions and access to power and privilege. Since oppression breeds on highlighting difference and building barriers based on those differences, by identifying with others, we can break down those divisions. However, this poses the danger of thinking "We're all alike."

Consider when a White person tries to empathize with the experience of an African American person in an all-White environment. The White person may recount how she also felt uncomfortable and marginalized as the only White person in an all-Black gathering. On the one hand, it may be helpful to focus on the similarities in order for her to relate to the experience of the Black person. However, she may ignore the particularities of the Black woman's experience and the differences between their experiences, given the larger context of racism. For example, the White woman can generally choose whether or not to be in the situation of being a racial minority and it is an exception to her usual interactions where her Whiteness is the norm.

While encouraging empathy, we need to be careful not to obscure differences as we emphasize similarities. We must acknowledge and discuss differences in power and social position. In addition, some people feel that by empathizing they are "doing something". Empathy itself is not action; it is the starting place, not the end product.

Impediments to Empathy and Empathic Responsiveness

The potential of empathy as a positive social force can be diminished in many ways. There are many factors that reduce people's ability to be empathic, as well as to act on their empathic responses. I will identify several of these and offer some brief suggestions for how to address them.

Lack of Cognitive Ability

First, people need a certain level of cognitive ability to engage in perspective-taking. While there are different kinds of empathy displayed by children, the type of empathy discussed here requires the ability to have a differentiated sense of self and the cognitive flexibility to imagine the perspective of someone else. Most teenagers and adults have that cognitive ability, though many still have a difficult time with the cognitive flexibility that is required. People who are "dualistic thinkers" (see Chapter 3) tend to see things as either-or, and have difficulty considering experiences or perspectives that differ from what they consider the "truth." For these individuals, it may be helpful to stress that being empathic does not mean condoning someone else's behavior. Since abstract connections may be more difficult, we can provide opportunities for them to concretely put themselves in the position of another which requires them to take on a different way of seeing the world (i.e. through a role play).

Lack of Emotional Flexibility

In addition to cognitive flexibility, people need emotional flexibility.

> One who cannot tolerate his own feelings, or who is essentially a stranger to himself, is unlikely to forge an affective connection to someone else. A degree of self-knowledge and comfort with one's own affective life facilitates both knowing and being known to others. (Kohn, 1990, p. 152)

Generally, people who have difficulty acknowledging and experiencing their own feelings have difficulty perceiving and understanding the feelings of others. Although there is no conclusive research on gender differences and empathy (varying with how empathy is measured), it tends to be more challenging for males to make empathic connections. Male socialization usually does not foster the development of emotional self-knowledge, expressiveness, or sensitivity to others. As a result, men often have underdeveloped empathic abilities and overdeveloped emotional "armor" to protect themselves against feelings that might make them vulnerable and uncomfortable. In educational contexts, we can consistently model empathic behavior toward them and others, and provide opportunities for them to develop and practice empathic skills.

Lack of Psychological or Emotional Freedom

Third, people are less likely to feel empathy if their own needs feel more pressing than those of others. It can be hard to be empathic when feeling stressed or in pain. If people are self-absorbed, anxious, or lack the psychological/emotional freedom to attend to another's needs, their empathic abilities will be decreased. As previously discussed, this can be the case when individuals are focused on their own victimization as a member of a subordinate group. We can provide the safety and opportunity for them to share their feelings, concerns, or experiences, so they feel heard and validated. Once they feel recognized and no longer need to defend their own pain or disadvantage, they may have more psychological space to connect with another. (Also, review the suggestions in Chapter 4 for reducing resistance.)

Blaming the Victim

Individuals often have little or no empathy for victims they see as accountable and deserving of their fate. Blaming the victim may, in fact, lead to feelings of indifference or hostility. Through a variety of educational strategies—providing information, role plays, personal stories, researching facts, critical analysis—people can develop a more informed perspective which may shift their understanding or interpretation of the situation. This, in turn, can alter the way they see the victim and allow for some empathic connection. People who believe in a "just world", which assumes a close relationship between one's fate and one's merit, are more likely to react with compassion, if they are asked to imagine themselves in the same situation as the victim (Rubin & Peplau, 1975).

Empathic Bias

People also tend to have difficulty empathizing with others who seem too different from themselves. There tends to be an *empathic bias* when individuals feel less empathy for those they perceive as different and more empathy for those they perceive as more like themselves. Empathic bias is reinforced by the stereotypes and prejudices people learn. It can be reduced by providing people with opportunities to increase familiarity with individuals or groups they see as different and encouraging a focus on the similarities between themselves and the others—shared characteristics, feelings, and experiences. Ultimately, despite all other differences, we share a common humanity.

Psychological threat. Lastly, while similarity of experience can promote empathy, it can also impede it when the situation is experienced as too psychologically threatening. It may touch on one's own unresolved issues, unconscious conflicts, or disappointments. A heterosexual woman may resist empathizing with an angry lesbian woman due to her inability to acknowledge her *own* anger about the sexism *she* faces. A man may have difficulty empathizing with a battered woman if he has not dealt with his own feelings of seeing his mother in an abusive relationship. We may be able to help him empathize with women in other situations involving sexism or the domination of women by men that do not stir up such feelings. And even though we are not therapists, we can appropriately allow people to express their feelings and/or to help them understand why they are unable to empathize in this situation. We can also recommend referrals for counseling or other assistance.

Limitations of Using Empathy to Promote Prosocial Activism

Not all empathy leads to prosocial action or activism. Even when people do feel empathy, there are several factors that reduce their motivation to act on this empathic connection. One reason is *empathic overarousal*. People can be overwhelmed by their own feelings of distress that are generated from being empathic. The level of guilt or anxiety can be immobilizing. Allowing people to process their feelings—through writing, talking, emoting, movement, art— helps reduce the intensity of the feelings so they can consider acting more constructively.

The second reason for not acting on empathy is *feelings of powerlessness*. When people are unable to relieve the suffering of other individuals or groups, they may rationalize the failure to act by derogating the victim. After an empathic connection with a homeless man, a person who feels powerless to help this man or to deal with homelessness might find ways to blame him for being in his situation (i.e. not trying to find a job, not going into rehabilitation). We can assist people in dealing with their sense of disempowerment by helping them to learn about and develop strategies for positive intervention and action. In this case, someone could talk with the person who is homeless to see what would be helpful, find out what services are available in his or her community, or work with an organization that addresses issues of housing and homelessness.

Third, we live in an *unsupportive social context*, in a culture where people are encouraged to see victims as deserving their plight. Empathic abilities and the motivations to act are not commonly taught, encouraged, or valued in this society. What motivates people to help others is determined more by the social system in which they live than their basic nature. Absence of genuine altruism in the US should not be attributed to a fundamentally egoistic human nature, but to the highly individualistic, competitive, and success-oriented nature of our social system (Sampson, 1991, p. 275). Even though we cannot simply change the dominant culture, we can continue to help people develop their empathic abilities, to highlight the benefits of caring for others, and to provide examples of people who do act on their sense of empathy and connection to improve the lives of others.

To use empathy as a motivation for progressive social action, we need to 1) help people emotionally and intellectually relate to others' experiences, 2) understand that people may be motivated by their own personal needs as well as altruism, and 3) be able to address the various individual and societal impediments to people developing and then acting on their empathic responses. As expressed by J. T. Trout in the *Empathy Gap* (2009), "Empathy can trigger the urge to help others, sure enough; but it cannot be the ultimate guide to alleviating human suffering. It can be a place to start, but not to finish" (p. 26). Since the effective use of empathy generally requires that people see the victim's situation as somehow wrong, to this I turn next.

Moral and Spiritual Values

By invoking moral principles and spiritual values, people can be motivated to live up to and according to their values, and to right what they perceive as a wrong. For people to act on moral or spiritual principles, they need to be aware that a certain situation is, in fact, a violation of their values. If they see that there is an injustice, this can generate concern and investment to address it. Although not everyone has the same interpretation of justice or fairness, in this country, notions of equal opportunity, meritocracy, and equal rights are commonly touted as national ideals.

First, it can be helpful to have individuals identify and articulate their moral and spiritual values. This provides a standard from which to judge situations. It can also provide educators with useful information about how to speak to their concerns.

Next, we can educate people about the inequity of a given situation. People often have little accurate knowledge about social inequities. In addition to providing facts, statistics, personal stories, and theories, individuals can be asked to conduct research themselves and to gain awareness from first-hand experiences. Often, students are more persuaded by information they uncover themselves. If people think that a life on welfare is one of luxury and an easy, free ride, we can ask them to research the amount of the allowance, to live on that amount for a couple of weeks, or to try to apply for welfare to see how they are treated.

Once people are aware of an inequity, we can help them see that it is unfair, that it violates their moral/spiritual principles. People may recognize that people's situations are not equal, but see that as deserved and thus not unfair or problematic. Unless they perceive the discrepancy as an injustice, they will not feel that a moral wrong has been committed. For example, even if someone recognizes a racial educational achievement gap but believes it is due to a lack of inherent intelligence, deficient cultural values, or laziness, then there is no moral problem.

Because there is pressure to cognitively distort situations in ways to justify the status quo, educators need to be able to challenge those distortions. We need to help people question the dominant ideology that make inequities seem fair and to offer alternative explanations. People can be encouraged to reexamine their assumptions and beliefs that tend to blame the victim, deny discrimination, and presume a level playing field. Educators can help elucidate how institutional structures and practices violate stated principles of fairness and equity. Often when myths, such as that there is equal opportunity for all, are exposed and a greater understanding of systemic inequality is gained, people are more likely to feel that their values have been breached, that something isn't right. As in the aforementioned example of welfare, if students realize how inadequate most public assistance is in supporting families and in providing the necessary job training, transportation, day care, and employment opportunities for people can get decent-paying jobs with medical benefits, they are more likely to feel that people are being denied the opportunity to live a reasonable life off welfare and that this is detrimental to those individuals and society at large. A study by Smith and Tyler (1996) with people who were economically advantaged found that the more respondents viewed market procedures and outcomes for the disadvantaged to be unfair, the more they supported redistributive policies.

Because an ethic of justice tends toward an intellectual or cognitive orientation, providing information and facts is a useful strategy. An ethic of care tends to be more feeling or affectively oriented. In this case, an effective approach is to illustrate the harm of social injustice, thereby promoting empathy. This appeals to values of caring for others and alleviating suffering. The strategies discussed earlier to foster empathy—such as personal stories, relationships, and perspective-taking—are useful with people who have a care-based morality.

After people recognize moral injustice, the next step is motivating them to take some action to remedy the situation. For some, the clarity of a moral wrong might be enough to elicit their support. For others, more particular appeals may be needed. We can be more effective at appealing to moral values, if we understand the process through which people determine what is just and why they would act morally. I think one common impediment to motivating others based on moral/ spiritual values is that we often speak in language from our own frame of reference, not necessarily in the terms of those we're trying to reach. As I discussed previously, what morally motivates me, may not be what motivates you. For example, in one of my workshops a professor expressed her frustration of not being able to convince her White students at a Catholic college to care about racism. It wasn't until she spoke about it in terms of what Jesus would do, did she get a response.

When we are unaware of an individual's perspective or are trying to reach a group, we can offer a range of reasons that will appeal to people with different moral orientations and motivations. The developmental sequences within each moral framework can provide a guide for how to speak to particular types of moral thinking. Also, although individuals tend to be predominantly in one stage, they may use reasoning from other stages, depending on the circumstances.

I have often been asked to conduct diversity and sexual harassment training in schools with teachers, administrators, and other staff. Frequently, this is initiated by a teacher who sees a problem and wants to garner the support from the administration and fellow teachers. There are usually several ways to appeal to people's moral values. I will tend to include a variety of reasons, both to appeal to the range of concerns as well as to provide examples of more principled and caring considerations.

Those using moral reasoning from Pre-conventional or Survival perspectives may be most concerned with protecting themselves from accusations and legal liability. For them, addressing sexual harassment can reduce their personal or institutional liability and negative public exposure that could jeopardize their careers. For those concerned with being able to teach without as many discipline problems and conflicts, the training can reduce negative behavior and tensions among students.

Those at the Goodness or Conventional Level tend to be interested in having policies and laws to ensure that people are treated fairly or are not subject to behavior that interferes with their right to an education. They want to follow and enforce established rules that help maintain order in the school and allow people to be treated respectfully. For those concerned with being good and caring teachers, the training can help them better meet the needs of their students, ensure their safety, and prepare them to deal with differences.

To speak to the concerns of people at the Truth or Post-Conventional Level, I try to appeal to shared or stated values. These may include wanting all children to be able to reach their full potential or wanting to create a caring community where people are not subjected to hurtful or demeaning behavior. These individuals are seeking ways to create an environment in which everyone can learn and work effectively.

Deciding whether to address a moral injustice is more than a simple instrumental decision, a rational assessment of the costs and benefits of a certain course of action. Emotional reactions may be the most important influence on *whether* or not people take actions. The *type* of action is more a function of cognitive judgments (Wright, et al., 1990). Therefore, eliciting emotions, such as anger or moral outrage enhances one's likelihood of acting. Since people are more likely to act to restore justice when there is a clear injustice and when there is a particular set of actions that could correct the injustice. It is important that people have specific ideas of how to act that they feel will make a difference. Otherwise, they may feel hopeless and powerless, and resort to psychological distortion.

Limitations of Appealing to Moral Principles and Spiritual Values

Equity theory suggests that recognizing an injustice produces an uncomfortable and distressing emotional state (Tyler, et al. 1997). People attempt to restore a sense of justice 1) behaviorally, by changing their behavior or the situation and 2) psychologically, by changing their interpretation of events (such as assuming people are lazy, incompetent, undeserving). The psychological solution allows people to justify their advantage. People who view themselves and others as personally responsible to their success or failure are more likely to assume that societal inequities are legitimate (Martin, 1995). They accept the "just world hypothesis" that people get what they deserve in life and consequently, deserve what they get. Therefore, there is no motivation to remedy the situation.

Even when people do recognize an injustice, people will decide whether to act based on two main factors. The first is practical concerns (e.g. the likelihood of success or of retaliation, the amount of self-sacrifice). People may want to see justice occur, but may not be willing to incur the consequences of the imagined change. The second is the ambiguity of the situation—how clear it is that an injustice has occurred and what needs to be done to address it. If people are not convinced that there is an unfair inequity or do not believe that what is proposed will remedy it, they are less likely to act.

In addition, there may be some groups of people who are seen as nonentities, undeserving or expendable, and thus are morally excluded from one's scope of justice (e.g. migrant workers, the Japanese during WWII, gays) (Opotow, 1990). This allows people to see the harm to these groups as acceptable, appropriate, or just. Moreover, the less one's sense of self is rooted in a moral identity, the less persuasive moral arguments will be.

Self-Interest

Most change agents know that you need to be able to answer the question, "What's in it for me?" People are concerned with how things will affect them. The previous chapter outlined how people may construe that question differently; yet in some form, people want to have their needs met.

A basic principle of conflict resolution is to identify underlying concerns and interests and to try to develop a solution that meets the needs of both (all) parties. This requires letting go of preconceived solutions and being willing to think creatively to come up with alternatives that would be satisfying to both. Often, conflicts persist because people cannot imagine alternatives to the present situation or do not believe that their needs would be met by the currently proposed solutions. Similarly, with issues of oppression, people often do not support efforts to eliminate oppression because they feel it doesn't affect them, that nothing can really change or they cannot imagine how it could be different and not threaten their well-being. Ultimately, we need to help people from dominant groups expand their sense of possibilities to see how social justice really can meet their long-term interests and needs. In the meantime, we may need to identify their present and short-term interests, and find ways to address those while engaging them in actions for equity.

Some appeals to self-interest can be targeted toward a specific issue or action. In this context, self-interest is used as a strategy toward a particular end (at least for the moment). We are interested in getting support for a given program or project. It can also be used in a more educational or theoretical way to help change people's ways of thinking about social justice and to help them understand how oppression is harmful to all. In this case, the goal is two-fold: consciousness-raising and changing attitudes and behavior. Strategic and consciousness-raising approaches can be used separately or in conjunction with each other.

Strategic Approaches

First, we need to find out what people are concerned about. Then we can *integrate people's concerns into the social justice agenda*. Try to show how those interests can be addressed by supporting social change efforts. For some people, these concerns may be very self-focused; for others, they may be more inclusive of other people. The examples along the continuum of self-interest illustrate what might appeal to people with different conceptions of self-interest. The most important thing is to understand their viewpoint and to speak to their needs. From there, we can make the link to issues of equity and show how their needs can be compatible with social justice.

Even while appealing to more individualistic types of self-interest, we can offer a more interdependent perspective. This is a chance to raise consciousness, provide alternative ways of viewing the situation, and challenge the win-lose mentality. Because we do not want to reinforce individualistic thinking, the goal is to start where people are and help expand their perspective toward consideration of the common good. While providing additional examples of how to use self-interest to garner support for a current issue or project, I will also illustrate how we can expand on narrow self-interest, help people see their personal concerns in a larger context, and link their short-term and long-term interests.

As a University Affirmative Action Officer, I needed to enforce affirmative action guidelines that many people felt were unfair and interfered with their right to hire whomever they wanted. To get their cooperation, I often pointed out ways in which hiring a person from a underrepresented group benefited them—not only were they more likely to get permission to actually fill the position, but that person might also help attract and retain students in their department, especially from underrepresented groups (which was important for maintaining or increasing the viability and resources for their department). I also included how this new person's experience or perspective might enhance their own scholarship and thinking about their discipline and how diversity makes the campus a more vibrant and attractive place to students and faculty. Finally, I challenged them think about what it meant to be "most qualified" (especially, when diversity is a goal) and provided information about how to more fairly evaluate qualifications. Regardless of the real reason for their compliance, I felt I needed to expose them to broader ways of thinking about and justifying the hiring of an underrepresented candidate.

Another approach is to *link personal concerns to larger issues of equity and justice*. This shifts the dynamic from blaming the victim to blaming the system. Many college students, particularly at public universities, are concerned about paying for college and experience the stress of working and worrying about expenses. I have heard White students complain about the perceived "special treatment" some students of color receive and the scholarships that are set aside just for them (though this is minimal and quickly changing). This tends to lead some White students to blame students of color for White students' lack of financial support for college. The economic concerns of White students are valid. However, the real problem is not students of color. Some White students realize this, and instead of working against scholarships for minority students, they have organized to challenge the larger system that does not make college accessible to all who want to attend. They have enlisted the support of other White students by addressing their concerns about college costs, but focus on the bigger issue of educational funding and opportunity. Through collective action and lobbying with students of color (and other allies), they have been more successful in addressing access to a college education (e.g. through lower tuitions and more state and other aid). So although their concerns may be about their own college tuition, the solution may be to address the larger issue of economic and social equity. Their self-interest is better served by more systemic change.

Lastly, we can *link people's short-term and long-term interests with the social justice agenda.* We can help people see that they will be better off both in the short-term and in the long-term by supporting efforts toward equity. Most people are concerned with juvenile crime and drug-dealing. Some people believe that building more prisons is the answer. Alternatively, in many communities, people are trying to create comprehensive programs for youth that include education, training, and constructive involvement in recreational and community activities. One strategy to enlist support for these efforts is to help people see how these types of programs reduce violence, are far more cost-effective, and improve their quality of life. In the short run, young people are less likely to be involved in illegal activity and create problems on the street. In the long term, they are more like to become productive, contributing citizens as opposed to adult criminals, prison inmates, or welfare recipients who require further government money. It also maintains the integrity of the community and property values. Instead of some "quick fixes", people's short-term as well as longer-term concerns can be addressed.

Theoretical/Consciousness-Raising Approaches

The strategic use of self-interest clearly provides some opportunity for consciousness raising. Learning environments often offer us greater latitude in how we can educate people from privileged groups about their self-interest in social change. We can help them to explore the costs of oppression, the benefits of justice, and how to move toward the kind of world they would like to live in.

There are many ways people can be given the chance to *consider the costs of oppression to themselves and others from dominant groups.* I have engaged students in thinking from this perspective, by asking them to identify the ways they feel negatively affected by some form of oppression in which they are part of the privileged group. This makes most sense once they have already done some exploration of oppression and multicultural issues. After considering this question individually, they then listen to the responses of peers, provoking further reflection and discussion. This may be one of the few times when the pain of people in privileged groups has been acknowledged and validated. For people who have never named or discussed the costs, it can be a powerful experience and provide great relief to let go of the secrets or the feeling that they were the only ones. When I have conducted this exercise with groups, simply viewing the list of costs generated by the group has had a significant impact. It vividly illustrates the pervasive detrimental ramifications of oppression for members of dominant groups.

For some groups, responding to a general list of costs (see Chapter 6) will be much easier and more effective than trying to develop their own since it requires less original thought. You can ask them which items they can relate to on the list and to add their own examples. Even for people who have a difficult time identifying costs, it encourages them to think in a different way, it allows them to hear the stories of others, and it begins to broaden the way they think about oppression and their role in it.

People from oppressed groups may have difficulty seeing themselves as members of a privileged group. As discussed previously (Chapters 3 and 4), people tend to be most identified with their subordinated identities where they experience the most pain. I particularly have found that people of color initially tend to find this type of exercise challenging. They tend to be most aware of their experience as targets of racism and less able to see themselves as members of a privileged group in another "ism". Some of this is may be due to their stage of identity development. It may also be related to the fact that the existence and impact of racism is so often minimized, that people of color feel they need to consistently remind people (especially White people) of its significance. I have found it helpful to acknowledge the pervasiveness of racism and its widespread effects as well as how it mitigates other areas of privilege. However, since the focus of this exercise is not on privilege but on the costs of oppression to all, I encourage them to think about how they might also be harmed by a form of social inequality where they are not the direct target. In addition, before I begin the discussion of costs to the dominant groups, I review how oppression affects those in disadvantaged groups and some of the privileges for those in advantaged groups. I then add the parts about negative effects on people from dominant groups, suggesting it as a way to provide a more complete and complex understanding of oppression, not to equate it with the experiences of people from targeted groups. Naming oppression and recognizing privilege at the outset allows some people from oppressed groups to then feel more comfortable considering costs to the privileged group.

People may suggest situations in which they see themselves as the victim of "reverse racism" or another form of oppression. Affirmative action is often a favorite example of how White people are negatively affected by racism. First, it is helpful to dispel the myths that there is currently a level-playing field and that affirmative action has taken away so many jobs from White men. Then it's important to help them reframe this situation and understand it, not as a victim of racism but as a result of racism in our society. A system of racial discrimination has motivated the establishment of these kinds of programs and supports. If there were no racism, there would be no need for affirmative action and special consideration given because of race.

Encourage students to imagine what it would be like if there were no racism, sexism, or other forms of oppression and how that would be beneficial to them. Ask them to consider questions such as: How would their lives be enhanced if they did not have to deal with the results of systemic injustice? What would it be like if the list of costs were obliterated? What would it feel like to be rid of the limitations, pressures, conflicts, guilt, moral ambivalence, and ignorance? Visualizations, drawing, writing, discussion, and list-making can make these imaginings more concrete.

A related approach is to *have people compare their vision of an ideal world with our current reality*. Ask people to imagine and describe the kind of world they want to live in—How would society be organized? What would work, housing, education, the environment, neighborhoods, or recreation look like? Then have them compare that ideal to this reality. They can consider the following questions: how is the vision different from our reality? What gets in the way of attaining that vision? How does structural inequality undermine this ideal? How might greater social justice help to reach those ideals? Since most people want to live in a world with peace, positive social relations, and material well-being, this can lead to discussions of various forms of oppression, as well as the larger dominant/subordinate power structure upon which injustice is based. This exercise can also be focused on a particular aspect of society, for example one's community, school, or workplace. Similar questions and discussion could ensue. These types of discussions can help people think about their investment in social justice and lead them to consider ways to move toward that vision.

We can also *help people to identify and experience more equal and satisfying relations in everyday life*. Imagining a total transformation of society can seem too unrealistic or abstract to be useful. Yet, in most of our daily lives we have the kinds of experiences that would be more available in a just and caring society. Encourage people to notice how they feel when they do have emotionally honest and mutually-satisfying relationships with others; when they are behaving in accordance with their values; when they feel that they are acting out of their deeper sense of humanity and love; when they have positive, enriching relationships with people who are different from themselves; and when they feel a sense of personal integrity and moral consistency. Help them verbalize these situations and positively reinforce these kinds of connections and ways of being. We can provide opportunities in the class for these types of relationships and experiences through how we structure the class, the activities we do, and the kind of processes we use. This activity can be used to discuss how to create more of these kinds of experiences in our lives, how to change the systems and structures which undermine these ways of being, and how to replace them with ones that foster a more just and caring world.

Another way to address self-interest may be to *highlight the psychological benefits of engaging in political activism*. Psychologists maintain that well-being encompasses feelings of pleasure, a sense of life purpose and direction, and social well-being— feeling connected to others and to society. Political activism, even short-term actions, can enhance all three of these qualities (Kasser & Klar, 2009). Activists report a sense of satisfaction, an experience of pleasant emotions, connections with others, and a feeling of aliveness as some of the positive results of being politically engaged. (An exception was when people participated in "high risk" behaviors, such as getting arrested or physically injured.) We can use this research to motivate people to take action for social justice and/or to encourage them to participate in some activity that fosters equity and note how they feel.

Pros and Cons of Appealing to Self-interest

Intentionally appealing to self-interest can be a controversial strategy. It has advantages as well as dangers. Although it can be a useful and necessary approach, we need to be thoughtful and careful in its use. I will first discuss some of its possible pitfalls and then consider some of its positive uses and benefits.

One of the major dangers of using narrow self-interest to motivate support is the distrust it breeds from people (both allies and people from oppressed groups) who are genuinely committed to the action. Appropriately, people may not trust the motives or the depth and longevity of the support of individuals, who they suspect are acting on individualistic self-interest. If the motivation stays only at the level of narrow, individualistic self-interest, their support may be withdrawn when self-interest is reassessed as circumstances change. By appealing to individualistic self-interest, without trying to broaden the perspective or commitment, we may be reinforcing a way of thinking that is counter to our ultimate goals.

Additionally, someone may engage in superficial involvement or low-risk commitment while undermining a more serious examination of the issues or more meaningful change. This often results in mere lip service or it can trivialize or co-opt the issue. Many people are familiar with the token committee and unread report, or diversity training that never goes beyond understanding cultural differences to address inequities in organizational policies and practices. Sometimes strings are attached; support will be given as long as the work is not too radical or it avoids certain topics.

Using self-interest to develop support also has advantages. Appealing to narrow, individualistic self-interest is probably most problematic; however, it starts where people are and addresses them in a way that makes sense to them. "Speaking their language" initially may be more effective than appealing to issues that hold little interest. While we might prefer that people engage in actions from more lofty ideals and commitments, this is not always immediately possible. Obtaining support, even if it is with selfish motives, may allow a positive project to move forward instead of being blocked or impeded.

Joining narrowly self-interested people where they are can also provide an opening for more genuine change, a first step in real engagement. Involvement with an issue may expose people to individuals, situations, or information that they otherwise might not have encountered. That in turn, may change attitudes and subsequent behavior. A White manager may initiate a program to address the hiring and promotion of people of color primarily because she sees this as a way to get more financial resources for her department. Yet, in the process of participating in the task force, she may develop actual relationships with people of color, learn some important information about racism, and encounter people who challenge her stereotypes. This can result in a more genuine commitment to racial equity.

If the social justice-oriented behavior is inconsistent with currently held beliefs or behavior, it may create cognitive dissonance and the need to rationalize the new behavior. Attitude change may occur in order to justify the behavior to oneself and others. For example, a heterosexual leader of a fraternity decides to be a representative on a committee to examine the treatment of gay and transgender students on campus and to play a role in educating about homophobia and transphobia.

While initially participating to deflect criticism of fraternities, through this experience, he might gain some new awareness and justify his involvement by explaining to his friends that this really is something to take seriously.

Furthermore, recognizing one's self-interest, particularly from a mutual or interdependent perspective, can foster a more long-term commitment to social justice. Shifting the focus from only doing it for "them" to also doing it for oneself enhances the investment. It can be hard to maintain a commitment to social change, particularly when some issues are framed as against one's immediate self interest. Acting for oneself, not just for others, can help deepen and sustain support for social justice efforts. If people recognize the collective benefit, it may reduce potential condescension and thus, make them more trusted by the oppressed group.

Drawing on Empathy, Moral and Spiritual Values, and Self-Interest

In the previous chapter, I described how empathy, moral and spiritual values, and self-interest could be used in conjunction to strengthen the motivation to act for social justice. Similarly, when we try to implement strategies to foster support for equity, we can intentionally try to integrate these three dimensions. We can consider how we can appeal to these various aspects and have them build on each other.

After a workshop in which I presented this framework, a participant, Tim, developed an action plan that illustrated this integration. Tim was interested in creating interracial dialogues on campus, particularly between White fraternity members and other students of color on campus. There had been some incidents of racial prejudice from some fraternities. First, Tim would appeal to the fraternities' self-interest. He knew that the fraternities were concerned about their image on campus. (Another participant said that on his campus the self-interest would be to increase the membership in their fraternity.) He would propose a day-long retreat with representatives from the fraternities to discuss how they could improve their reputation of being racially insensitive. During this retreat, Tim would also do some consciousness-raising about racism, attempting to help these students become more sensitive to, and empathic toward the experiences of students of color. Just as the fraternity members hate to be stereotyped, so do the students of color. By the end of the day, Tim expected to have some fraternity members willing to participate in racial dialogues, both as a mechanism to improve their racist image, and as a way to actually better understand the issues for students of color. Through these dialogues, he hoped to foster their sense of empathy and their moral commitment to eliminate behavior that is racially offensive.

Another way empathy, moral/spiritual values, and self-interest can work together to create change is illustrated in a situation that occurred in Salt Lake City (Canham, Jensen & Winters, 2009). The City Council was considering ordinances that would protect lesbian, gay, bisexual, and transgender (LGBT) residents from discrimination in housing and employment. The Church of Jesus Christ

(LDS/Mormon) initially opposed these measures. The Church also had previously backed a California proposition barring gay marriage (Prop 8) that had eroded relations between the church and the LGBT community. Yet, after more than two months of secret, and sometimes difficult meetings between church officials and gay leaders, rapport and understanding was built. "You start to see the humanity" one church leader reported as she told of hearing the stories of discrimination faced by the LGBT participants (empathy). The ordinances were passed with the Church's backing. The Church officials explained their support by stating that the statutes were "fair and reasonable" and consistent with Mormon teachings, which advocate treating people with respect (moral and spiritual values). They talked about having compassion and the fact that Church members have gay sons and daughters (empathy and self-interest). A gay activist who was involved in the dialogues also suggested that the Church was trying to show what a caring and concerned institution it is and to put some of the Prop 8 tensions behind it (self-interest).

Offering Alternatives to our Current System

So far, I primarily have focused on how to encourage people to support actions for social justice. In order for people to buy into change that is more ideologically and structurally transformative, their sense of possibility and self-interest need to be addressed. It is important that people learning about diversity and oppression realize how our notion of reality is socially constructed and can be transformed. If people accept the dominant worldview and our present system as the way things are, have been, and will always be, there is little reason to imagine or work for significant change. As long as people accept systems of domination as inevitable and assume that it is human nature to want to control others, there is little motivation for creating a just society. If they believe that efforts to promote equity will diminish their lives, they will resist altering the status quo. Therefore, to engage people from dominant groups to support systemic change, they need to know there are positive alternatives to our present system.

While there are many ways to describe our current reality and alternative ways of organizing society, I'll focus on two frameworks described by Riane Eisler (1987, 1996; Eisler & Loye, 1990/98; www.partnershipway.org). I offer these models as tools to expand people's frame of reference, to suggest new ways to conceptualize reality, and to challenge the assumption that human nature or innate differences alone are responsible for inequities. These paradigms also help people to evaluate current systems and envision alternatives.

By identifying underlying social patterns, Eisler has depicted two different types of social organization. She describes a dominator model and a partnership model that have very different assumptions about human beings, social relationships, and social structures. Her descriptions of these models are based on extensive cross-cultural and historical evidence from anthropology, archaeology, religion, history, art, and social sciences. I find these constructs helpful in educational contexts for several reasons. First, they are based on actual human societies, not imagined realities. Second, they present models of social organization in a fairly neutral and accessible way. Third, they help people look at the connections between social structures and underlying cultural and personal patterns. Rather than just describing particular elements of more egalitarian societies or human relationships, they illustrate a comprehensive social *system* with interrelated aspects.

According to Eisler, the main characteristics of a dominator model include:

- Ranking and inequality, in which differences are systematically converted into superior and inferior (beginning with men and women);
- Hierarchical and authoritarian social structures;
- Institutionalized social violence;
- The widespread infliction of or threat of pain.

Since the dominator model relies on fear and force to maintain the system, trust is systematically undermined. Power is often used to dominate and destroy—people as well as nature. A sense of scarcity is created to justify exploitive economic policies and a politics of fear. Planning is short-term with little thought for future generations.

Our current social organization with its various forms of oppression resembles the dominator model in many ways. This is reflected in our high rates of incarceration (especially of poor, males of color), the grossly unequal distribution of wealth, widespread incidents of rape and domestic violence, the exploitation of human and natural resources, the competitive individualism within our institutions, and the threat of job loss or physical harm if one is too much a threat to the status quo.

In contrast, the partnership model highlights:

- Linking, in which differences (beginning with males and females) are valued and respected;
- A low degree of social violence where violence is not a structural component of the system;
- Generally egalitarian social structures;
- Interactions based on mutual respect and empowerment.

In the partnership system, human relations are held together more by trust and pleasure than by fear and pain. Equality is actively nourished. Power is generally used to give, nurture, and illuminate life. A sense of abundance is created with a value on ensuring that people are taken care of. Planning includes long-term concern for present and future generations.

Eisler cautions that these models are not mutually exclusive. Both models operate within a given society, within a given institution, and within a given individual. Yet, societies tend to orient more toward one than the other. Nor is a partnership pattern of social relations a utopian model. According to Eisler, it is unrealistic to assume that there would be no violence, pain, or cruelty, since these seem to be part of the human condition (Eisler & Koegel, 1996). However, in partnership societies, these modes of relating are neither idealized nor institutionalized.

The research by Wilkinson and Pickett (2009) also shows how our beliefs and actions related to social justice are shaped by the larger culture and social arrangements. They found that growing up in societies with varying degrees of equality affect our social relations, beliefs about human nature, and the kinds of behavior that is elicited. People have the potential for conflict and domination, as well as love, cooperation, and assistance. The social arrangements can affect how these are expressed. (The growing work in social neuroscience demonstrates that human brains are hard-wired for caring and cooperation.) People in more equal societies have a greater level of trust which leads to greater cooperation. They are more likely to feel that they are part of a shared culture and that everyone should be treated with respect and tolerance. People who trust are more likely to donate time and money to helping other people. Greater material equality leads to a more cohesive and cooperative community. On the other hand, people in unequal societies tend to see human beings as narrowly self-interested which affects their ability to trust and to feel that they are part of a community. It undermines their sense that they're in this together and that they need to do things for the common good.

Many social scientists have voiced concerns about our "cultural ethos of selfishness and materialism" (Lerner, 2002, 2006, www.tikkun.org) and how the dominance of corporations and free-market capitalism have promoted a preoccupation with self, money, and the accumulation of things, eroding a sense of morality, social responsibility, and community (Daly & Cobb, 1994; Derber, 2009; Korten, 2001, 2007; Kasser, 2003; Putnam, 2000). With a zero-sum mentality, people feel that there's not enough for everyone and that others are getting something at their expense. We are expected to look out for ourselves, view others in terms of what they can do for us, and pursue our own short-term gains. As a result, people feel unrecognized, disconnected from others, and a lack of a sense of meaning in their lives. People are angry, frustrated, and confused about this lack of meaning in their lives and the range of social problems they encounter (crime, job loss, violence, homelessness, the breakdown of families). However, instead of blaming the impact of the competitive marketplace and systems of inequality for these problems, some blame the "traditionally demeaned Others"—feminists, people of color, gays and lesbians, immigrants, etc. Many people assume that immigrants are taking jobs away from US citizens, that White women and people of color are taking opportunities away from White men, and that gays and lesbians are demanding "special rights" beyond the equal rights afforded to everyone else. This diverts their attention away from corporate greed and concern for the bottom line, and focuses their scorn on groups struggling for full participation in society (Pharr, 1996). They support anti-democratic agendas that limit access to social and economic justice for marginalized groups.

In his book *The Racist Mind*, Raphael Ezekiel explores the psychological foundations of Neo-Nazis and Klansmen. He found that many of the youth who join

Nazi movements are poor and high-school dropouts. Meaning, not ideology, was the most compelling reason they joined these right-wing groups. They longed to be "seen" by an adult and feel a sense of purpose and importance. Even though they come from an oppressed group (the poor), they identified with their dominant identity, White (and male). They then acted against certain subordinated groups—people of color, gays and lesbians, Jews, etc. Many of these young men became involved in attacks or supported public policies that limited the rights and resources of oppressed groups.

People who support policies that systematically disadvantage others often do so to increase their own sense of self-worth and self-protection, yet often at personal and spiritual cost. Social movements that have most successfully motivated people have framed the issues in a broader moral and meaning context (e.g. the New Deal, civil rights and Martin Luther King, Jr.), not narrow individual rights. If people came to see their own needs as best served by a society with a concern for the common good, they would be more open to policies that better provided for more people. If people can see how their needs for meaning and connection are better met by challenging rather than accepting the dominant ethos and blaming marginalized groups, there is the potential to create allies for change. Increasingly, people are seeking more meaning and spirituality in their lives (The Higher Education Research Institute, 2010; The Pew Forum on Religion, 2009), yet they tend to focus on individual solutions that are not tied to an analysis of the larger culture.

Even when people believe in fairness and equity, they are less likely to support practices and changes they feel pose a threat to their well-being. Therefore, along with educating for critical consciousness, we need to create the social and economic conditions that allow people to more easily make choices that move us toward social justice. Changes in the policies and structures of the dominant culture can make it safer for people to support greater meaning and equity in our world. People need opportunities to act according to their highest ideals and not feel like a fool or self-destructive.

We can question systems and policies that set up a zero-sum game and value profits over people, ensure greater democratic participation, create more cooperative arrangements, demand more accountability from those who create situations of unnecessary scarcity, and challenge practices that put people in "us or them" situations. We can explore how to expand the pie and to utilize resources in ways that do not pit people against each other. We can highlight shared goals, collective well-being, and mutual responsibility. For example, a controversy arose in New York City as to whether wealthy parents should be able to raise money to fund teachers' salaries and school programs. The Chancellor was concerned that this would just further disparities in a public education system. Through letters to the editor in the local newspaper, I followed some of the discussion and the proposed solutions. Some parents, taking a very individual rights orientation, argued that it was their right to support their child's education. Other parents offered a more collaborative, interdependent approach. I read a few letters that recognized that it was in everyone's best interest for all of the children in their city to have a decent education. There was the suggestion that half of the money raised by the economically advantaged parents be shared with poorer schools. A couple of people suggested that the parents could be using this energy and skill to be lobbying together to demand more adequate educational funding that would benefit all the schools. Even further, they could rethink how education is financed and supported. Many social scientists and activists have been advancing in theory and practice more egalitarian, collaborative, and democratic organizations and policies that allow for people to experience greater meaning and purpose. (See appendix for some examples.)

In conclusion, there is no one right way to engage people in social change efforts. We need to know our audience and our context. We can motivate people to support small actions as well as larger efforts to shift the dominant paradigm. I have suggested a variety of approaches that can help develop people's sense of concern and possibility, and encourage their support and involvement. Often, multiple tacks are most effective. We can build on the interconnections among empathy, moral and spiritual values, and self-interest to broaden people's perspective and strengthen their commitment. Overall, we can continually reinforce how supporting equity and diversity offers benefits to themselves and others and serves our collective well-being.

10

ALLIES AND ACTION

After consciousness-raising and motivating, we need to help people from privileged groups find ways to create change. When students feel empowered to challenge bias and inequality, it reduces feelings of guilt and helplessness, and channels their energy in constructive ways. Yet, just as unlearning oppression is an ongoing process, so is becoming an effective ally. In this chapter, I explore what it means to be an ally, how to develop efficacy as an ally, and options for promoting social justice. I draw on my own experiences and what others have modeled and written (cf. Albrecht & Brewer, 1990; Bishop, 2002; Kivel, 2002; Leondar-Wright, 2005; Raible, 2009; Reason, Broido, Davis & Evans, 2005). Since many of these issues pertain to us as social justice educators as well as the people we work with, I will address the reader directly in several of the sections that offer ideas about taking and sustaining action.

What is an Ally?

In previous chapters, I discussed how empathy, moral/spiritual values, and self-interest can motivate people from privileged groups to support efforts for social justice. Appealing to these factors may get individuals engaged, but it does not mean they will necessarily share the larger goals of social justice. Some people will continue to operate out of narrow self-interest; others will act out of a commitment to equity and fairness. Allies are people with a genuine desire to create justice. They are individuals from a privileged group who make intentional choices to support or work for the rights of those from the oppressed group. They are committed to eliminating a form of oppression from which they benefit. Allies are not just acting for others, but for themselves as well. They recognize that social justice is about their own liberation and humanity, not solely about the liberation of people from the subordinated group. Allies act from their own values, not for the approval of the members of the oppressed group.

Qualities of an Effective Ally

There are numerous things that make someone an effective ally, encompassing a range of awareness, knowledge, skills, and behavior. Below, I describe several characteristics that that I think are central. These are the ideal; even the best allies fall short at times. Yet, allies can strive to embody these qualities with increasing depth and consistency.

Knowledge of the oppression. Allies understand the oppression in its various forms and contexts which allows them to recognize and address it. They are aware of how it impacts people from the oppressed group and from the dominant group, and how it intersects with other forms of oppression.

Self-awareness. Allies have insight into how their own socialization and experiences impact their attitudes, beliefs, and behaviors. They maintain vigilance about how their privilege, sense of entitlement, and internalized dominance gets enacted. This includes the ability to honestly self-reflect and assess their strengths and areas for growth.

Humility. Allies can let go of their internalized sense of superiority and value others' wisdom and ways of doing things. They are able to work *with* people from the oppressed groups in equitable and supportive ways without needing to rescue or dominate. They are willing to admit what they do not know and continue to learn.

Non-defensiveness. Allies are able to hear critical feedback and use this to continue their own learning and development as an ally. They can acknowledge mistakes and view feedback as "gifts" toward their growth.

Ability to choose appropriate action. Allies are able to analyze situations and their own competence in order to choose strategies appropriate to the situation. They recognize the power of collective action, rather than just individual efforts, for creating social change.

Commitment to stay conscious and engaged. People from privileged groups can too easily "forget" to think about inequality, fail to recognize the urgency for change, or walk away from challenging situations. Allies continually remind themselves to pay attention to the dynamics of privilege and oppression, and recognize the exigency for addressing inequities. They are committed to trying to work things out when relationships or efforts get difficult, and to hang in there for the long haul in working for social justice.

Accountability. Allies develop relationships with people from the oppressed group and others from their dominant group to debrief and get honest feedback. They check in with themselves and others to ensure they are acting in ways consistent with their values and in solidarity with the efforts of the oppressed group.

It takes commitment and vigilance to develop and sustain these qualities. This is not to say that allies are never ignorant or make mistakes. They do and will. But *how* they deal with those situations is what is telling. When confronted with acting in an oppressive way, can they resist becoming defensive and rationalizing their behavior, instead of listening, apologizing, and reflecting on the feedback? When someone from the oppressed group expresses her disappointment that they did not notice or speak up, do they point to others who also did nothing or do they acknowledge their lapse and do better the next time? At times, I still struggle with not beating myself up or with wanting to curl up in a corner when I have done something that falls short of my ideals as an ally. However, I know that ultimately that does no one any good. It is better to get over myself, remember my ability to be an ally, and figure out how to improve.

Ally Development

Social identity development theory describes evolving understandings of the nature of oppression, the meaning of social identities, and the types of action required for change. Like identity development, the capacity to be an ally can be viewed as a process. The awareness, motivations, and competencies to be an effective ally grow and evolve along with one's identity development. Even with good intentions to address inequality, people may not have the consciousness or capability to do so effectively. In some cases, they may be replicating the same oppressive dynamics they seek to change.

Drawing on theories of identity development and my continuum of self-interest, Edwards (2006) theorizes about a model of ally development. His interest is in creating allies that are effective, consistent, and sustainable. Looking at underlying motivations, he suggests three types of aspiring allies for social justice.

Aspiring allies for self-interest are motivated by selfishness to protect people they know or care about from individual perpetrators. Their actions reinforce their feelings of power as they see themselves as rescuers and protectors. They lack a systemic analysis of oppression and do not challenge structural inequities. Given their narrow focus, when they are not trying to help an individual they know, they may engage in oppressive behaviors. For example, a man may volunteer to be a campus escort for women but not be concerned about the larger issues of violence against women and make sexist jokes in other contexts.

Aspiring allies for altruism seek to help people from the target group, often out of guilt. While well-intentioned, actions are paternalistic, usually in the role of rescuer or hero. These allies have an intellectual understanding of systemic inequality but usually focus on individual perpetrators. They seek to be the "exceptional member" of their dominant group, are dependent on approval from the oppressed group, and tend to be defensive when confronted. Aspiring allies are vulnerable to feelings of burn-out since their motivation is based on "helping" others. For example, in one elementary school, some administrators, teachers, and parents were concerned about the achievement gap, in particular the low performance of many of the low-income students of color. They began to come up with ideas to address it—more tutoring, more access to computers—generally ways to help individual students and their families. However, they did not actively seek the students'and families' perspectives on the barriers to academic achievement and what would be useful, nor collaborate with them on a plan. Nor did the administrators, teachers, and parents consider the need to examine the school structures, policies, and practices (and other systemic factors) that might be contributing to this gap.

These first two types of aspiring allies reflect different kinds of good intentions but are not yet able to be fully effective, consistent, or sustainable agents for change. The last type of ally is an ally for social justice, which reflects the qualities I discussed earlier. People in this group understand their own socialization and privilege, the oppression experienced by the targeted group, and the intersecting nature of systems of inequality. They seek social justice for the liberation of all, working *with* members of the oppressed group to create systemic change.

By describing different understandings of oppression and motivations to act, this framework can be used to foster the growth of allies. We can encourage students to self-assess regarding their goals, behaviors, and readiness for particular actions. It provides us with indicators of where we might be able to assist people in their ally development. For example, we can help allies for self-interest learn more about the systemic nature of oppression. Allies for altruism can be encouraged to explore their internalized dominance and see their self-interest in eliminating inequalities.

In their desire to be an ally, there are a few things I often see people do, especially when they first have their consciousness raised and are excited about taking social action. The first is approaching others with a missionary zeal. After taking a course or workshop that has been enlightening, students may be eager to share their new learnings with people who have not had this experience. In their desire to help others "see the light", they can develop an intensity that comes across as overbearing and self-righteous. They try to convince others to change their views and show little respect, patience, or humility. This can alienate the very people they are trying to engage. We can talk with students about how they can appropriately share their new understandings, without trying to convert or judge others. We can encourage them to gradually share their new perspectives, focusing on their own process, not on what others should know or do. They can let their actions speak for themselves, modeling what they are trying to convey. Help them find contexts where they can share and express their energy where it will be more welcomed.

The second issue is a rushing to intervene. There can be an impulse to address every situation of inequality without adequate analysis, skill, or planning. Running around trying to save the world can lead to efforts done haphazardly, prematurely, or incompetently. Clearly, there is no need to wait until they feel completely skilled and knowledgeable, but people should be sufficiently self-aware to assess what they need to be effective. If people tend to just jump in, it is probably good for them to take time to more thoughtfully choose how they intervene and ensure that their efforts are supported by and align with the efforts of the oppressed group.

The third related issue is assuming they can personally "fix" things. People may believe that they alone can solve the problems of inequality. This can stem from internalized superiority that leads people from privileged groups to believe they have the intellect and power to single-handedly "take care of things." In these cases, it is wiser and more effective for them first to get input from and strategize with others and consider how working collectively might strengthen their efforts.[1]

Everyone makes mistakes and learns along the way, but we need to try to limit the damage to the people and causes we seek to support. If the people someone is trying to organize feel patronized, they may not engage now and may be less willing to do so in the future. If a training becomes an opportunity for attacks due to poor design and facilitation, people will avoid attending other sessions. Being an ally is not simply about meeting one's own needs, but considering what is best for advancing social justice. We can encourage students to develop the tools to intervene in thoughtful ways that will enhance the likelihood of having a positive impact.

Creating Change and Options for Action

Once people have developed some awareness, have assessed their strengths and limitations, and are motivated to take some action, they need to decide what steps to take. Often, people feel confused or uncertain about they can do. According to one research study (Broido, 2000), college students are more likely to take social justice action if they are specifically invited to do so or if it is expected as part of their role. This may be true for others as well. Although they may not be ready to take on a high-profile leadership role, they can still be involved with actions requiring less visibility or risk. We need to respect where people are, while encouraging them to think broadly and be courageous.

Having people reflect on their spheres of influence is one way to assist them in looking at where they could affect change (Adams, Bell & Griffin, 2007; Tatum, 2003). Beginning with themselves in the center circle and moving out to other concentric circles, individuals can think about how they can affect their immediate family and their friends, their neighbors and colleagues, their community and organizational affiliations, their political and elected leaders, and national and international groups. They can explore how they can use their influence in any one of these areas to promote social justice.

Encourage people to think about actions that target oppression on individual-interpersonal, and institutional-cultural levels. At the individual-interpersonal level, actions are primarily focused on changing the consciousness and behaviors of individuals—oneself and others. These can include, attending meetings and events related to social justice issues, interrupting comments and jokes, taking classes and workshops, having intentional conversations about diversity and social justice issues, broadening one's diversity of relationships, and pointing out inequitable group or classroom dynamics.

Institutional and cultural level change involves changing institutional structures, policies, laws, practices, cultural images, language, and media. This can occur through petitions, boycotts, lobbying, letters to the editor, organizing or attending marches and demonstrations, speaking up at meetings about diversity issues, phone/e-mail/letter-writing campaigns, community organizing, joining boards of organizations, voting, being on committees that influence institutional personnel decisions and policies (hiring committees, curriculum committees), organizing educational events, working on legislative or political campaigns, monitoring practices (e.g. racial profiling, school suspension rate), or filing lawsuits.

Because most people tend to focus on addressing individual actions and attitudes without a systemic perspective, we need to continually encourage people to hold a more comprehensive understanding of oppression and a larger vision of change. Help them see the structural roots of individual problems. For example, feeding hungry people at a soup kitchen is important but what are the underlying reasons for hunger in their community and this country? Remind them to consider how their individual actions can be joined with collective action to contribute to more fundamental societal change.

As people try to develop plans for action, it can be helpful to first have an analysis of the problem or issue that they want to address and a vision of a successful outcome. What are the root causes and manifestations of the inequality? What would it look like if they accomplished their goal? The more they understand the dynamics of the current situation, the better they can strategize about how to change it. The more conscious people are about what they want to create, the better they can assess if they are moving in the right direction. Having a thoughtful analysis and clear vision enables people to more successfully develop the strategies and steps for effective interventions. I often have individuals create action plans that include a concrete goal, the resources they need (human and material), the obstacles they might face, how they might overcome those obstacles, specific steps to achieve the goal, some form of assessment to see if the goal was met and a reflection on what they learned from the process. If their action is directed at changing conditions for people from the oppressed group, they need to ensure they are working in partnership with people from that group. The role of an ally is not to decide for people from the oppressed group what their needs and desires are.

Moreover, instead of focusing on how they can help people from the targeted group, encourage individuals to consider how they could work with people from their own privileged group. I have heard repeatedly individuals from oppressed groups tell people from dominant groups, "Stop worrying about how to fix us, go work with your own people." A critical role allies can play is to educate people from their own social group and assist them in understanding and addressing inequality. Often, people from the marginalized group are tired of having that job or expectation.

Barriers to Taking Action

Even with good intentions and a desire to see greater justice, many things can prevent people from dominant groups from actually doing something to address inequities. There are several common impediments to action. Often, people feel *overwhelmed, powerless, or hopeless* due to the enormity of the task. Given the extent and complexity of systems of oppression, people do not know where to start to make a dent. They may feel there is little they could do that would have an impact since systems of oppression seem so vast and entrenched. People may feel hopeless because of how long oppressive structures have been in place and how intractable they can seem. They may feel that there is little chance that anything will change.

Often, there are other more personal reasons. Individuals may *feel inadequate*, that they lack the knowledge or skills to do anything constructive. They believe that they need to be better informed, more courageous, or more "something" before they are ready to take any action. For some, *guilt or shame about their privilege* keep them from taking action. People may be embarrassed by aspects of their identities, lifestyle, or access to resources. Therefore, to avoid having others, especially those from the subordinated group, find out about who they are or their lives, they stay removed from social action. Many also may worry about the *risks* and the responses to their social change efforts. Concerns may be about physical safety, job security, losing relationships, being seen as crazy, making mistakes, hurting people from the oppressed group, or seeming ignorant. There certainly can be real risks to engaging in social change, yet some people may exaggerate the potential negative consequences and imagine the worst.

In addition, most people's lives are busy and rarely do they feel that they can do all the things they would like to do. People may feel that there is a *lack of time* for social change work. Individuals from dominant groups have the privilege to opt out and decide not to address issues related to inequality. Lastly, on the other hand, people may feel *burnt out*. In their zeal to create greater equality, people may become involved in too many different efforts or have been involved in efforts that feel draining and ineffective. They lack the energy or motivation to continue working for social change.

Overcoming Barriers to Action

There is always a reason why people from privileged groups may balk at being involved in social change work. As recounted earlier, there are many blocks to actually doing something. Yet, there are also many ways to promote and maintain action. The following points can be useful to share with our students to encourage their activism. These suggestions can also be useful for ourselves as we struggle to sustain our work for social justice.

Maintain an historical perspective on social change. Looking to history reminds us that while change is possible, it takes time. Significant social change is a long-term process with both forward movement and setbacks. Very often, people do not see the result of their efforts or their impact seems limited. Big shifts occur after the groundwork has been laid for years and there have been countless small efforts that chip away at the attitudes and beliefs that hold unjust policies and practices in place. Think of your efforts as adding another brick to the road for social change. Not only does history provide us with a long-term perspective, it also provides role models and sources of inspiration. As the quote from Rabbi Tarfon reminds us, "It is not upon you to finish the work. Nor are you free to desist from it."

Find examples of successes. While achieving equality does not happen overnight, there are many important changes people do make that foster equity and significantly improve people's lives. Whether in their schools, communities, workplaces, or government, people create practices, structures, policies, or laws that advance social justice. These victories need to be recognized and celebrated.

See yourself as and be part of a larger community of social change agents. Advocating for social justice can feel lonely and more risky if you are acting alone or are ridiculed for your efforts. Finding others who share your commitment not only reduces isolation and fears, it also helps keep you motivated and thoughtful about what you do. Realize that your social justice work is part of a larger network, community, movement, and history. You are building on the work of others from the past and extending the work that is happening now. Coordinate and network with others with shared goals. In fact, it is through collective social action that major social changes occur.

Start small if necessary. No one can eliminate oppression single-handedly, but everyone can have a positive impact. Think about where you can make a difference. Reflecting on your spheres of influence can be useful in identifying the various places in your life where you can create change. Find some action that feels doable, even if it is just educating yourself, to build momentum for further efforts.

Have some success or positive experiences. Even though we do not always see the results of our efforts, having a bit of success is certainly motivating. It enhances our sense of efficacy and empowerment. Engage in some actions with a small goal where there is a high likelihood it will be achieved. In addition, make the experience of working for change a positive one—work with people you enjoy, build new relationships, or learn new information and skills.

Choose activities or issues that speak to your passion and feel morally compelling. It is easier to find the time and energy when something feels rewarding, renewing, and exciting, rather than like a burden or obligation. There is plenty of social justice work that needs to be done. Find the things that most call to you at different points in your life.

Choose appropriate levels of risk. It is important to think through the risks before taking action and to consider how much risk you are willing to take, given your life circumstances. There are a wide range of actions for social justice that can range from very low to very high risk. However, do not let any possibility of risk immobilize you. Do some reality testing—How risky is this really? What's the worst thing that could happen? How could I minimize the risks? Build in support and develop back-up plans in case some of the feared consequences do occur.

Find ways to evolve as an ally. Seek out activities, classes, workshops, projects, and collaborations with others to expand your knowledge and skills to be a more effective ally. Join groups or organizations to learn from others with more experience or expertise while contributing in appropriate ways. Work to develop your confidence and competence so that you have greater options for action.

Shift guilt into constructive action. Guilt is a natural feeling but being mired in it serves no one. Instead of feeling guilty about or trying to hide your power and privilege, use it in the service of social justice. Share your knowledge and skills; support and help develop the leadership of people from oppressed groups. Use your access to open doors for others.

Get personal support. Having a support system is critical for taking and sustaining change efforts. In addition to actually working with others, have people in your life who can nurture and encourage you—supporting you through the ups and downs of doing social justice work.

Consider the benefit. Think about how you will benefit from taking some action. These can range from greater self-esteem, feelings of empowerment, greater moral integrity and reduced guilt, to expanded personal relationships, new knowledge and skills, and a better work/school environment. There is much to be gained by acting in accordance with your values and knowing you are working toward your own and others' liberation.

Take care of yourself. There is no need to be a martyr. There is often an ebb and flow in the extent and types of social justice work people are engaged in. Instead of disengaging, find other ways to be involved that feel more nourishing and more appropriate for this point in your life. Set boundaries and make sure you're doing things for yourself that are healthful, healing, and rejuvenating.

Responding to Biased or Offensive Comments

One important role for allies is interrupting biased comments. Yet, one of the more challenging moments can be when they hear a prejudiced or stereotypical comment. Often, there is the momentary "freeze" and an anxious feeling of "what do I do now?" To do nothing generally leaves them feeling angry, guilty, or disappointed in themselves. If they have a repertoire of different responses, and have practiced them, they are more likely to be able to say something in the moment.[2]

I describe a range of strategies we can suggest to others, as well as use ourselves, to address offensive comments, whether they were made intentionally or unintentionally. These approaches can be used in conjunction with each other and often are most effective if they are. *There is no one right way to respond.* Deciding how to respond depends on the situation, the context, the people involved, and your mood, among other things. Part of the challenge in responding effectively is determining what is right for you and the other person in that situation. We all have different personal styles and comfort levels. We have various types of relationships with people. The context varies. The choices you make will depend on these variables.

First, there are several things to keep in mind as you consider how to respond. What is your *goal*? Do you simply want the behavior to stop or also to educate the person? Sometimes, all you can do or may want to do is to have the person stop the offensive behavior. Given the situation or your investment in the relationship, you may not have the time, energy, or opportunity to educate and help them understand why their behavior is problematic. Other times, it is important that we try to raise consciousness and sensitivity. We want the other person to become more informed and more thoughtful about how their behavior affects others. So, in deciding how to respond, we need to consider what our goal is.

The *tone* of your response affects how you are heard. How we say it is as important as what we say. When people feel attacked, blamed, and judged, they are likely to get defensive and angry. They stop listening. Keep your tone non-confrontational and non-judgmental if you want people to listen to you.

Think about your *relationship with the person*. Is this someone with whom you have a close relationship and will continue to interact? Is it your boss or someone with whom there is a power difference that puts you more at risk for speaking up? Is it a stranger you will never see again or a co-worker you need to work with every day? The kind of relationship, your investment in the relationship, the ongoing nature of a relationship, and the risks involved need to be considered.

The context or setting influences how you might want to handle the situation. Is it a more formal setting which expects more restrained or professional behavior or an informal social setting which allows for more latitude in interaction? The location does not excuse offensive or biased comments, but it can affect how you choose to respond. You also need to decide if the behavior warrants *a public and/or private response*. If a comment is said in front of others, you need to weigh embarrassing the person versus needing to publicly acknowledge the inappropriateness of the comment. Private conversations often provide more opportunity for education, but public responses can educate others and make a broader statement. Another option is to speak to the individual privately but to talk to the group more generally about appropriate language or stereotypes. Whether in public or private, you have a responsibility to interrupt harmful behavior.

Last, think about *age-appropriateness*. These strategies can be used with people of different ages—children and adults. Again, you need to carefully consider with whom you're dealing and what is most suitable. How we respond needs to be done in age-appropriate ways. Children's comments often reflect ignorance and the need for education.

Bearing all that in mind, these are some approaches that may be helpful:

Paraphrase or Repeat Back What They Said

Restating their comment clarifies it for you and for them. Either, it can help them hear how biased or silly they sound or it ensures that you are understanding them correctly and can respond appropriately. "So, you're saying that all people on welfare are just lazy and looking for a free ride?"

Ask For More Information

This can be a follow-up to paraphrasing. Try to understand why people hold those views. As people try to explain their comments, they often realize how what they are saying is unfounded or does not make a lot of sense. It also provides you with more information so you can address the misconceptions. Keep asking clarifying questions to unravel the web of assumptions. Point out contradictions in their statements. In order for people not to feel attacked or ridiculed, you need to do this non-judgmentally with genuine interest.

For example, "I'm wondering what's led you to believe this about people on welfare?" Further questions might include: "How many people do you know that are on welfare? Do you know how much assistance people actually get who are on welfare?"

Express Empathy First

Listen for the feelings behind the statement. People may make biased comments when they are feeling frustrated, disappointed, or angry. Often, if you can initially acknowledge the underlying feelings, it provides an opportunity to address the bias later. First allow someone to be heard, then challenge the beliefs.

If someone says, "I'm tired of losing jobs to those unqualified Blacks just so they can meet their affirmative action quota." Instead of immediately launching into a lecture about his assumptions that the Black person was unqualified, that they were just hired to fill a quota and clarifying what affirmative action is, first acknowledge the feelings. "You sound pretty frustrated about not getting that job. You've really been working hard to find a new job. I know job hunting can be really difficult and disappointing."

Play Dumb

Even if you understand what they are saying, pretend that you don't and ask them to explain. It forces them to think more about their statements.

If someone refers to the race of the person (most likely, a person of color since White people don't usually refer to White people by race), you can say, "I'm not sure what their race had to do with the story. Did I miss something?" This can also be used with jokes. When people have to explain the punchline, it often loses much of its humor.

Challenge the Stereotype

Give information to correct the assumptions underlying the stereotype and share your own experience that contradicts the stereotype, and offer alternative perspectives.

Comment: "I can't believe they're going to let those gay people adopt kids. That's not providing a good home—kids need a mom and dad."

Response: "Actually, I know many gay couples who are wonderful, loving parents with great kids. In fact, research says that kids raised in gay homes are just as well-adjusted as kids raised in heterosexual homes. Sexual orientation really has nothing to do with it."

Encourage Empathy

Ask them how they would feel if someone said something like that about their group or their friend/partner/child. Remind them of a time when they complained about similar comments directed at them.

Comment: "Man, is she built. I wouldn't mind having to work late with her".

Response: "How would you feel if someone said something like about your wife/girlfriend/sister/daughter? I'm sure she doesn't like it either. We're here to work."

Or, "I know you hate it when people make Italian jokes. It's not OK to make jokes about other ethnic groups either."

Tell Them They're Too Smart or Good to Say Things Like That

When someone says something that you doubt the person really believes or at least doesn't hold strongly, you can say: "You're too smart to say something like that." "You're too good/caring a person to say something that offensive/insulting." It's hard to reply, "No I'm not."

Highlight Commonalties

Point out shared interests, values, experiences, and concerns between the person making the comment and the person they are referring to.

Comment: "I heard our new neighbor down the street is Muslim. I hope we're not going to be living in a neighborhood of terrorists."

Response: "Come on. Actually I met him last week and he seems like a nice guy. He works in technology like you. He also was asking about local golf courses. I thought you might be able to tell him."

Consider W. I. I. F. T. (What's In It For Them)

Explain why diversity or that individual can be helpful or valuable. Often someone can bring new resources, skills, and perspectives that can enhance the group's effectiveness, increase clients/students/members, and improve services. Individuals may also learn new things that can foster their personal or professional growth.

"I know you didn't support her being hired, but our students have been asking for more diversity in our staff and for more people who share their experiences. I think she will be an important addition and will enhance our department and enrollments."

"She will really help us work with some of our clients. She understands the culture and can help reduce the distrust."

Express Your Feelings

Tell the person how you feel and if possible, explain why you're offended or uncomfortable. Offer an alternative, if appropriate. "I'm uncomfortable when I hear you talk about a person (or a specific group) in that way. I'd like you to stop." "I find that language offensive and don't appreciate hearing it. I know you know other more appropriate words to use." "I find it offensive when you call him that. He is a Sikh." "I know you may not intend it this way, but I cringe when I hear you refer to grown women in service roles as 'girls' because it sounds so demeaning. They can be called 'women' just like you call the females in the senior staff."

Use Humor

Sometimes exaggerating the comment or using gentle sarcasm makes the point. However, you need to be sure that it is heard as humor or sarcasm, not a reinforcement of prejudice. This is where tone is particularly important.

When people are operating out of stereotypes, you can use humor to highlight the inappropriate assumptions. For example, if a woman is being considered for a leadership position but someone is concerned that it might be a better job for a man, consider saying with light sarcasm, "Oh, we can't hire Ann to lead the team, she might cry when the negotiations get tough. We need a big strong man to do the job. Let's just keep women making the coffee. They're so good at that."

Appeal to Values and Principles

Individuals and organizations often espouse particular values and principles. Refer to these when challenging their comments. "I know you want to have a respectful and inclusive workplace; those kinds of statements just aren't consistent with that." Or frame it as a question: "In the past you've talked about wanting to raise open-minded kids. How do you think having them hear those comments might impact them?"

Share Your Own Process

Talk about how you used to say, think, or feel similar things but have changed. Avoid sounding self-righteous or holier-than-thou. It might be useful to share what caused you to change or to offer alternative language or perspectives. "I used to laugh or tell jokes like that, but then I realized how hurtful they are to people. I don't do it anymore and I would like you to stop too." "I used to make those assumptions too but then I learned that those are untrue generalizations or stereotypes and I try to catch myself when I start to think that." "I used to use those terms, but them I heard that those can be offensive (because—). Better language I've learned to use is … "

Point Out Policies or Laws That Prohibit Such Conduct

In workplaces, remind people of their obligation and liability. Note the policies and laws that prohibit such conduct and the consequences. "That behavior could be considered sexual harassment and you know we have a policy against that. You could end up in big trouble." In workplaces or public settings (e.g. stores, hospitals, businesses, etc), you may witness behavior or overhear comments being made. In these cases, consider reporting the behavior to a supervisor. Employers are responsible for creating workplaces free from harassment and such behavior, especially if it is part of a pattern of conduct, may be violating policies and laws. Also, if you are a customer or client, offensive behavior impacts the service you receive and the desire to engage with this organization. If it was directed at a person, you can also acknowledge to the target that you saw the offending behavior and offer your support.

Jokes

Jokes and humor can be complicated; what is funny can depend on when it is told, by whom to whom and with what intent. Sometimes a joke can affectionately poke fun at a stereotype; other times it can use the stereotype to hurt and reinforce prejudice. As a rule, I do not think it is appropriate for people from privileged groups to be making jokes at the expense of the oppressed group. If you're unsure about whether a joke is acceptable, ask yourself if you would tell this joke in front of people from the subordinated group.

Even if people from the target group say they doesn't mind, it does not mean it is harmless. Very often, people feel uncomfortable saying how they feel and will go along with it, even if it is offensive to them. Not only is this hurtful, it can erode trust. It forces people to wonder, "What do you really think of me and others like me?" Nor is it acceptable to tell an offensive joke if you believe no one from that group is around. It still perpetuates stereotypical and harmful messages. You can never be sure who people are, what people may hear in passing, or what others may hear you have said. People who are the target of the joke may feel that they cannot trust you—you'll say one thing to their face but another behind their back.

Consider these responses if you do hear an offensive joke:

> "I know you meant it as a joke, but I still find if offensive. It's not funny when other people tell jokes about that group."
>
> "You may have heard it from (the subordinated group), but it's different when we tell it."
>
> "I'm sure you can find jokes that don't put down other people."
>
> Offer your own joke that doesn't rely on making fun of others.

As the preceeding list indicates, there are many ways people can respond to prejudiced or offensive comments. As we expand our repertoire and practice, we usually will be better at finding something to say. Even if we miss the moment, we often have the chance to address it later. Undoubtedly, there always will be another opportunity.

Challenges of Being an Ally

Ally Balancing Acts

As people try to be allies, they may face situations they are unsure how to handle. They may struggle with balancing two different impulses or perspectives. In the actual circumstance, individuals need to use their best thinking, analysis, and personal reflection to discern the most appropriate course of action. There is nuance and complexity that is not easily reduced to a simple answer. These are some examples of ally dilemmas others and I have faced and ways to think about them.

1. *Wanting to appropriately personalize comments made about themselves or their privileged group by someone from an oppressed group but not wanting to overpersonalize.*

In a meeting, Joyce starts talking about how fed up she is with the arrogance of men. She turns to a Steve in the group and says "You guys think you know what's good for everyone." Steve wonders if she is talking about him specifically or about men in general. Should he personalize it or should he depersonalize it and dismiss it as an angry rant that has nothing in particular to do with him?

Sometimes allies will wonder, "Is this really about me or not really about me?" Generally, it is neither useful to overpersonalize nor discount sentiments shared by members of oppressed groups. When people take remarks too personally, it tends to lead to self-absorption along with paralyzing guilt or defensiveness. Automatically distancing denies one the opportunity to learn and take responsibility. Particularly if the statement is not made to the person as an individual, dominant group members do not need to own all comments about their group. Sometimes, remarks or feelings will be directed at a person because of the social group they represent, not because of who they are as an individual. However, people from the privileged group need to consider how the statement relates to their behavior. If they have concerns that they might in fact be implicated and have a relationship with the person who made the comment, it might make sense to check it out. See if the other person has some feedback s/he would like to share. Honest self-reflection and checking in with trusted people can help discern how to assess the situation.

2. *Recognizing the significance and pervasiveness of oppression but wanting to see someone as just a fellow human being.*

Alicia, a heterosexual woman meets a new student in class, Joe, and they begin to develop a casual friendship. She realizes he is a gay. She becomes hypervigilant about not saying anything that assumes heterosexuality. Alicia is unsure if she should talk about what she and her boyfriend did that weekend or if that would seem like flaunting her heterosexual privilege. She thinks of Joe as her new gay friend. She realizes that her constant self-monitoring is impeding the development of their friendship and wishes she could just relax and treat him like any other male friend.

On the one hand, it is important to be aware of heterosexism (or any form of oppression) and how it affects people's experiences and interpersonal dynamics. Not being "colorblind" or "sexual orientation blind"—recognizing one's social identity and its significance—is appropriate. However, people are not simply that single social identity nor is that oppression the only aspect of people's lives. The challenge is to recognize the significance of social identities and oppression while not reducing people to just that part of themselves, making then one-dimensional.

One of my favorite poems that speaks to this paradox is called "For the white person who wants to know how to be my friend" by Pat Parker, a Black poet. The first two lines are, "The first thing you do is forget that I'm black. Second, you must never forget that I'm black." Ideally, we can do both of these at the same time. Early in the process of unlearning oppression, many people feel extremely conscious and self-conscious about social identities and the dynamics of oppression. Like learning any new content or skill, people may overthink or overcompensate. As they internalize their new understandings of themselves and others, they do not need to reduce individuals to a particular identity but can more comfortably see themselves and others as more multifaceted people. It is important to stay cognizant about how our social locations impact us and our relationships. Yet, we also have a shared humanity and numerous similarities and differences beyond our social identities. Moreover, often multiple dynamics of oppression are at play. While a heterosexual person may be focused on their straightness, the other's gayness, and heterosexism, if they are different sexes then there are also gender dynamics and sexism at play (along with all the other social identities).

3. *Wanting to articulate a marginalized person's point of view but not wanting to speak for/as a person from a marginalized group.*

Kathy is at a meeting with only other White folks trying to come up with fundraising ideas for a community center. As they discuss various options, Kathy is concerned that these ideas might not appeal to the African American people in their community. The themes and locations seem to be based on White, middle-class experiences. Kathy wants to raise these concerns but doesn't want to sound as if she is representing how Black people feel.

It's important that different viewpoints on an issue are considered, particularly those from marginalized groups. People from privileged groups do not need to speak *for* people from the oppressed group. Mostly important, people from dominant groups need to find ways for people from marginalized groups to speak for themselves—by ensuring they are present or by including their voices in their own words. If they are not present, people from dominant groups can articulate perspectives held by people from the subordinated group. People from privileged groups do not need to speak as if they are an expert on others' experiences, using phrases such as "—people think/feel/believe ... ". Instead, they can speak from their own experience, describing what they have heard or learned from people from the oppressed group. Consider language such as, "In my experience, I've seen/heard. ... ", "From what I've learned, ... ", or "If I were a—(member of an oppressed group) I might think/feel. ... "

In a group situation, if a person from a marginalized group makes a point that gets ignored, a person from the privilege group can note that the comment got passed by and that they'd like to reconsider it. Or they can briefly paraphrase what the person said and redirect the conversation back to the person to repeat and elaborate on their point. "I heard so and so say—. I'd like to go back to that." Since people are more likely to pay attention to or take seriously comments made by people from the privileged group, be sure that they are not incorrectly being credited with the idea.

4. *Wanting to share one's opinions, resources, and expertise but not wanting to dominate.*

Tom is a White, United States born man who is part of a multi-racial group working on immigration reform and issues affecting the Latino immigrants in their community. The group meets at a local Latino center and is headed by a Latina. Tom runs his own company and has a long history as a community activist. He often feels he has a lot to contribute but worries that if he says or does too much he will be seen as overpowering; if he remains quiet, he feels he is withholding useful information.

It is often easy for members of privileged groups to dominate. After all, they are often in leadership roles and have knowledge, skills, experience, resources, and connections that may be useful. On the other hand, in their effort not to be over-bearing or oppressive, they may hold back from sharing what they can offer. It can be a delicate balance to fully contribute without overpowering. The goal is to respect the leadership and direction set by people from the oppressed group, offer-ing one's resources in ways that will support those goals. People from privileged groups can talk with members of the subordinated group about how their con-tributions can best be used. Instead of imposing their views, they can offer their thoughts and ask questions that will help advance the process. Checking in with others for feedback on how they are coming across can help allay concerns.

5. *Wanting to respect the perspective of someone from the subordinated group but wanting to disagree.*

At a parents' meeting at school, Bill, who is African American, recounts a story about a Black student being treated unfairly by a teacher. Andrea, a White woman, thinks racism was a factor. Bill feels that race had nothing to do with it. Andrea feels uncertain about disagreeing with Bill because it involves race.

Start from the assumption that everyone has a piece of the truth and that people from the oppressed group know more about their experience than someone from the dominant group. When in the dominant group, I think it's best to first listen and try to understand the perspective of the person from the subordinated group. But critical thinking skills should not be set aside. Not everyone from the oppressed group thinks or sees things the same way. Just as people from privileged groups are at different places in their identity development and analysis of oppression, so are people from the oppressed group. As with any individual, people's views are affec-ted by their particular background, experiences, and personalities. After listening respectfully, and carefully considering what s/he is saying, an individual from a privileged group can certainly come to a different opinion. It's useful to talk with others, especially from the subordinated group, to check out one's views, and get other perspectives. Think about if, how, and when to differ with his/her opinion. Depending on the relationship and context, open discussion may be fine. In other settings, doing this privately might be more appropriate.

6. *Wanting to challenge oppression and be an ally but feeling inadequate to speak up or intervene.*

Jamila recently completed a course that addressed disability oppression. As she arrives at a gathering at a friend's house, she notes all the steps to get in. Upon entering, she notices a person who is vision-impaired at the foodtable struggling to serve himself. Jamila wants to help but is not sure what to do and doesn't want to be patronizing. Instead of offering assistance, she decides to join a conversation with some acquaintances she knows from school. A man remarks that there are some students who just started his graduate clinical psychology program who are hearing-impaired and blind. He says it's inappropriate for them to become therapists since they cannot adequately see or communicate with clients. He feels this is political correctness gone too far. Jamila doesn't agree and finds his views ableist but realizes she doesn't know that much about disability issues and isn't sure how to refute what he is saying. When she leaves the party, she is feeling guilty and frustrated with herself for not doing anything but still unsure of what she should have done.

The more people begin learning about oppression, the more aware they become of what they don't know or how much they have internalized oppressive attitudes and beliefs. They may be torn between feeling ignorant and wanting to address situations. Some people may feel immobilized because they fear they will make a mistake or hurt someone from the oppressed group. They worry that if they do not know exactly what to say or do, they don't want to do anything. Instead of waiting until they feel they have it all together (which will never happen), they can start doing something they feel reasonably prepared to do and their confidence and skill will grow. If it's responding to a comment, some of the aforementioned suggestions can be useful, even if it's just expressing disagreement or discomfort with those assumptions. If it is a recurring situation, people can do their homework and be prepared the next time the opportunity arises. If someone does make a mistake when trying to positively intervene, be humble, apologize, and learn from it. In addition, consider addressing a situation with others. This shifts the onus off of just one individual and allows others, with additional skills and knowledge to help develop an effective response.

Finding the right balance in various circumstances warrants ongoing attention. It tends to get easier as people get more comfortable in their role as an ally. As we heard from people in the unlearning oppression chapter, their ability to feel more empowered, relaxed and authentic in situations with people from oppressed groups grew as they gained more consciousness and experience. Having people to be accountable and debrief with also helps make sure people are on the right track.

Working Collaboratively With People From The Oppressed Group

In the course of social justice work, people from dominant groups will be working with people from oppressed groups. As the aforementioned situations indicate, allies need to be thoughtful about what they say and do. Working with any group of people has its challenges. When groups addressing social issues include people from the dominant group and subordinated group, additional dynamics are at play. From my experience working with allies as a subordinated group member, being an ally as a dominant group member, and reading about efforts at collaboration, I have learned that people from privileged groups are more likely to successfully collaborate if they avoid the following:

Taking over. As discussed previously, individuals from dominant groups are often in positions of power and have confidence in their knowledge, skills, and ability to get things done. Add to this internalized (often unconscious) superiority. Many people from privileged groups may lack the experience or comfort in taking direction from people from the marginalized group. However, people from the subordinated group need to take leadership in addressing their own oppression and be supported in that role. People from privileged groups can share their resources in ways that enhances rather then controls or diverts the group.

Wanting things to be done according to the norms of the dominant culture. Just as allies cannot expect to be in charge, they cannot expect the group to function in the ways they are most accustomed to. When people from the oppressed group get to set the norms, whether it be about communication, conflict, food, time, or process, it may be different from how the dominant group usually does it. This requires people from privileged groups to value other ways of thinking, being, and doing. They need to be willing to be flexible and out of their comfort zone.

Trying to be one of them. Whether out of shame, lack of rootedness in one's own culture or wanting to be accepted, people from privileged groups cannot pretend to be someone they are not. Dressing certain ways or adopting certain language or speaking styles does not make one part of the oppressed group. More likely, people will be seen as "wannabes", making it more difficult for trust to develop. People from dominant groups can be sensitive to their enactment of privilege, while being clear about who they are and their values.

Seeking emotional support. People who work together ideally can develop relationships that are mutually caring and respectful. However, people from the privileged group should not expect emotional caretaking from people from the oppressed group. Usually, people from the subordinated groups spend their lives taking care of or worrying about the feelings of people from the privileged group. People from the marginalized groups are not there to help people from dominant groups deal with their guilt, hurt, or fear. Emotional support can be gotten from others from one's dominant group and from individuals from the oppressed group where a relationship of this type has been established.

Expecting to be taught. People from dominant groups can learn a lot from working with people from marginalized groups. However, this can be done without looking to people from the oppressed group to teach them. While asking questions can certainly be appropriate, people from the subordinated group should not be expected to spend their time and energy educating. There are many ways to gain information and understanding, including listening and observing.

Expecting gratitude or praise. Everyone likes to feel that her/his efforts are recognized and appreciated, but as an ally in social justice work, that is not the purpose. Social justice work is done for one's own and others liberation, not as charity or to be seen as a good person.

In describing qualities he looks for in an ally against racism, Raible (2009) states, "The main goal is to develop relationships of solidarity, mutuality and trust, rooted in a praxis of intentional anti-racist thought, action and reflection." The more people from privileged groups are able to develop consciousness and analysis, the less relationships will be limited by particular social identities and social locations. The greater the ability to create relationships of solidarity, mutuality, and trust, the better people can work toward shared social justice goals.

Relationships with Members of One's Dominant Group

Clearly, having relationships with people from the oppressed group is essential for allies in numerous ways. However, relationships with people from one's privileged group are also central. Instead of just turning to a person from the subordinated group, people from privileged groups can turn to each other for support, accountability, debriefing, and information. People from a dominant group can educate and interrupt oppressive attitudes or behavior from other dominant group members, instead of relying on people from the subordinated group to do so. Sometimes, individuals can hear feedback more readily when it comes from someone like themselves.

Yet, one of the dangers for those seeking to be allies is distancing themselves from others from their social group—seeing themselves as special, exceptional, or better. Sometimes, they want to separate themselves from other "oppressors". Other times, there is competition with other allies from their privileged group about who is more enlightened or more connected to people from the oppressed group. Allies from the same dominant group can be especially hard on each other and overly critical. This may arise from feelings of insecurity. Ultimately, we need to embrace rather than distance ourselves from others in our social group, even if at times we find their attitudes or behaviors repugnant. We have the responsibility to affect change and the opportunity to find fellow travelers on this journey.

Conclusion

Throughout this chapter, I have offered ideas that I hope will help people find avenues for action and ways to be more effective and consistent agents for change. The possibilities and opportunities for being an ally are endless. In summary, I'd like to highlight some key points:

- Continually develop your awareness, knowledge, and skills.
- Speak up when you see or hear something that perpetuates inequality.
- Educate others (appropriately) about privilege and oppression.
- Be humble: be willing to listen to feedback and learn from mistakes.
- Be courageous: take risks and do what you think is right to advance social justice.
- Get and give support, and act with others to create social change.

In groups:

- Notice who's present or included and who's not, then work to be more inclusive as needed.

- Make sure all voices are heard.
- Think about how a decision or policy might affect privileged and oppressed groups differently, then make sure its impact is equitable.
- Notice who's in power or in charge and who's not, then work to more equitably share power.
- Support the leadership of people from marginalized groups.
- Make connections among different forms of oppression; don't let oppressed groups be pitted against each other.

Yet, being an ally is not simply choosing to engage in a particular activity. Being an ally means bringing a social justice lens to all situations. It is utilizing an awareness and analysis about oppression no matter where one is, what one is doing, or what role one is in. It's asking, "Are these actions further marginalizing people from oppressed groups and reinforcing inequity or are they advancing inclusion and fostering justice?" As people move through their lives, it's thinking critically, speaking up, and taking action. It's continually reflecting on their actions and enacting a consciousness that is always evolving.

Barbara Love (2010) refers to living with "liberatory consciousness" which "enables humans to live their lives in oppressive systems and institutions with awareness and intentionality rather than on the basis of the socialization to which they have been subjected"(p. 470). She suggests four key elements to developing a liberatory consciousness: awareness—noticing what is happening; analysis—analyzing what's happening and considering possible actions; action—taking and accomplishing an action; and accountability/ally-ship—accepting responsibility and accountability to self and community for the consequences of the action or non-action. We can all strive to live with "liberatory consciousness" as we endeavor to create the conditions that truly allow us all to be liberated.

11

ISSUES FOR EDUCATORS

We can't teach what we don't know, we can't lead where we won't go.

Malcolm X

Throughout the book, I have reiterated the importance of creating a supportive and "confirming" environment, of offering appropriate challenge, and of embodying respect and acceptance. As I have said numerous times, our own perspectives, attitudes, and behaviors are central to our educational effectiveness. Yet, thus far, the primary focus has been on gaining insight into the students or people we work with. Characteristics of privileged groups, various developmental theories, reasons for resistance, motivations for supporting social justice, and how these affect educational strategies or pedagogy have been discussed. I have emphasized how more knowledge and insight about our students allows us to be better educators. However, our students are not the only ones we need to understand. So, I now turn to the spotlight on us as educators.

In Chapter 3, I referred to the qualities identified by Rogers (1980) that are necessary for growth-promoting relationships—genuineness, unconditional positive regard, and empathy. People need to be able to trust us in order to take intellectual and emotional risks. Stephen Brookfield (1990) refers to the trust between teachers and students as the "affective glue" that binds educational relationships together (p. 163). We need to be perceived as authentic—as human beings, in our regard for the students, and in our commitment to equity. Students need to feel that we really do care about them and are their allies in the learning process. They also need to believe that we are genuine in our interest in the issues and in our desire to promote social justice. In addition, trust is gained when people see us as credible and congruent: when we have sufficient knowledge and experience, and when our actions match our words. If we talk about valuing individuals and cultural differences, we had better reflect that in our practice.

Furthermore, through our own reactions and interactions with students, we have the opportunity to model the principles of equity, democracy, and respect that we espouse. Our classrooms are microcosms of the larger systems of social relations and can be laboratories for alternative ways of relating. On the one hand, we can engage in classroom dynamics that mirror the societal dynamics of domination, competition, and win-lose conflict. We do this when we treat students disrespectfully, overpower their voices, or show off our expertise at their expense. Or, on the other hand, we can demonstrate how power can be used in ways that enhances others and how conflict can be a productive process. Our own behavior is a powerful educational tool.

In a similar vein, Shelley Kessler (1991) describes the "teaching presence", the qualities in the classroom that allow students to be vulnerable and discover new things, to be authentic and fully alive. She identifies three components for generating this teaching presence: being present, an open heart, and discipline. When a teacher is fully present, she or he is "alert to the circumstances of what is happening *right now*, attentive to what is happening inside him-herself and what is going on in the room" (p. 13, italics in the original). A teacher with an open heart is willing and able to care, and willing and able to be vulnerable—to feel deeply and to be moved. Discipline refers to creating the safety needed to allow students to take risks and be authentic with one another. The teacher ensures that students follow the class guidelines and are not allowed to hurt each other. These qualities transcend any particular methods or activities. Although she writes about her work with young people in a program to foster spiritual development, these ways of being correspond to the non-judgmentalness and compassion I have stressed are needed when educating people from dominant groups about social justice.

Without a doubt, cultivating this "teaching presence" is easier said than done. When educating about diversity and social justice, who among us has not at some point gotten our buttons pushed or gotten hooked? How many of us have never disliked a person and found it hard to work with that individual, become aware of our biases, or felt very judgmental toward a student? Who has not at some point lost their ability to think clearly, respond flexibly, really listen, and be understanding?

As we become aware of our own issues and reactions, we can better manage and transform our responses. Self-awareness is essential for any good teacher. There are many things we should know about ourselves in order to be competent and compassionate educators. Because of the intellectual and emotional complexity of educating about diversity, it is even more critical for social justice educators to be self-reflective. Insight into our own inter- and intrapersonal dynamics allows us to better monitor our behavior and address areas of limitation (see Bell, Love, Washington, & Weinstein, 2007). We then can more successfully create educational experiences that meet our goals.

In this chapter, I will first examine several common attitudes and behaviors that may diminish our effectiveness in educating people from privileged groups. After considering these challenges, I will then suggest some ways to deal with them. Throughout this discussion, my focus will be on how to develop and sustain the patience, flexibility, and open-heartedness needed for social justice education. I will explore how to cultivate the qualities that can enable educators to develop trusting relationships and offer constructive challenge.

Social Identity Development

Theories of social identity development are one way to develop insight into our attitudes and behaviors in educational contexts. Our stage of social identity development affects our views of self and our own social group, of others and their social group, and of social oppression. In Chapter 3, I described the process of social identity development for people from privileged groups. These models were presented in the context of understanding the thinking and behavior of students at different stages. Those same theories applied to us can help us to understand our own actions and reactions.

I will briefly review each stage of the Hardiman and Jackson model (1997), this time with emphasis on the social identity development of people from targeted groups. I will then explore how our levels of awareness, in both our dominant and subordinated identities, affect our work with people from privileged groups. Even though I will focus on work with people from advantaged groups, it is essential to consider how our social identities and levels of awareness impact our work with people from oppressed groups, especially when we are part of privileged groups. I hope readers will use this discussion as an impetus to further explore these issues.

We simultaneously go through the process of identity development in each of our dominant and subordinated identities. We also tend to be at different stages of development in our different identities. Moreover, no one is simply in one stage or moves neatly from one stage to the next. People tend to have a predominant stage or worldview, although they will incorporate perspectives from other stages depending on the issue and situation.

I doubt any social justice educator would be in the first stage, *Naive*, where people are unaware of structural inequities and of the social significance of our identities. This stage is most typical of young children; older individuals would have little interest to engage in such work. In *Acceptance*, people (actively/consciously or passively/unconsciously) accept the current social arrangements and dominant ideology, along with its stereotypes and notions of subordinated group inferiority and dominant group superiority. People from oppressed groups in Acceptance will attempt to ignore, deny, or rationalize the inequities they face. They will also internalize the negative messages about themselves and their social group.

Educators who are primarily in Acceptance are not ready to be teaching about social justice. They have not yet developed a critical consciousness about power relationships and institutional oppression or the ability to offer more equitable alternatives. People in Active Acceptance are firmly committed to our present social relations. People in Passive Acceptance are less aware of how they perpetuate systems of oppression and maintain the supremacy of the privileged group. "Good Liberals" are generally in Passive Acceptance and might teach about diversity with good intentions. Nevertheless, they will tend to point to individual reasons for inequities and imply that people from the oppressed group should be more like the dominant group. Even if this is not the educators' predominant perspective, they may still hold beliefs indicative of this stage. They need to continue to deepen their awareness of this form of oppression and make conscious efforts to check their assumptions about the privileged and oppressed groups. Students in Acceptance may feel very comfortable with instructors who are also at this stage. However, educators are unable to offer sufficient challenge or contradiction to facilitate the participants' growth, and may instead reinforce the status quo. They may lose credibility with and frustrate the students who are in Resistance or Redefinition.

In *Resistance*, people become highly attuned to the dynamics of oppression. They are invested in unlearning the misinformation they believed in Acceptance and in challenging unjust behaviors and social structures. People in Active Resistance tend to do this more publicly and vehemently than people in Passive Resistance. People from dominated groups attempt to purge themselves of the negative images they have internalized about themselves and their group. They generally want to associate with others from their social group and have little interest or tolerance for people from the privileged group. As people become aware of their oppression and attempt to change it, they often experience strong feelings of pain, anger, and hostility.

In this stage, people often want to help others "see the truth" and to rally support for social change. Thus, they are motivated to be educators. Resistance is probably the most common stage of social identity development of social justice educators and the most challenging one from which to do this work. Someone from a dominant group in Resistance may glorify people from the oppressed group and excuse their inappropriate behavior, yet have little compassion for people from their own group. They may feel particularly punitive toward those who are in Acceptance who lack an understanding of the oppression or a commitment to address it. People in this stage, may project their own negative feelings about themselves as a privileged group member onto others from their group. Since most would prefer to be with people from the oppressed group, they may not want to deal with people from their dominant group, especially if they are not at a similar stage of consciousness.

These feelings are likely to be even greater for educators from a subordinated group. They tend to be highly invested in having people "get it" and may become overly emotionally involved in class discussions or in student outcomes. These educators will often be perceived as having their own agenda or a chip on their shoulder. They may find it hard not to stereotype or dehumanize people from the privileged group (i.e. "those White men") or to value any aspects of the dominant group's culture. It is particularly difficult for educators in Active Resistance to have patience with the educational process and to maintain respect and empathy for people from the privileged group.

People in Resistance also may have difficulty educating about other forms of oppression. In this moment in time, their "ism" feels the most important and compelling. Since they are most focused on this issue and their own experiences, they may not have the depth of understanding of other "isms" or the same level of commitment to address them. (Even though understanding one form of oppression can help in understanding others, most people in this stage are not yet making those strong connections. It also depends on their level of awareness in their other social identities.) In general, educators in Resistance need to assess whether they are ready to be in an educational role.

This occurred with a colleague of mine in graduate school. Michael was from an upper-middle class family and recently, became very interested in class issues. He was reading a lot about class exploitation and working people's movements. He was an activist on campus, particularly in efforts to ensure greater accessibility for poor and working-class students. He was into "downward mobility" and looked the part. Michael was anxious to teach the classism weekend workshop. After doing so a couple of times, it become clear to Michael as well as the other trainers that this was not a good match. He had a constant edge of anger in his voice, students found him overbearing, and co-trainers found him too inflexible. At this point in time, Michael needed to be able to immerse himself in the literature about and struggles against class inequality. Being a trainer was not most productive for him or the participants. Being an organizer was more appropriate.

People who are moving out of Resistance and into *Redefinition* are grappling with redefining their social group identity, independent of the oppressive system. People from privileged groups are trying to develop a positive identity that is not based on superiority. Instead of rejecting and reacting to the dominant culture, people from oppressed groups are seeking and reclaiming aspects of their own culture. The intensity of feelings has usually subsided.

Since educators from privileged groups are developing an affirmative sense of their social identity, they may have fewer negative feelings about others from their group. Educators from oppressed groups are still most interested in being with others from their group with a similar consciousness in order to forge a new social identity. However, they are in a proactive as opposed to a reactive mode. As they develop strength in their own social identity and efficacy at dealing with oppression, they tend to be better at managing their own feelings in order to educate others.

In *Internalization*, people have internalized this new sense of their social identity. While people may still feel passionately about social justice, they have more emotional and psychological space to deal with others. They are less immersed in their own issue and are more able to take a broader perspective. People are able to see themselves as individuals with multiple social identities and make links among different manifestations of oppression. This makes it easier for them to relate to people who are from dominant as well as subordinated groups. They tend to have more tolerance and understanding for people in privileged groups who are ignorant and/or resistant.

Ideally, it would be nice if we could all reach Internalization in all our social identities before being an educator. Needless to say, this is not the case, nor would it be practical. We cannot afford to wait until we have it "all together" to educate others about issues of social justice. However, we can do some honest self-assessment and then make responsible choices about what we do. We can create ways to manage our feelings and behavior. Later in this chapter, I'll suggest some ways to do this.

Other Factors that Affect our Educational Effectiveness

Social identity theory is just one way to understand our thinking and reactions. Just as there are many forces that affect students' openness to learning and growth, there are many things that affect our educational responses and abilities. I will now highlight a few other factors that in addition to or conjunction with our stage of social identity development impact how we work with people from privileged groups.

Triggers

Most of us can think of words or behaviors that push our buttons—that make our stomachs tighten, our fists clench, our hairs stand up. There may be things that make us freeze and feel paralyzed. I call these triggers. Some common triggers are, "You're being too sensitive", "Those people … ", "They all look alike to me", "Why do they have to be so obvious?", "She asked for it", as well as eye rolling and other body language. Triggers can cause us to lose our composure, our clarity, and our ability to respond appropriately. People from privileged groups can trigger educators from both advantaged and disadvantaged groups. (People from subordinated groups can also push our buttons, though I'll confine my discussion to dominant group members.)

I remember walking into a room to do a training on oppression issues, after a week of dealing with several incidents of rape and sexual harassment of women on campus. I said to my male co-trainer, "If any of these guys say that men are as oppressed as women, I may strangle him. You have to deal with it." Of course it came up, and fortunately Jim could address it. By knowing how I was feeling, I could avoid acting inappropriately. Even if I was not fortunate enough to have a skillful co-trainer, I would have been somewhat better prepared to respond realizing that I would have to carefully watch my response.

Usually, the trigger hits upon our own issues. Often there is something in our own experience that makes these words or actions so potent. Sometimes, it touches on our unresolved issues. This occurred when I was co-leading a weekend work-shop on classism at a university. One woman in the group consistently said classist, insensitive things. People in the workshop tried to engage her, but she remained narrow in her perspective. As people became more frustrated with her, she became more entrenched. During a break, a professor who was observing suggested that one of us (the trainers) talk to her since she seemed to be boxing herself into a corner. I said I didn't want to be the one to do that—I didn't like her and I wasn't feeling at all empathic. She was an upper-middle class, Jewish woman who pushed my buttons about materialistic, spoiled Jews, of whom there were many in the town where I went to high school. I still had my own issues about my experiences there and my own identity as an upper-middle class Jew. Fortunately, my co-trainer had more presence of mind and was able to speak with the student, who was in fact feeling judged and attacked. The student was able to return to the workshop more open and better able to participate productively. (I used the break to try to deal with my feelings.)

Other times, our reactions may be related to transference. This occurs when we project our feelings about an individual who is close to us onto another person (in this case, someone from a privileged group). A certain appearance, tone, comment, or interpersonal style may set us off because it restimulates our emotional reaction to someone else. It seems that people frequently have difficulty with individuals that remind them of their parents. Very often, transference occurs unconsciously. We may end up in a strange dynamic with a person, not quite understanding what is going on or why we are feeling so intensely. (Students also engage in transference, which sometimes explains their reaction to us.) A female colleague had an especially hard time with men who were condescending. While few women appreciate this kind of conduct, it really set her off; that dynamic always seemed to hook her. When we discussed it, she began to realize how this was reminiscent of her relationship with her father and her struggle to be seen as an adult in his eyes.

Another kind of triggering situation occurs when educators from disadvantaged groups are working with groups of people from advantaged groups. In the course of educating about diversity issues, many educators ask people to identify stereotypes or prejudices they have about different social groups. How this is done warrants serious thought since the intent is not to inflict pain but to increase awareness. People from oppressed groups, including trainers, may find it particularly painful to hear negative things said about their social group by dominant group members since it replicates oppressive societal dynamics.

In one situation, I was co-leading a day-long workshop on racism and anti-Semitism with a relatively inexperienced trainer, an African American woman who I'll call Denise. The group was made up of highly motivated and concerned White psychologists from various religious backgrounds. As the day progressed, several participants shared some of their racist prejudices and misconceptions—this was done appropriately, honestly, and with an investment in overcoming these beliefs and attitudes. I (and others) began to notice Denise becoming more and more quiet and withdrawn. When I asked her what was going on, she explained how over-whelmed she felt hearing the negative things such nice, caring professional people felt about people of color.

Another time, I was co-training with a lesbian, who I'll call Patty, who was not out to all members of the group. The two-day workshop was on diversity issues with a group of people, who were committed to social justice and (mostly) het-erosexual (from what we knew). On the second day, we were planning to do sev-eral role-plays to help participants develop skills to interrupt oppressive comments and behaviors. Together we developed a role-play about homophobic name-calling. I would be the one doing the name-calling, a participant would try to intervene, and Patty would process (discuss and debrief) the role-play. We enacted the role-play and when it was time for Patty to facilitate the discussion, she sat there silently. I looked at her, waiting for a response, indicating that we were ready to end the role-play. When it became clear to me she was not responding, I began to debrief what we had just done. When we spoke about it afterwards, she said she just froze when she heard the homophobic remarks.

I do not think that anyone really becomes impervious to hearing negative things about one's group, especially from a dominant group toward a target group. Per-haps we become more used to it, develop ways to cope with it, and find ways not to absorb it. It can be easier to deal with when it is clearly done in the context of raising consciousness—bringing things to light for examination, instead of keeping them hidden and allowing them to grow and fester. Many people say that people from disadvantaged groups have heard all these words before and know that people have these thoughts. However, there is something very powerful about hearing them all at once, especially from the mouths of nice, caring people. The educator is even more vulnerable when s/he is one of the few people (if not the only person) from that targeted group present. Becoming immobilized may be related to inex-perience or one's stage of social identity as well as what else is going on in one's life at that time. While we can't always anticipate our reaction, we can try to think through the impact of our activities on both our participants and ourselves.

Becoming the Advocate or Missionary

Another common pitfall in educating for social justice is falling into the role of missionary. This is when we try to convert people to our point of view or argue with them in an attempt for them to "see the light". When we feel strongly about an issue, it can be quite easy to slip into this role. When we start trying to convince people, we take on the role of advocate and lose our ability to be an educator who assists people in their own learning process.

I think this reflects one of the central challenges for social justice educators. Generally, people do this work because they care deeply and have a personal stake in the issues. This energy can be crucial to creating exciting educational experiences and to persevering through all the difficulties and risks. Yet, there is a difference between passion and overzealousness, commitment and dogmatism, and integrity and self-righteousness. I couldn't teach without passion, but it needs to be tempered with respect and openness. Otherwise, when we act in ways that overpower or negate the views and feelings of others, we jeopardize our credibility as educators and our relationships with students. If people feel that something is being forced upon them, they are likely to resist or withdraw. This becomes counterproductive to our intentions.

Stereotypes and Biases

Just like everyone else, we educators have our own prejudices and assumptions about individuals from different social groups, including privileged groups. Appropriately, many educators are sensitive to and concerned about stereotypes about people from marginalized groups. However, they are often less aware of or take less seriously stereotypes about people from privileged groups. Like biases about people from oppressed groups, prejudices about people from dominant groups can grow out of messages from our environment (e.g. family, peers, media) and our own experiences. The same principles regarding stereotypes about oppressed groups hold true for stereotypes about privileged groups—even when there may be a kernel of truth, it is exaggerated and applied to all members of that group, regardless of their individual qualities. Moreover, one or more experiences with individuals from a particular group does not give us license to then assume that those qualities fit all members of that groups. Our stage of social identity development (especially Resistance) may heighten our tendency to hold negative views about individuals from privileged groups.

Even though knowledge about particular cultural groups and social positions (see Chapter 2 on privileged groups) can be useful, we lose our ability to really see an individual if we make blanket generalizations. Furthermore, when we objectify or dehumanize people from an advantaged group, we are doing just what we are asking them not to do with people from a disadvantaged group. We are distorting and diminishing their sense of humanity. We are perpetuating the very notion of "us and them" that we are attempting to overcome by social justice work. When our hearts and minds are clouded by biases, our ability to be open and fair is impeded. Our capacity to be empathic and accepting is diminished.

Increasing our Educational Effectiveness

Educating about diversity brings together our own issues with our students' issues. This interplay is embedded in the context of the larger social dynamics. This highly charged mix creates opportunities for great stimulation and learning as well as frustration and challenge. In order to navigate and grow from this work, we need to engage in praxis—action and reflection (Freire, 1970). As we engage in teaching and reflect on our practice, we will encounter difficulties and disappointments.

Instead of seeing these situations as negatives, we can try to view them as gifts. They provide an opportunity for growth. We can ask: What can I learn from this? How can this make me a better educator? How can this experience help me develop as a person? And even when it's hard to view the situation in such a way, we can always consider it an AFGO (Another F—ing Growth Opportunity).[1]

Ongoing Personal Work—Content and Consciousness

Being an effective social justice educator and having the qualities required for the "teaching presence" requires ongoing personal work. Educators need a commitment to personal and professional growth. We need to continually raise our consciousness, work through our issues, and stay current on the topics. There are numerous things we can do to improve our ability to be present, open, and informed.

We become more comfortable and flexible as we increase our knowledge of the content we teach and enhance our skills in managing the process. The better informed we are about our subject(s) the more easily we can respond to stereotypes, provide accurate information, and challenge misconceptions. The more skilled we are at dealing with conflict, working with emotions, and handling group dynamics, the more we can enjoy the process rather than dread it. These skills allow us to foster the conditions for safety and the development of trust. We also become better able to structure sessions to enhance the potential for learning and decrease the likelihood of resistance. When we feel competent and well-informed, we can be less self-conscious, anxious, or defensive. Information and skills can provide us with a confidence that allows us to be more relaxed and more present. We are less likely to be in situations where we feel, "I didn't know what to do!"

As important as it is to be knowledgeable about the content and able to manage the process, it is just as important to be aware of and able to manage ourselves. Some honest self-evaluation is a key starting point. We need to determine if we are ready to educate about certain issues, and if so, how, with whom, and in what context. As suggested previously, models of social identity development provide one tool for this type of self-reflection. We need to understand the impact our identities and stages of development have on our self-awareness and our work with others. If we haven't done our own work around an "ism", we won't be ready to educate others. If we are going to be working with people on an emotional as well as a cognitive level, we need to have had the opportunity to do this ourselves. As I have stated throughout, consciousness-raising is not just an intellectual endeavor. In addition to having the content knowledge and the process skills, we need to have explored our own baggage. Part of this exploration of readiness includes assessing our strengths and limitations. As much as possible, we need to try to anticipate our reactions and the situations that might be challenging for us.

Once we have determined what we are ready to do and how we might behave, we can create structures to support us. If we are unsure of our readiness, emotionally or intellectually, to educate about a topic we can try to work with a co-trainer/teacher for the whole session or for parts of it. We can bring in guest presenters who can more skillfully address and facilitate discussion on an issue. It is very helpful to have people with whom we can debrief and share support and advice. Many people find it useful to keep a journal to record and process their thoughts and reactions.

Another aspect of our personal work is being conscious of and able to deal with our biases. We need to monitor the thoughts in our heads, check the assumptions that we make, and reflect on our behavior to ensure that we are being non-judgmental, caring, and fair. When we notice our prejudices infiltrating, we need to take responsibility to address them. This might mean gathering more information to enhance our understanding, speaking with the students to get to know them as an individuals, exploring why we hold such views, or just being extra vigilant in our interactions. Certainly, the more we can rid ourselves of our stereotypes and biases, the less energy we need to spend worrying about them and the freer we can be. We can remain self-aware, without being self-conscious.

We also need to examine our areas of resistance or defensiveness. One way to become aware of these is to notice which feedback we automatically reject or rebut. If a male student claims that we were being unfair to men, do we automatically dismiss it as male privilege speaking, or do we take time to see if there is some truth in what he is saying? If a student claims that we are portraying people of color as victims, do we justify our curriculum by claiming we're just trying to illustrate the depth of racism, or relook at our syllabus to see if it is imbalanced? If a colleague comments on the fact that the authors of our books are not diverse or appropriately representative, do we immediately claim that we can't have something by everyone or do we ask for recommendations? We do not need to accept what everyone says as the unadulterated truth, but we can use it as an opportunity for reflection.

We can also notice the events, discussions, or workshops that we make time to attend and those that we never seem to fit in. We can consider how these choices reflect what we consider more or less important or issues we want to avoid. If we pride ourselves on being more sensitive and socially conscious than others, or committed to equity and fairness, we can find it more difficult to acknowledge the ways in which we do not live up to these ideals. Yet, to truly achieve these goals, we need to explore the places where we fall short.

In general, we need to know our triggers. While there is always the chance to be surprised, we can pay serious attention to the people or situations that push our buttons. We can explore when we feel most vulnerable and what gets us most angry. We can reflect on why we have certain reactions to certain people. As we become more conscious of our triggers, we can find ways to manage and eliminate them; we can look to address their source. This may mean working on healing some of our own pain and wounds, or overcoming conditioned responses.

The Triggering Event Cycle (O'Bear, 2007) offers a way to understand and manage triggering situations. The seven steps of the cycle include: 1) the stimulus occurs, 2) the stimulus triggers an intrapersonal "root" (memory, past trauma, or experience of fear or prejudice), 3) the intrapersonal issue forms a lens through which a facilitator creates a "story" about what is happening, 4) the story a facilitator creates shapes the cognitive, emotional, and physiological reactions s/he experiences, 5) the story s/he creates influences the intention of a facilitator's response (to intimidate, prove them wrong, be liked, avoid conflict), 6) the facilitator reacts to the stimulus, and 7) the facilitator's reaction may be a trigger for participants and/or another facilitator. The goal is for facilitators to recognize early in the process that they are being triggered, utilize self-management tools to change how they interpret the situation, deal with their reactions, and be able to choose effective responses.

One useful tool is self-talk. Before a class or in the moment when a triggering event occurs, we can silently talk to ourselves to get through the situation. These self-statements can relate to how we are viewing the other's behavior as well as our own reactions. We might think things like, "Remember, they're speaking out of pain or ignorance", "He's just trying to get my goat, and I'm not going to fall for it", "She's just showing off for her friends, but she's probably scared underneath", "I can handle this calmly and rationally", "Just keep breathing". If we know in advance the kinds of things that tend to push our buttons, we can develop and practice in advance what we could say to ourselves to keep us centered.

Another strategy that more broadly helps us to be present and to deal with our triggers and prejudices is to practice mindfulness. Mindfulness is the "art of conscious living". It means "paying attention in a particular way: on purpose, in the present moment, non-judgmentally. This kind of attention nurtures greater awareness, clarity and acceptance of present-moment reality" (Kabat-Zinn, 1994, p. 4). Mindfulness is being awake and aware and able to "look deeply". In situations where we feel we are not being conscious or are immersed in negative reactions, it can help us return to a more centered way of being and to deepen our understanding of what is really going on. By developing mindfulness, we are less likely to be caught in conditioned responses and unproductive thoughts. During the times we do get stuck, it provides a way out. When we are able to be present and conscious in the moment, it expands our understanding and choices; it puts us in touch with our wisdom and creativity. Mindfulness helps us to develop awareness, calm, and joy in our lives, and by extension, in our educating. We can move away from dualistic thinking and better appreciate our interconnection. Kabat-Zinn suggests a way to check to see if we are really awake—look at other people and ask yourself if you are really seeing them or just your thoughts about them.

Essentially, mindfulness practice is conscious breathing. You tune into and follow your breath. A helpful way to stay focused on your breathing is to say "In" as you breathe in and say "Out" as you breathe out. You do this silently without trying to control your breath. Mindfulness meditation is a way to systematically cultivate present-moment awareness and to connect our body and mind. Mindfulness meditation (as well as other forms of mediation) can be a "path for developing oneself, for refining one's perceptions, one's view, one's consciousness" (Kabat-Zinn, p. 264). In many ways, mindfulness is similar to other meditative practices. For these purposes, I will not go into a comparison or explain in-depth the philosophy and practice of mindfulness. There are currently many helpful and accessible books about mindfulness meditation available. (See, for example; Braza, 1997; Hanh, 1991; Goldstein and Kornfield, 1987; Kabat-Zinn, 1994.) Although mindfulness grows out of Buddhism, it is not a religious practice and can be done alone or along with other spiritual traditions.

Developing and Maintaining Respect and Compassion

Engaging in the process of self-development and reflection tends to expand our capacity for being open-hearted and non-judgmental. Nevertheless, developing and maintaining respect and compassion for people from privileged groups can still be highly challenging. When people act resistant, treat others (or us) in hurtful ways, express offensive views, or presume entitlement it generally strains our ability to be empathic. Dealing with deep levels of ignorance or defensiveness can be frustrating.

It can be even more challenging when we are in the subordinated group working with people from the dominant group. So often in our lives, when we are in an oppressed group, we are expected to educate, to not be angry, and to be accommodating. We are forced on a daily basis to deal with the bias and discrimination from people from the dominant group. In a workshop or classroom, we are once again being asked to be understanding and tend to the needs of the privileged group. We are also more likely to have our authority and credibility challenged. No one should be expected to take on this role. It takes enormous strength and clarity. But if we do choose to be an educator in this capacity, we have the responsibility to do our job effectively.

For any of us, if we seek to create "the teaching presence" and relationships which support growth and change, we need to be able to sustain feelings of respect and compassion. Writing from a Buddhist perspective, Sharon Salzberg (1995) defines compassion as,

> ... the strength that arises out of seeing the true nature of suffering in the world. Compassion allows us to bear witness to that suffering, whether it is in ourselves or others, without fear; it allows us to name injustice without hesitation, and to act strongly, with all the skill at our disposal. To develop this mind state of compassion ... is to learn to live with sympathy for all living beings, without exception. (p. 103)

Her description contains several important components that I will address in more detail. First, compassion encourages us to have sympathy. Her use of sympathy is akin to my use of empathy in that it requires us to be able to sense what another's experience is like. It enhances our sense of interconnection. One thing that blocks these feelings is our inability to see the full humanity or human dignity within each person. As I noted earlier, when we objectify or demonize individuals, we undermine our ability to be empathic and accepting. "Process can be destructive when we lose sight of the person's potential for learning, growth and change" (Romney, Tatum, & Jones, 1992, p. 98). When we deepen our understanding, we deepen our capacity to really see others, and thus to care about them. There are several ways we can try to gain or recapture this sense of human connection.

We can draw upon our own experiences of being a member of a privileged group in order to understand the feelings and behaviors of others from dominant groups. Whenever I feel angry or frustrated with men who are unable to see their privilege, are oblivious to common acts of sexism, behave in condescending ways, or belittle the concerns of women, I think of all the times I've heard people of color accuse White people of these same things. When I see men being defensive, feeling self-conscious about how to act and what to say or tired of being made aware of all the things they do as men that perpetuate male dominance, I can see my own struggles in unlearning racism. It is humbling for me to think about how difficult it has been for me to look at parts of myself that I wish did not exist (and some that I still avoid), how painful it has been to acknowledge the ways that I and other White people have systematically oppressed others, and how hard it is to try to rid myself of ingrained and sometimes unconscious attitudes, beliefs, and behaviors. Yet, it is by drawing on these similar feelings that I can develop more compassion for others in privileged groups. As described in Chapter 2, there are common social forces that produce some shared characteristics of dominant groups. I realize that my consciousness and responses are not so different from theirs. I can appreciate the difficulty and effort involved in grappling with issues of oppression as someone from a privileged group.

When I am having difficulty feeling patient and compassionate, I've started to do a version of a Buddhist meditation, Metta, which is used to help cultivate compassion for oneself and others. (This is described in detail in Salzberg). I will repeat to myself, "May I be happy, May I be healthy, May I be safe, May I be at ease." Depending on the time I have, I will do this several times. I will then think of someone that I like and repeat the phrases directed at her/him, "May you be happy, May you be healthy, May you be safe, May you be at ease." I'll continue doing this as I think about someone I have neutral feelings for, and finally toward someone with whom I'm having difficulty liking or accepting. I've been amazed how this meditation has allowed me to be more calm and open. I will also do it silently, while looking around at the students, as I sit waiting for a session to begin. I tried it one day with a class that was experiencing a lot of tension and conflict. I felt that they were getting into rigid positions and conceptions of each other and I wanted to do something before we engaged in further hard conversation. At the beginning of class, I invited the students to close their eyes and go through this process with me: thinking first about themselves, then someone in the class they had a good relationship with, then someone they felt neutral about, and then someone they were having difficulty with. While it didn't completely change the class dynamics, it did seem to soften some of the animosity and it certainly allowed me to be more present.

Another strategy to develop a sense of connection is to try to look for something good in the person. As trite as this may sound, it is not uncommon for educators to get fixated on the ways an individual is unpleasant or difficult and lose sight of all else. As long as we perceive the individual only in these terms, we are unable to see the complete person and will be unable to feel openly toward her/him. Intentionally, look for admirable characteristics and behaviors. I have yet to be unable to identify some redeeming quality. This can provide an opening to expand our view of the person, develop some positive feelings, and begin to see him/her as a more full human being.

Another related approach is to separate the humanness of the person from their actions. Regardless of what people do or who they are, we need to remember that they are a human being with innate human dignity. It can be helpful to remember that they are someone's son or daughter or to imagine them as young children, before they became so damaged. Non-violent activists have this perspective at the core of their philosophy and practice.

As Martin Luther King, Jr. (1981) advised,

> When we look beneath the surface ... we see within our enemy-neighbor a measure of goodness and know that the viciousness and evilness of his acts are not quite representative of all that he is. We see him in a new light. We recognize that his hate grows out of fear, pride, ignorance, prejudice and misunderstanding, but in spite of this, we know God's image is effably etched in his being. Then we love our enemies by realizing that they are not totally bad. (p. 51)

The second component of Salzberg's definition states that to be compassionate means to recognize the pain and suffering in ourselves and others, and to bear witness to it. As Henry Wadsworth Longfellow said, "If we could read the secret history of our enemies we should find in each man's life sorrow and suffering enough to disarm all hostility" (as quoted in Salzberg, 1995, p. 125). If we can truly acknowledge someone's suffering, it can profoundly shift our perspective and feelings. We can see them as wounded individuals, not just as destructive or "evil" people. Often the pain is not apparent, especially when people have material comforts or positions of social power. As I discussed earlier in the context of resistance, people who have not dealt with their own pain are the ones most likely to be resistant to acknowledging or addressing someone else's suffering; they are more likely to mistreat others. In social justice education, we often need to help people heal from their pain, especially that caused by systems of domination. This requires that we ourselves are able to be an "enlightened witness" in their process. Bearing witness means accepting people where they are and being with them as they struggle through unlearning and relearning. We may need to work through some of our own issues in order to have the emotional capacity and understanding to do this.

Lastly, as Salzberg states in her definition, compassion enables us to take action and change the things that cause suffering and injustice. This is a critical point since being compassionate is often misinterpreted as being passive and inactive. We can "accept" individuals as people with human dignity and acknowledge their suffering while working to change their behaviors and the conditions that create suffering. King reminds us that we can oppose the unjust system, while at the same time loving the perpetrator of that system. Compassion does not mean condoning harmful action, denying injustice, accepting abuse, or allowing inequity. Salzberg asserts that to develop compassion it is important to consider the human condition on every level: personal, social, and political, and then try to change the conditions that create the social problems and cause suffering (p. 114). When we act with compassion, we are able to act with clarity, centeredness, and love, rather then out of anger, fear, and pain. We can make better choices and implement them more effectively. Martin Luther King, Jr. proposed that "Love is the only force capable of transforming an enemy into a friend" (1981, p. 54). He was referring not to sentimental, affectionate love but to "understanding, redemptive, creative good will for all men" (p. 52).

Terms like "evil" and "enemy" might seem harsh or extreme when thinking about students and workshop participants, or even others we encounter in our social change efforts. And while I hope that we don't see the people we work with in this way, I have heard (and have said) things that reflect this type of thinking and feeling. When we are derisive, dismissive, insulting, or disdainful about individuals because of what they have done, their social identity or their social position, I think we begin to take on this negative view. And while the term "love" may seem a bit overblown, it is this spirit that I think is crucial to our work. It encompasses the respect, non-judgmentalness, presence, and empathy deemed central to creating relationships that foster change. A quote I heard at a conference has stuck with me, "Do you love them enough to teach them?" (Unfortunately, I do not know who originally said it.)

I believe this orientation toward others is beneficial in all aspects of our lives. Especially when we are in an educational role, it is incumbent upon us to act in a responsible manner. In the rest of our lives we may choose not to associate with certain individuals, avoid engaging in certain types of conversations, or treat people less thoughtfully. (Sometimes I feel like I just want to be "off-duty".) Yet when I'm in an educational capacity, I am accountable to *all* the students/participants. I need to do my best to do whatever I can to help facilitate each person's learning and growth. While I cannot make some people think critically or change, neither can I just ignore them or write them off.

In a discussion about diversity training, a former student/colleague exclaimed, "How can anyone do this work without a sense of spirituality?" I know that many people do so, drawing on other moral or philosophical frameworks. However, various spiritual traditions provide philosophies and practices that aid us in cultivating love, compassion, and mindfulness as we work for social justice. (See Ingram,

1990 as one of many examples.) I have described what I personally have found most helpful. I encourage readers to draw upon whatever frameworks and practices are most meaningful and useful to them. We need all the strength, wisdom, and inspiration we can get.

Getting Support

The thrust of this chapter has been on our own process and issues as educators. Yet, we can't really do it alone. For some, doing education about social justice may feel like, and in fact may be, a solitary and isolating process. Whether or not we have people near us who share our work and passion, there are many others around the country and world who are engaged in similar efforts. Whether in person or through technology—conferences or social networking media, we need to find each other. Connecting with other social justice educators and social change agents helps us to continue to learn and improve—challenging our thinking and offering new resources. We need each other for encouragement when we feel discouraged and for emotional support as we deal with situations in our classrooms, institutions, and communities. In my own experience, many wonderful people committed to social justice have personally and professionally sustained me. Developing clarity, being centered, and staying sane are all more likely with the support of others.

Maintaining Hope

Last but not least, we need to maintain hope—for ourselves and for our students that individuals and society can change. If we as educators become cynical and jaded, we undermine our ability to help others on their journey to embrace and act for social change.

We may find hope from many sources: When we see individuals grow and evolve, when we witness people taking risks, when we accomplish a goal that fosters equity, when we have authentic, collaborative relationships across differences, when we hear about the many others who every day are working for social justice, and when we see changes in the larger society that collectively move us toward liberation. Like support, we need a sense of hopefulness to nurture our minds, bodies, and spirits to do this work.

For all the signs I see of hope and possibility, there are as many barriers. Yet when we become pessimistic about people from privileged groups and the possibility of change, we fall prey to the culture of cynicism that undermines social change. Surplus powerlessness (Lerner, 1998) is our tendency to see ourselves as more powerless than we really are. It makes us feel that it is impossible or unrealistic in the face of real power inequities to try to create fundamental change. Surplus powerlessness is not based on a realistic assessment of the political situation, but the internalization of messages from the dominant culture that tell us that nothing can really change and that we had better do what we can to protect ourselves.

However, we have a history rich with examples of people who had the courage to expect and demand change, and in the process inspired and empowered others to join them.

I often think of the words of Elie Wiesel, Holocaust survivor, writer, and peace activist. He had just finished speaking about his trips to various places in the world that were beset with war, conflict, and human cruelty, and his efforts to promote peace and healing. An audience member asked, "In light of all that you've seen, how do you keep going?" He responded, "What choice do I have?" For those of us who carry a commitment to a caring and just world in our hearts and souls, what choice do we really have but to continue the struggle? For ultimately, *justice frees us all.*

APPENDIX

Resources for Teaching/Training about Diversity and Social Justice

There are innumerable organizations and educational materials that address different aspects of diversity and social justice. These are a few suggested resources offering activities and workshop designs for educating about diversity and social justice in general and about individual forms of social inequality.

Teaching for Diversity and Social Justice: A Sourcebook (2nd ed.)
Maurianne Adams, Lee Anne Bell, & Pat Griffin (Eds.). New York: Routledge, 2007.

Has curriculum designs for racism and white privilege; racism, immigration, and globalization; sexism; heterosexism; transgender oppression; religious oppression; anti-Semitism and anti-Jewish oppression; classism; ableism; and ageism and adultism as well as sections on theoretical foundations and principles of practice. It also has lists of references and resources.

Readings for Diversity and Social Justice (2nd ed.)
Maurianne Adams, Warren Blumenfeld, Carmelita Rosie Castaneda, & Heather Hackman (Eds.). New York: Routledge, 2010.

This companion book to *Teaching for Diversity and Social Justice* has a website with discussion questions, extensive lists of further resources, activities and assignments, and next steps and action for each of the forms of oppression previously mentioned. http://www.routledge/textbooks/readings for diversity and social justice.

Beyond Heroes and Holidays: A Practical Guide to K-12 Anti-Racist, Multicultural Education and Staff Development

Enid Lee, Deborah Menkart, & Margo Okazawa-Rey (Eds.). Washington, DC: Network of Educators on the Americas, 2006.

Primarily focuses on anti-racism, but also addresses multiculturalism in general and other forms of oppression.

Dealing with Differences: Taking Action on Class, Race, Gender, and Disability
Angeles Ellis & Marilyn Llewellyn. Thousand Oaks, CA: Corwin Press, Inc. (A Sage Publications Co.), 1997.

Has training designs on class and classism; race, racism, and xenophobia; gender, sexism, and heterosexism; and disability and ableism. Geared for young adults but also useful for adults.

110 Experiences for Multicultural Learning
Paul B. Pederson. Washington, DC: American Psychological Association, 2007.

Uprooting Racism: How White People Can Work for Racial Justice (2nd ed.)
Paul Kivel. Gabriola Island, BC. New Society Press, 2002.

Teaching/Learning Anti-Racism: A Developmental Approach
Louise Derman-Sparks and Carol Brunson Phillips. New York: Teachers College Press, 1997.

Understanding Whiteness, Unraveling Racism: Tools for the Journey
Judy Helfand and Laurie Lippin. Cincinnati: Thomas Learning Custom Publishing, 2001.

The Source
http://thesource.diversityworks.org
An online sortable database of diversity, anti-oppression, and community-building activities.

The Diversity Factor
http://diversityfactor.rutgers.edu
Articles and resources for geared for workplace diversity.

Diversity Central: Cultural Diversity at Work
http://www.diversitycentral.com

Anti-Defamation League (ADL)
http://www.adl.org

Teaching Tolerance
http://www.tolerance.org

Witnessing Whiteness
http://www.witnessingwhiteness.org
Companion website for the book *Witnessing Whiteness: The Need to Talk about Race and How to Do It* (2nd ed.) by Shelly Tochluk, Lanham, MD: Rowman & Littlefield

Education, 2010. Has a series of workshop agendas and handouts on racism and white privilege.

United for a Fair Economy
http://www.faireconomy.org
Provides outlines and materials for a number of workshops on wealth/income inequality and economic/class issues. Also publishes books for educating about these issues.

Class Action
http://www.classism.org
Resources to explore class and dismantle classism

Tranformations: A Journal of Inclusive Scholarship and Pedagogy
http://www.njcu/sites/transformations

Resources for Progressive Social, Political, and Economic Alternatives

Center for Partnership Studies
http://www.partnershipway.org

The Equality Trust
http://www.equalitytrust.org

Yes! Magazine
http://www.yesmagazine.org

Institute for Policy Studies
http://www.ips-dc.org

Applied Research Center
http://www.arc.org

Tikkun Magazine/Network for Spiritual Progressives
htpp://www.tikkun.org

NOTES

Chapter 2: About Privileged Groups

1 I first saw this exercise done by Jackson Katz at the University of Rhode Island in 1993.

Chapter 8: Why People from Privileged Groups Support Social Justice

1 I wish to acknowledge the work of Steve Wineman (1984) which suggested a framework for these responses.

2 Kimmel (1993) found that one reason why men have supported the women's liberation movement was that it simply made logical sense. While this may be true for some individuals, in my own research, I have found that this reason has rarely arisen, and therefore do not include it in my discussion.

Chapter 10: Allies and Action

1 Thank you to Tema Okun for raising this point.

2 *Speak up! Responding to Everyday Bigotry* by Teaching for Tolerance, Southern Poverty Law Center, Montgomery, AL, 2005. (http://www.tolerance.org) is a great resource for how to respond in different situations.

Chapter 11: Issues for Educators

1 I have found this expression very helpful, as have the people I've shared it with. So, at the risk of offending some readers, I wanted to share it here.

BIBLIOGRAPHY

Adair, M. & Howell, S. (1988). *The Subjective Side of Politics*. San Francisco: Tools for Change.

Adams, M., Bell, L. A., & Griffin, P. (2007). *Teaching for Diversity and Social Justice* (2nd ed.). New York: Routledge.

Albrecht, L. & Brewer, R. (Eds.) (1990). *Bridges of Power: Women's Multicultural Alliances*. Gabriola Island, BC: New Society Press.

Allsup, C. (1995). What's All This White Male Bashing. In R. Martin (Ed.), *Practicing What We Teach: Confronting Diversity in Teacher Education*. Albany: State University of New York Press.

Alperowitz, G. (1996). The Reconstruction of Community Meaning. *Tikkun Magazine*, 11(3), 13–16, 79.

Anderson, M. & Collins, P. H. (2010). *Race, Class and Gender: An Anthology* (7th ed.). Belmont: Wadsworth.

Andrzejewski, J. (1995). Teaching Controversial Issues in Higher Education: Pedagogical Techniques and Analytical Framework. In R. Martin (Ed.), *Practicing What We Teach: Confronting Diversity in Teacher Education*. Albany: State University of New York Press.

Apple, M. (1982). *Education and Power*. London: Routledge and Kegan Paul.

Ayvazian, A. (1995). Interrupting the Cycle of Oppression: The Role of Allies as Agents of Change. *Fellowship*, January/February, 6–9.

Banks, J. (1991). *Teaching Strategies for Ethnic Studies*. Boston: Allyn and Bacon.

Bate, W. (1997, April 10). To Learn about Inner-city Plight, Walk in Their Schools. *Poughkeepsie Journal*, A11.

Batson, C. (1989). Prosocial Values, Moral Principles and a Three-Path Model of Prosocial Motivation. In N. Eisenberg, J. Reykowski, & E. Staub (Eds.), *Social and Moral Values: Individual and Societal Perspectives* (pp. 2–28). Hillsdale: Lawrence Erlbaum Associates.

Batson, C., Polyarpou, M., Harmon-Jones, E., Imhoff, H., Mitchner. E., Bednar, L., Klein, T., & Highberger, L. (1997). Empathy and Attitudes: Can Feeling for a Member of a Stigmatized Group Improve Feelings Toward the Group? *Journal of Personality and Social Psychology*, 71(1), 105–18.

Baxter, M. M. (1992). *Knowing and Reasoning in College: Gender-related Patterns in Student Development*. San Francisco: Jossey-Bass.

Belenky, M., Clinchy, B., Goldberger, N., & Tarule, J. (1986). *Women's Ways of Knowing: The Development of Self, Voice and Mind*. New York: Basic Books.

Bell, L., Love, B., Washington, S., & Weinstein, G. (2007). Knowing Ourselves as Social Justice Educators. In M. Adams, L. Bell, & P. Griffin (Eds.), *Teaching for Diversity and Social Justice: A Sourcebook* (2nd ed.) (pp. 381–93). New York: Routledge.

Bellah, R. N., Madsen, R., Sullivan, W. M., Swidler, A., & Tipton, S. M. (1985). *Habits of the Heart: Individualism and Commitment in American Life.* New York: Harper and Row, Publishers.

Bennett, M. & Bennett, J. (1992). "Defensiveness"—A Stage of Development. *Cultural Diversity at Work.* Seattle: The GilDeane Group, 5(1), 4–5.

Berger, M. & Guidroz, K. (Eds.) (2009). *The Intersectional Approach: Transforming the Academy through Race, Class & Gender.* Chapel Hill: The University of North Carolina Press.

Berman, S. (1997). *Children's Social Consciousness and the Development of Social Responsibility.* Albany: State University of New York Press.

Bingham, S. (1986). The Truth about Growing Up Rich. *Ms. Magazine,* 14, 48–50.

Bishop, A. (2002). *Becoming an Ally: Breaking the Cycle of Oppression in People.* New York: Zed Books.

Blumenfeld, W. (Ed.). (1992). *Homophobia: How We All Pay the Price.* Boston: Beacon Press.

Blumenfeld, W., Joshi, K., & Fairchild, E. (2008). *Investigating Christian Privilege and Religious Oppression in the United States.* Rotterdam, The Netherlands: Sense Publishers.

Bowser, B. & Hunt, R. (Eds.). (1981/1996). *Impacts of Racism on White Americans.* Beverly Hills: Sage Publications.

Braza, J. (1997). *Moment by Moment: The Art and Practice of Mindfulness.* Boston: Charles E. Tuttle, Co, Inc.

Brookfield, S. (1987). *Developing Critical Thinkers: Challenging Adults to Explore Alternative Ways of Thinking and Acting.* San Francisco: Jossey-Bass, Inc.

Brookfield, S. (1990). *The Skillful Teacher.* San Francisco: Jossey-Bass, Inc.

Broido, E. M. (2000). The Development of Social Justice Allies during College: A Phenomenological Investigation. *Journal of College Student Development,* 41, 3–18.

Butler, J. (1990). *Gender Trouble: Feminism and the Subversion of Identity.* New York: Routledge.

Butler, J. (2004). *Undoing Gender.* London: Taylor & Francis.

Califa, P. (1997). *Sex Changes: The Politics of Transgenderism.* San Francisco: Cleis Press.

California Newsreel (2003). *Race—The Power of an Illusion.* http://www.pbs.org/race (accessed on July 6, 2010).

Canham, M., Jensen, D., & Winters, R. (2009). Salt Lake City Adopts Pro-gay Statues—with LDS Church Support. *The Salt Lake City Tribune,* November 11.

Capossela, T. (1993). *The Critical Writing Workshop: Designing Writing Assignments to Foster Critical Thinking.* Portsmouth: Boynton/Cook.

Carter, R. (1997). Is White a Race? Expressions of White Racial Identity. In M. Fine, L. Weis, L. Powell, & L. Mun Wong (Eds.), *Off White: Readings on Race, Power, and Society* (pp. 198–209). New York: Routledge.

Catalyst (2010). *Women CEO's of Fortune 1000.* Available online at: http://www.catalyst.org/publication/322/women-ceos-of-the-fortune-1000 (accessed on July 15, 2010).

Clark, A. (1991). The Identification and Modification of Defense Mechanisms in Counseling. *Journal of Counseling and Development,* 69(3), 231–36.

Colby, A. & Damon, W. (1992). *Some Do Care.* New York: The Free Press.

Cose, E. (1995). *A Man's World.* New York: Harper Collins.

Critchell, S. (2010, May 17). What Color is "Nude"? Fashion Debate a Loaded Term. http://www.nola.com/fashion (accessed on July 23, 2010).

Crowfoot, J. & Chesler, M. (1996). White Men's Roles in Multicultural Coalitions. In B. Bowser & R. Hunt (Eds.), *Impacts of Racism on White Americans* (pp. 202–44). Beverly Hills: Sage Publications.

Crum, T. (1987). *The Magic of Conflict*. New York: Touchstone.

Cruz, N. (1990). A Challenge to the Notion of Service. In J. C. Kendall & Associates (Eds.), *Combining Service and Learning: A Resource Book for Community and Public Service*. Vol. 1 (pp. 321–23). Raleigh: National Society for Internships and Experiential Education.

Curry-Stevens, A. (2007). New Forms of Transformative Education: Pedagogy for the Privileged. *Journal of Transformative Education*, 5(1), 33–58. http://jtd.sagepub.com/cgi/content/abstract/5/1/33 (accessed on April 12, 2010).

Daly, H. & Cobb, J. (1994). *For the Common Good*. Boston: Beacon Press.

Daly, H. & Cobb, J. (2007). *The Great Turning: From Empire to Earth Community*. San Francisco: Berrett-Koehler.

Daloz, L. P., Keen, C., Keen, J., & Parks, S.D. (1996). *Common Fire: Leading Lives of Commitment in a Complex World*. Boston: Beacon Press.

Delpit, L. (1995). *Other People's Children: Cultural Conflict in the Classroom*. New York: The New Press.

De Graaf, J., Wann, D., Naylor, T., Horsey, D., & Robin, V. (2005). *Affluenza*. San Franciso: Berrett-Koehler.

Derber, C. (1979). *The Pursuit of Attention: Power and Individualism in Everyday Life*. Boston: G.K. Hall and Co.

Derber, C. (2009). *The Wilding of America: How Greed and Violence are Eroding our Nation's Character*. New York: St. Martin Press.

DiTomaso, N. (2003). An interview with Nancy DiTomaso. Online. *California Newsreel*. Race—The Power of an Illusion. http://www.pbs.org/race (accessed July 5, 2010).

Dill, B.T. & Zambrana, R. (Eds.) (2009). *Emerging Intersections: Race, Class and Gender in Theory, Policy and Practice*. New Brunswick: Rutgers University Press.

Domhoff, G. W. & Zweigenhaft, R. (1998a). *Diversity in the Power Elite: Have Women and Minorities Reached the Top?* New Haven: Yale University Press.

Domhoff, G. W. & Zweigenhaft, R. (1998b). The New Power Elite: Women, Jews, African-Americans, Asian-Americans, Latino, Gays and Lesbians. *Mother Jones*, 22 (2), 44–47.

Dovidio, J. & Gaerner, S. (2005). Color Blind or Just Plain Blind? The pernicious nature of contemporary racism. *The Non-profit Quarterly* 12(4), 22–27.

Duke, L. (1992). Blacks, Whites Define "Racism" Differently. *The Washington Post* , June 8.

Edwards, K. (2006). Aspiring Social Justice Ally Identity Development: A Conceptual Model. *NASPA Journal*, 43(4), 39–60.

Eisler, R. (1987). *The Chalice and the Blade: Our History, Our Future*. New York: HarperCollins Publishers.

Eisler, R. (1996). *Sacred Pleasure: Sex, Myth, and the Politics of the Body*. New York: HarperCollins Publishers.

Eisler, R. & Koegel, R. (1996). The Partnership Model: A Signpost of Hope. *Holistic Education Review*, Spring, 9(1), 5–15.

Eisler, R. & Loye, D. (1990/98). *The Partnership Way*. New York: HarperCollins Publishers.

Elliot, A. & Devine, P. (1994). On the Motivational Nature of Cognitive Dissonance: Dissonance as Psychological Discomfort. *Journal of Personality and Social Psychology*, 67(3), 382–94.

Ezekiel, R. (1996). *The Racist Mind: Portraits of American Neo-Nazis and Klansmen*. New York: Penguin Books.

Feagin, J. & Vera, H. (1995). *White Racism*. New York: Routledge.

Fernandez, J. (1996). The Impact of Racism on Whites in Corporate America. In B. Bowser & R. Hunt (Eds.), *Impacts of Racism on White Americans* (pp. 157–78). Beverly Hills: Sage Publications.

Frankenberg, R. (1993). *White Women, Race Matters: The Social Construction of Whiteness.* Minneapolis: University of Minnesota Press.

Freire, P. (1970). *Pedagogy of the Oppressed.* New York: Herder and Herder.

Freire, P. (1994). *Pedagogy of Hope: Reliving Pedagogy of the Oppressed.* New York: Continuum.

Friedman, V. J. & Lipshitz, R. (1992). Teaching People to Shift Cognitive Gears: Overcoming Resistance on the Road to Model II. *Journal of Applied Behavioral Science*, 28(1), 118–36.

Fromm, E. (1941). *Escape from Freedom.* New York: Avon.

Gaertner, S. & Dovidio, J. (1986). The Aversive Form of Racism. In J. F. Dovidio & S. L. Gaertner (Eds.), *Prejudice, Discrimination, and Racism* (pp. 61–89). Orlando: Academic Press.

Gallagher, C. (1997). Redefining Racial Privilege in the United States. *Transformations*, 8(1), 28–39.

Gates, D. (1993). White Male Paranoia. *Newsweek*, March (29), 48–53.

Gilligan, C. (1980/1993). *In A Different Voice.* Cambridge: Harvard University Press.

Giroux, H. (1983). *Theory and Resistance in Education: A Pedagogy for the Opposition.* South Hadley: Bergin and Garvey.

Glyn, A. & Miliband, D. (Eds.) (1994). *The Economic Cost of Social Injustice.* London: Ippr/ River Oram Press.

Goldberger, N., Clinchy, B., Belenky, M., & Tarule, J. M. (1998). *Knowledge, Difference and Power: Essays Inspired by Women's Ways of Knowing.* New York: Basic Books.

Goldstein, J. & Kornfield, J. (1987). *Seeking the Heart of Wisdom: The Path of Insight Meditation.* Boston: Shambala.

Goodman, D. (2010). Helping Students Explore their Privileged Identities. In *Diversity and Democracy* (13(2), 10–12. Spring 2010), Washington, DC: AACU. Available online at http://www.aacu.org (accessed on May 14, 2010).

Gramsci, A. & Forgacs, D. (2000). *The Antonio Gramsci Reader: Selected writings 1916–1935.* New York: New York University Press.

Greenfield, P. M. & Cocking, R. R. (1996). *Cross-cultural Roots of Minority Child Development.* Hillsdale: Lawrence Erlbaum Associates.

Grossman, D. (1995). *On Killing: The Psychological Cost of Learning to Kill in War and Society.* Boston: Little Brown.

Handy, C. (1998). *The Hungry Spirit: Beyond Capitalism: A Quest for Purpose in the Modern World.* New York: Broadway Books.

Hanh, T. N. (1991). *Peace is Every Step: The Path of Mindfulness in Everyday Life.* New York: Bantam Books.

Hardiman, R. & Jackson, B. (1992). Racial Identity Development: Understanding Racial Dynamics in College Classrooms and on Campus. In M. Adams (Ed.), *Promoting Diversity in College Classrooms: Innovative Responses for the Curriculum, Faculty, and Institutions* (pp. 21–37). San Francisco: Jossey-Bass Publishers.

Hardiman, R. & Jackson, B. (1997). Conceptual foundations for social justice courses. In M. Adams, L. A. Bell, & P. Griffin (Eds.), *Teaching for Diversity and Social Justice: A Sourcebook* (pp. 16–29). New York: Routledge.

Hawkesworth, M. E. (1993). *Beyond Oppression: Feminist Theory and Political Strategy.* New York: Continuum.

Helms, J. (1990). *Black and White Racial Identity: Theory, Research and Practice.* Westport: Greenwood.

Helms, J. (1995). An Update on Helm's White and People of Color Racial Identity Models. In J. G. Ponterotto, J. M. Casa, L. A. Suzudi, & C. M. Alexander (Eds.), *Handbook of Multicultural Counseling.* Thousand Oaks: Sage Publications.

Helms, J. (2008). *A Race is a Nice Thing to Have* (2nd ed.). Hanover: Microtraining Associates.

Higher Education Research Institute (2010). National Study of College Students' Search for Meaning and Purpose. UCLA. Available http://spirituality.ucla.edu (accessed July 25, 2010).

Hilfiker, D. (1994). *Not All of Us Are Saints: A Doctor's Journey with the Poor.* New York: Hill and Wang.

Hoehn, R. A. (1983). *Up from Apathy: A Study of Moral and Social Involvement.* Nashville, TN: Abington.

Hoffman, M.(1989). Empathy and Prosocial Activism. In N. Eisenberg, J. Reykowski & E. Staub (Eds.), *Social and Moral Values: Individual and Societal Perspectives* (pp. 65–85). Hillsdale: Lawrence Erlbaum Associates.

Hooks, B. (1989). *Talking Back.* Boston: South End Press.

Ignatiev, N. (1995). *How the Irish Became White: Irish-American and African-Americans in Nineteenth Century Philadelphia.* New York: Verso.

Ingram, C. (1990). *In the Footsteps of Gandhi: Conversations with Spiritual Social Activists.* Berkeley: Parallax Press.

Johnson, A. (2005). *The Gender Knot: Unraveling our Patriarchal Legacy.* Philadelphia: Temple University Press.

Jones, J. & Carter, R. (1996). Racism and White Racial Identity: Merging Realities. In B. Bowser & R. Hunt (Eds.), *Impacts of Racism on White Americans* (pp. 1–23). Beverly Hills: Sage Publications.

Kabat-Zinn, J. (1994). *Wherever You Go, There You Are: Mindfulness Mediation in Everyday Life.* New York: Hyperion.

Katznelson, I. (2006). *When Affirmative Action Was White: An Untold Story of Racial Inequality in Twentieth Century America.* New York: W.W. Norton and Co.

Kasser, T. (2003). *The High Price of Materialism.* Cambridge, MA: MIT Press.

Kasser, T. & Klar, M. (2009) Some Benefits of Being an Activist: Measuring Activism and its Role in Psychological Well-being. *Journal of Political Psychology.* 30(5), 755–77. Wiley International. International Society of Political Psychology.

Kaufman, M. (1993). *Cracking the Armor: Power, Pain, and Lives of Men.* New York: Penguin Books.

Kegan, R. (1982). *The Evolving Self: Problems and Process in Human Development.* Cambridge: Harvard University Press.

Kelman, H. D. & Hamilton, V. L. (1989). *Crimes of Obedience.* New Haven: Yale University Press.

Kendall, J. C. (1990). *Combining Service and Learning: A Resource Book for Community and Public Service* (Vols. 1 & 2). Raleigh, NC: National Society for Internships and Experiential Education.

Kessler, S. (1991). The Teaching Presence. *Holistic Education Review,* Winter, 4–15.

Kimmel, M. (1993). The Struggle for Gender Equity: How Men Respond. *Thought and Action,* 8(2), 49–76.

Kimmel, M. (2010). Toward a Pedagogy of the Oppressor. In M. Kimmel & A. Ferber, *Privilege: A Reader* (2nd ed.) (pp. 1–10). Boulder: Westview Press.

Kimmel, M. & Messner, M. (Eds.) (1989/95). *Men's Lives.* New York: Macmillan.

King, M. L., Jr. (1981). *Strength to Love.* Philadelphia: Fortress Press.

King, P. M. & Kitchener, K. S. (1994). *Developing Reflective Judgment: Understanding and Promoting Intellectual Growth and Critical Thinking in Adolescents and Adults.* San Francisco: Jossey-Bass.

Kivel, P. (1992/98). *Men's Work.* Center City: Hazelden.

Kivel, P. (2002). *Uprooting Racism: How White People Can Work for Racial Justice.* Philadelphia: New Society Press.

Kloss, R. (1994). A Nudge is Best: Helping Students Through the Perry Scheme of Intellectual Development. *College Teaching,* 42(4), 151–58.

Kochman, T. (1981). *Black and White Styles in Conflict.* Chicago: Chicago University Press.

Koegel, R. (1995). Responding to the Challenges of Diversity: Domination, Resistance and Education. *Holistic Education Review*, 8(2), 5–17.

Koegel, R. (1996). The Partnership Model: A Signpost of Hope—A Dialogue between Riane Eisler and Rob Koegel, *The Holistic Education Review* (now called *Encounter: Education for Meaning and Social Justice*), Spring, 9(1), 5–15.

Kohn, A. (1990). *The Brighter Side of Human Nature: Altruism and Empathy in Everyday Life*. New York: Basic Books.

Korten, D. (2001). *When Corporations Rule the World* (2nd ed.) San Francisco: Berrett-Koehler Publishers/Kumarian Press.

Korten, D. (2007). *The Great Turning: From Empire to Earth Community*. Berrett-San Francisco: Koehler Publishers.

Kreisberg, S. (1992). *Transforming Power: Domination, Empowerment, and Education*. Albany: State University of New York Press.

Kurfiss, J. (1988). *Critical Thinking: Theory, Research, Practice, and Possibilities*. ASHE-ERIC Higher Education Reports, New York: John Wiley.

Landrine, H. (1992). Clinical Implications of Cultural Differences: The Referential Versus the Indexical Self. *Clinical Psychology Review*, 12(4), 401–15.

Lappe, F. (2010). *Getting a Grip 2: Clarity, Creativity and Courage for the World We Really Want*. San Francisco: Small Planet Media.

Lappe, F. & Du Bois, M. (1994). *The Quickening of America*. San Francisco: Jossey-Bass.

Larew, J. (2010). Why are Droves of Unqualified Kids Getting into Our Top Colleges? Because their Dads are Alumni. In M. Kimmel & A. Ferber (Eds.), *Privilege: A Reader* (2nd ed.) (pp. 39–48). Philadelphia: Westview Press.

LaVeist, T, Gaskin, D., & Richard, P. (September 2009). *The Economic Burden of Health Inequalities in the United States*. Washington, DC: Joint Center for Political and Economic Studies.

Lazarre, J. (1996). *Beyond the Whiteness of Whiteness*. Durham: Duke University Press.

Leondar-Wright, B. (2005). *Class Matters: Cross-Class Alliance Building for Middle-Class Activists*. Gabriola Island, BC Canada: New Society Press.

Lerner, M. (1996). *The Politics of Meaning*. Reading: Addison-Wesley Publishing Co.

Lerner, M. (1998). *Surplus Powerlessness: The Psychodynamics of Everyday Life and the Psychology of Individual and Social Transformation*. Amherst, NY: Prometheus Books.

Lerner, M. (2002) *Spirit Matters*. Charlottesville, VA: Hampton Road Publishing Co.

Lerner, M. (2006). *The Left Hand of God: The Healing of America's Political and Spiritual Crisis*. New York: HarperCollins, Inc.

Lewis, Neil (2009, June 4). Debate on Whether Female Judges Decide Differently Arises Anew. *The New York Times*, pp. 16 & 18.

Lipsitz, G. (1998). *The Possessive Investment in Whiteness: How White People Profit from Identity Politics*. Philadelphia: Temple University Press.

Lorde, A. (1983). There Is No Hierarchy of Oppressions. *Interracial Books for Children Bulletin*, No. 14. Council on Interracial Books for Children,14 (3–4), 9.

Love, B. (2010). Developing a Liberatory Consciousness. In M. Adams, W. Blumenfeld, C. Castaneda, H. Hackman, M. Peters & X. Zuniga. *Readings for Diversity and Social Justice* (2nd ed.) New York: Routledge.

Lui, M., Robles, B., Leondar-Wright, B., Brewer, R., & Adamson, R. (2006). *The Color of Wealth: The Story Behind the U.S. Racial Wealth Divide*. New York: The New Press.

Luft, R. & Ward, J. (2009). Toward an Intersectionality Just Out of Reach: Confronting Challenges to Intersectional Practice. In Vasilikie Demos & Marcia Segal (Eds.), *Perceiving Gender Locally, Globally, and Intersectionally (Advances in Gender Research, Volume 13)* (pp. 9–37). Bingley: Emerald Group Publishing Limited.

Lynch, J., Kaplan, G., Pamuk, E., Cohen, R., Heck, K., Balfour, J., & Yen, I. (1998). Income Inequality and Mortality in Metropolitan Areas in the United States. *The American Journal of Public Health*, 88(7), 1074–80.

Lyons, N. (1988). Two Perspectives: On Self, Relationships and Morality. In C. Gilligan, J. V. Ward, & J. M. Taylor (Eds.), *Mapping the Moral Domain* (pp. 21–48). Cambridge: Harvard University Press.

Mandela, N. (1994). *Long Walk to Freedom*. New York: Little, Brown & Co.

MacKinnon, C. (1989). *Feminism Unmodified*. Cambridge: Harvard University Press.

Martin, R. (Ed.) (1995). *Practicing What We Teach: Confronting Diversity in Teacher Education*. Albany: State University of New York Press.

McIntosh, P. (1985). Feeling Like a Fraud. *The Stone Center Work in Progress Papers*, Working Paper No.18. Wellesley College, Wellesley: Center for Research on Women.

McIntosh, P. (1988). White Privilege and Male Privilege: A Personal Account of Coming to See Correspondences Through Work in Women's Studies. *The Stone Center Work in Progress Papers*, Working Paper No.189. Wellesley College, Wellesley: Center for Research on Women.

Miller, A. (1990). *For Your Own Good: Hidden Cruelty in Childrearing and the Roots of Violence*. New York: Farrar, Straus & Giroux.

Miller, J. B. (1976). *Towards a New Psychology of Women*. Boston: Beacon Press.

Miller, J. B. (1991). Women and Power. In J. Jordan, A. Kaplan, J. B. Miller, I. Stiver, & J. Surrey (Eds.), *Women's Growth in Connection: Writings from the Stone Center* (pp. 197–205). New York: The Guilford Press.

Minuchen, S. & Fishman, C. H. (1981). *Family Therapy Techniques*. Cambridge: Harvard University Press.

Mogil, C. & Slepian, A. (1992). *We Gave Away a Fortune*. Philadelphia: New Society Press.

Morns, E. (2007). "Ladies or Loudies": Perceptions and Experiences of Black Girls in Classrooms. *Youth and Society*, 38(4), 490–515.

Nestle, J., Howell, D., & Wilchins, R. (2002) (Eds.), *Genderqueer: Voices from Beyond the Sexual Minority*. New York: Routledge.

O'Bear, K. (2007). Navigating Triggering Events: Critical Skills for Facilitating Difficult Dialogues. *The Diversity Factor*, 15(3) http://www.diversityfactor.rutgers.edu (Last accessed May 14, 2010).

Oliner, S. & Oliner, P. (1988). *The Altruistic Personality*. New York: Free Press.

Opotow, W. (1990). Moral Exclusion and Injustice: An Introduction. *Journal of Social Issues*, 46(1), 1–20.

Orren, G. R. (1988). Beyond Self-Interest. In R. Reich (Ed.), *The Power of Public Ideas*. Cambridge: Ballinger.

Perry, W. (1968). *Forms of Intellectual and Ethical Development in the College Years: A Scheme*. New York: Holt, Rinehart and Winston.

Pettigrew, T. F. (1981). The Mental Health Impact. In B. P. Bowser & R. G. Hunt (Eds.), *Impacts of Racism on White Americans* (1st ed.) (pp. 97–118). Beverly Hills: Sage Publications.

Pew Forum on Religion and Public Life (2009). *Many Americans Mix Multiple Faiths*. Available at http://pewforum.org/Other-Beliefs-and-Practices/Many-Americans-Mix-Multiple-Faiths.aspx (accessed on July 25, 2010).

Pharr, S. (1996). *In the Time of the Right: Reflections on Liberation*. Berkeley: Chardon Press.

Powell, J. A. (2003). *An Interview with john a. powell*. Online. California Newsreel. Race—The Power of an Illusion. http://www.pbs.org/race (accessed July 5, 2010).

Putnam, R. (2000). *Bowling Alone: The Collapse and Revival of American Community*. New York: Simon & Schuster.

Raible, J. (2009). *Checklist for Allies Against Racism*. Online. Available at http://johnraible.wordpress.com (accessed on July 25, 2010).

Reardon, K. (1994). Undergraduate Research in Distressed Urban Communities: An Undervalued Form of Service-Learning. *Michigan Journal of Community Service Learning*, Fall, 1, 44–54.

Reason, R., Broido, E., Davis, T., & Evans, N. (2005). *Developing Social Justice Allies.* Summer, 110. San Francisco: Jossey-Bass.

Reimer, J., Paolitto, D., & Hersh, R. (1983). *Promoting Moral Growth.* New York: Longman, Inc.

Robb, C. (2007). *This Changes Everything: The Relational Revolution in Psychology.* New York: Picador.

Roediger, D. (1991). *The Wages of Whiteness.* New York: Verso.

Rogers, C. (1980). *A Way of Being.* Boston: Houghton Mifflin Co.

Romney, P., Tatum, B., & Jones, J. (1992). Feminist Strategies for Teaching about Oppression: The Importance of Process. *Women's Studies Quarterly,* 1 & 2, 95–110.

Rose, L. (1996). White Identity and Counseling White Allies about Racism. In B. Bowser & R. Hunt (Eds.), *Impacts of Racism of White Americans* (pp. 24–47). Beverly Hills: Sage Publications.

Rosenblum, K. & Travis, T. (1996). *The Meaning of Difference: American Constructions of Race, Sex and Gender, Social Class, and Sexual Orientation.* New York: The McGraw-Hill Companies, Inc.

Rubin, Z. & Peplau, L. A. (1975). Who Believes in a Just World? *Journal of Personality and Social Psychology,* 31(3), 65–89.

Ryan, W. (1970). *Blaming the Victim.* New York: Random House.

Sacks, K. B. (2010). How Jews Became White. In M. Kimmel & A. Ferber (Eds.), *Privilege: A Reader* (2nd ed.) (pp. 87–106). Philadelphia: Westview Press.

Sadker, M. & Sadker, D. (1994). *Failing at Fairness: How America's Schools Cheat Girls.* New York: Charles Scribner's Sons.

Sadker, D., Sadker, M., & Zittleman, K. (2009) *Still Failing at Fairness.* New York: Scribner.

Salzberg, S. (1995). *Loving Kindness: The Revolutionary Art of Happiness.* Boston: Shambala.

Sampson, E. (1988). The Debate on Individualism: Indigenous Psychologies of the Individual and Their Role in Personal and Societal Functioning. *American Psychologist,* 43(1), 15–22.

Sampson, E. (1991). *Social Worlds, Personal Lives.* New York: Harcourt Brace Jovanovich Publishers.

Santelices, M. V. & Wilson, M. (2010). Unfair Treatment? The Case of Freedle, the SAT and the Standardization Approach to Differential Item Functioning. *Harvard Educational Review,* 80(1), 106–34.

Schlosser, L. (2003). Christian Privilege: Breaking the Sacred Taboo. *Journal of Multicultural Counseling and Development,* 31, 44–51.

Sears, D. & Funk, C. (1990). Self-Interest in Americans' Political Opinions. In J. Mansbridge (Ed.), *Beyond Self-Interest* (pp. 147–70). Chicago: Chicago University Press.

Seifert, T. (2007). Understanding Christian Privilege: Managing the Tension of Spiritual Plurality. *About Campus,* May–June, pp. 10–17.

Shipler, D. (1997). *A Country of Strangers.* New York: Alfred Knopf.

Simon, L., Greenberg, J., & Brehm, J. (1995). Trivialization: The Forgotten Mode of Dissonance Reduction. *Journal of Personality and Social Psychology,* 68(2), 247–60.

Spelman, E. V. (1995). Changing the Subject: Studies in the Appropriation of Pain. In L. A. Bell & D. Blumenfeld (Eds.), *Overcoming Racism and Sexism* (pp. 181–96). Lanham: Rowman and Littlefield.

Staub, E. (1978). *Positive Social Behavior and Morality: Social and Personal Influences.* New York: Academic Press.

Staub, E. (1989). Individual and Societal (Group) Values in a Motivational Perspective and their Role in Benevolence and Harmdoing. In N. Eisenberg, J. & E. Staub (Eds.), *Social and Moral Values: Individual and Societal Perspectives* (pp. 45–61). Hillsdale: Lawrence Erlbaum Associates.

Steele, C., Spencer, S., & Lynch, M. (1993). Self-image Resilience and Dissonance. The Role of Affirmational Resources. *Journal of Personality and Social Psychology,* 64(3), 885–96.

Sue, D.W. (2010a). *Microaggressions in Everyday Life: Race, Gender and Sexual Orientation.* Hoboken: John Wiley & Sons.

Sue, D.W. (2010b) (Ed.). *Microaggressions and Marginality: Manifestations, Dynamics and Impact.* Hoboken: John Wiley & Sons.

Surrey, J. (1991). Relationship and Empowerment. In J. Jordan, A. Kaplan, J. B. Miller, I. Stiver, & J. Surrey, (Eds.). *Women's Growth in Connection: Writings from the Stone Center* (pp. 162–80). New York: The Guilford Press.

Tannen, D. (1990). *You Just Don't Understand.* New York: Ballentine Books.

Tatum, B. D. (1997). *"Why are All the Black Kids Sitting Together in the Cafeteria?" and Other Conversations about Race.* New York: Basic Books.

Tatum, B. D. (1994). Teaching White Students about Racism: The Search for White Allies and the Restoration of Hope. *Teachers College Record,* Summer, 95(4), 462–76.

Tatum, B. D. (1992). Talking about Race, Learning about Racism: The Application of Racial Identity Development Theory in the Classroom. *Harvard Educational Review,* 62(1), 1–24.

Terry, R. (1975). *For Whites Only.* Grand Rapids: William B. Eerdmans Publishing Co.

Terry, R. (1978). White Belief, Moral Reasoning, Self-Interest and Racism. In W. W. Schroeder & F. Winter (Eds.), *Belief and Ethics.* Chicago: Center for the Scientific Study of Religion.

Terry, R. (1981). The Negative Impact on White Values. In B. Bowser & R. Hunt (Eds.), *Impacts of Racism of White Americans* (pp. 119–51). Beverly Hills: Sage Publications.

Thompson, C. (1992). On Being Heterosexual in a Homophobic World. In W. Blumenfeld (Ed.), *Homophobia: How We All Pay the Price* (pp. 235–48). Boston: Beacon Press.

Trout, J. D. (2009). *The Empathy Gap: Building Bridges to the Good Life and the Good Society.* New York: Viking.

Tyler, T. R., Boeckmann, R. J., Smith, H. J., & Huo, Y. J. (1997). *Social Justice in a Diverse Society.* Boulder: Westview Press.

Viadro, D. (1996). Culture Clash. *Education Week.* April 10, 1996, 39–42.

Wachtel, P. (1989). *The Poverty of Affluence: A Psychological Portrait of the American Way of Life.* Philadelphia: New Society Publishers.

Wellman, D. (1977). *Portraits of White Racism.* New York: Cambridge University Press.

Wilchins, R. (1997). *Read My Lips: Sexual Subversion and the End of Gender.* Ithaca: Firebrand Books.

Wildman, S. (1996). *Privilege Revealed.* New York: New York University Press.

Wilkinson, R. & Pickett, K. (2009). *The Spirit Level: Why Greater Equality Makes Societies Stronger.* New York: Bloomsbury Press.

Wineman, S. (1984). *The Politics of Human Services.* Boston: South End Press.

Wolff, E. N. (2010). Recent Trends in Household Wealth in the United States: Rising Debt and the Middle-class Squeeze—An Update to 2007. *Working Paper No. 589,* Annandale-on-Hudson: The Levy Economics Institute of Bard College.

Wright, S. D., Taylor, D. M., & Moghaddam, F. M. (1990). The Relationship of Perceptions and Emotions to Behavior in the Face of Collective Inequality. *Social Justice Research,* 4, 229–50.

Young, I. (1990). *Justice and the Politics of Difference.* Princeton: Princeton University Press.

INDEX

Note: *Fig* following a page number indicates a figure.